HISTORICAL PROBLEMS

Volume 11

THE CROWN LANDS 1461–1536

THE CROWN LANDS 1461–1536
An Aspect of Yorkist and Early Tudor Government

B.P. WOLFFE

LONDON AND NEW YORK

First published in 1970 by George Allen & Unwin Ltd

This edition first published in 2021
by Routledge
2 Park Square, Milton Park, Abingdon, Oxon OX14 4RN

and by Routledge
52 Vanderbilt Avenue, New York, NY 10017

Routledge is an imprint of the Taylor & Francis Group, an informa business

© 1970 George Allen & Unwin Ltd

All rights reserved. No part of this book may be reprinted or reproduced or utilised in any form or by any electronic, mechanical, or other means, now known or hereafter invented, including photocopying and recording, or in any information storage or retrieval system, without permission in writing from the publishers.

Trademark notice: Product or corporate names may be trademarks or registered trademarks, and are used only for identification and explanation without intent to infringe.

British Library Cataloguing in Publication Data
A catalogue record for this book is available from the British Library

ISBN: 978-1-03-203925-1 (Set)
ISBN: 978-1-00-319296-1 (Set) (ebk)
ISBN: 978-1-03-204176-6 (Volume 11) (hbk)
ISBN: 978-1-03-204203-9 (Volume 11) (pbk)
ISBN: 978-1-03-204200-8 (Volume 11) (ebk)

Publisher's Note
The publisher has gone to great lengths to ensure the quality of this reprint but points out that some imperfections in the original copies may be apparent.

Disclaimer
The publisher has made every effort to trace copyright holders and would welcome correspondence from those they have been unable to trace.

TO MY WIFE

GENERAL INTRODUCTION

The reader and the teacher of history might be forgiven for thinking that there are now too many series of historical documents in existence, all claiming to offer light on particular problems and all able to fulfil their claims. At any rate, the general editor of yet another series feels obliged to explain why he is helping one more collection of such volumes into existence.

One purpose of this series is to put at the disposal of the student original materials illustrating historical problems, but this is no longer anything out of the way. A little less usual is the decision to admit every sort of historical question: there are no barriers of time or place or theme. However, what really distinguishes this enterprise is the fact that it combines generous collections of documents with introductory essays long enough to explore the theme widely and deeply. In the doctrine of educationalists, it is the original documents that should be given to the student; in the experience of teachers, documents thrown naked before the untrained mind turn from pearls to paste. The study of history cannot be confined either to the learning up of results without a consideration of the foundations, or to a review of those foundations without the assistance of the expert mind. The task of teaching involves explanation and instruction, and these volumes recognize this possibly unfashionable fact. Beyond that, they enable the writers to say new and important things about their subject matter: to write history of an exploratory kind, which is the only important historical writing there is.

As a result, each volume will be a historical monograph worth the attention which all such monographs deserve, and each volume will stand on its own. While the format of the series is uniform, the contents will vary according to need. Some problems require the reconsideration which makes the known enlighteningly new; others need the attention of original research; yet others will have to enter controversy because the prevailing notions of many historical questions are demonstrably wrong. The authors of this series are free to treat their subject in whatever manner it seems to them to require. They will present some of their evidence for inspection and help the learner to see how history is written, but they will themselves also write history.

G.R.E.

AUTHOR'S NOTE

In the documents spelling has been modernized except for surnames and unidentified place-names. Capitalization has also been modernized and the necessary minimum amount of punctuation inserted to make the sense clear. I have translated all original Latin except for isolated phrases appearing in documents which are otherwise entirely in English.

I am greatly indebted to Sir Goronwy Edwards for allowing me to discuss with him some of the unsolved problems of later medieval constitutional history with which this introductory essay attempts to grapple, and to Mrs Audrey Erskine for help with a number of awkward points of palaeography.

I also wish to thank the Public Record Office for permission to print nos. 2, 4, 5, 6, 7, 10, 12, 13, 15, 16, 17, 20, 22[1], 22[3] and 23 which are Crown copyright; the British Museum for permission to print nos. 14 and 22[2] and the Huntingdon Library, San Marino, California for permission to print no. 18.

B.P.W.

University of Exeter
March 1969

CONTENTS

INTRODUCTION	vii
AUTHOR'S NOTE	ix

INTRODUCTION

1	The significance of the royal demesne in English government before 1461	15
2	The crown lands in Lancastrian and Early Tudor government: comparisons and contrasts	29
3	The Yorkist land revenue experiment	51
4	The Court of General Surveyors and chamber finance under Henry VII	66
5	The decline of the General Surveyors, 1509-1536	76

DOCUMENTS

1	From *The Governance of England*	91
2	A lease of lands made by Henry VI, 1447	92
3	The Act of Resumption, 1450	92
4	Appropriations for household expenses, 1450	94
5	A sheriff 'declares' his account, 1451	95
6	Appropriations for household expenses, 1462	96
7	John Milewater's account, 1461-1463	97
8	The King's Speech to Parliament, 1467	102
9	The Act of Resumption, 1467	102
10	The management of Clarence's forfeited lands, 1470	103
11	The Croyland chronicler on Edward IV's financial policies from 1475	104
12	Yorkist prohibitions to the Exchequer, 1463-1484	106
13	Appointment of a treasurer of the Chamber, 1484	119
14	Extracts from a signet office docket book, 1483-1485	120
15	A prohibition to the Exchequer, 1493	140
16	The General Surveyors' declaration of accounts, 1503-1504	142
17	Extracts from the General Surveyors' docket book, 1505-1508	147

18 Minutes of Henry VIII's Council advising the abolition of the 'by-courts', 1509   162

19 John Heron designated general receiver of the king's revenues (Stat. I Hen. VIII, cap. 3)   164

20 The Court of General Surveyors absorbed into the Exchequer from June 1510   165

21 Statutory authority for the General Surveyors and the treasurer of the Chamber (Stat. 3 Hen. VIII, cap. 23)   173

22 The revenues administered by the General Surveyors (3 valors of 1509-1515)   179

23 Extracts from the General Surveyors' docket book, 1514-1537   183

INDEX   199

INTRODUCTION

The significance of the royal demesne in English government before 1461*

ENGLISH historians take it for granted that the successful development of English monarchy in the Middle Ages was based on the king's landed patrimony and obvious continental contrasts and comparisons in other countries of medieval Europe appear to strengthen this view. The early failures of the medieval German kings and the subsequent chronic weakness of the central institutions of the Empire, are, at least in part, attributable to the absence of any powerful, consolidated princely German *territorium,* while the *domaine* of the French Capetian house was the undoubted nursery of French monarchical and national government, law and finance. The prominent position of the *terra regis* in the greatest land register of all time, our own English Domesday Book, is taken to be sufficient in itself to demonstrate a parallel importance of the crown lands, crown estate, or 'royal demesne', as English medieval historians have dubbed it, in the history of our own monarchy. Since English constitutional history first became a serious professional and academic study, with the publication of William Stubbs's *Constitutional History of England in its Origin and Development* in the 1870s, this notion has lain behind some of the most fundamental generalizations of history textbooks: the revenues of the medieval English Crown are deemed to have been divided into ordinary and extraordinary and the king was traditionally expected to 'live of his own' on the ordinary revenues which were basically derived from the royal demesne, while the extraordinary revenues, derived from taxation, were of right reserved for extraordinary emergencies. Stubbs traced a continuous party of constitutional principle opposed to the alienation of the English royal demesne, running from the Anglo Norman baronage to the parliamentary knights of the shire in the national assemblies of the later

* The ideas put forward in this section will be more fully developed and documented in my forthcoming volume, *The Royal Demesne in English Medieval Government*.

Middle Ages,[1] and, by implication, to the constitutional opposition to Stuart tyranny in the seventeenth century. His generation also produced the only modern edition of the earliest treatise on the English constitution to be written in the English language, Sir John Fortescue's *Governance of England*, which its Victorian editor presented in support of Stubbs's thesis as a medieval exposition of these constitution theories.[2]

It is highly improbable that Stubbs could have evolved these basic generalizations from a profound and penetrating study of the surviving materials of medieval English history, as I hope to demonstrate in the course of this essay, but in any case their earlier appearances in law book and statute, which must have been known to him, suggest that they were originally the products of the minds of seventeenth and eighteenth-century politicians and lawyers, not of the distinguished nineteenth-century professional historian who gave them academic respectability among modern writers. They were in fact already succinctly formulated in the eighteenth century *Commentaries on the Laws of England* by Sir William Blackstone,[3] in an age notoriously lacking in sound scholarly knowledge of the English Middle Ages, and can be found in embryo still earlier in the preamble to a statute of the period following the Glorious Revolution.[4]

However, when we turn for confirmation to the late-medieval pages of Fortescue's text, as opposed to his Victorian editor's commentaries on it, we find there no mention of a division of the revenues of England into ordinary and extraordinary. The fifteenth century classified revenues as 'certain' or 'casual' and, in so far as the terms ordinary and extraordinary were understood at the date of Fortescue's treatise, they were, if applied to revenues, the equivalents of 'certain' and 'casual'. This signifies an important difference from what Stubbs or Blackstone understood by them. Extraordinary charges (i.e. the *expenditure* of English kings) were defined by Fortescue as those which 'be so casual that no man may know them in certainty',[5] which demonstrates the contemporary meaning of that word. Among land revenues a rent, farm or feefarm was an item of certain revenue, while the profits of a manorial court or a woodsale were casual revenue because they could not be estimated in certainty. The profits of justice,

---

[1] W. Stubbs, *Constitutional History of England*, 4th ed., Oxford, 1898, ii, 541 ff., chapter xvii, 'Royal Prerogative and Parliamentary Authority'.

[2] *The Governance of England*, ed. Charles Plummer, Oxford, 1885, second impression 1926, p. 250.

[3] W. Blackstone, *Commentaries on the Laws of England*, 7th ed., Oxford, 1775, i, 306.

[4] 1 Anne cap. 1, sect. V (An Act for the better Support of Her Majesties Household and of the Honour and Dignity of the Crown).

[5] Fortescue, *Governance*, p. 123.

the issues and profits of escheats, wardships and marriages, the feudal incidents, were casual revenues. On the other hand the proceeds of indirect taxation, in the eyes of a fifteenth-century Treasurer of England, were an item of certain revenue because it was possible to estimate them over a period of three years or so and to strike an average yield for current purposes, while the issues of direct taxation became an item of certain or ordinary revenue for the same reasons, the moment they had been agreed and granted by Parliament. Before that moment in time they had no existence at all. So much then for seventeenth-century political theories as a base for English medieval history.

If we turn to following out the medieval antecedents of the idea that the king should 'live of his own' we are soon confronted by similarly disconcerting facts. No historian has as yet quoted any instances of its use earlier than the Ordinances of 1311. There certainly is a complaint in the seventh ordinance of that year that the young Edward II's foolish grants of all kinds, including lands, to his favourites, were impoverishing the Crown, but, significantly, there is no reference in that context to the king being expected to 'live of his own'. The uses of this phrase actually occur in the fourth and eighth ordinances, in complaints against arbitrary 'prises': seizures of merchandize, cattle, horses, carts, etc., or of forced labour, perpetrated by Edward II's 'purveyors' for the maintenance of his Household. Thus the young king was being asked to stop arbitrarily taking away the livelihood of his subjects in this manner and to begin living on what was legally his, among which, it may be noted, the Ordinances included the proceeds of indirect taxation (the customs revenues). These evils of royal purveyance, a comparatively new grievance it seemed to contemporaries in the early fourteenth century because they dated its beginnings from the reign of Stubbs's hero Edward I, became so insupportable in the early years of Edward III's reign that around 1330 he was threatened with deposition because of them.[6] Thus when the king of England was first implored by his subjects to 'live of his own' they did not have in mind either the squandering of the royal demesne or the burden of parliamentary taxation.

The origins of a sentiment in condemnation of alienation of an English royal patrimony can now be similarly shown to be at variance with Stubbs's ideas. Liebermann, Schramm and others associated the particular recension of the so-called *Laws of Edward the Confessor,* where it first occurred, with the activities of the baronial opposition under King John as designed to limit the power of the Crown. More modern scholarship has now traced it back to devoted royal servants

---

[6] *De Speculo Regis Edward III*, ed. J. Moisant, Paris, 1891. For the correct dating of these tracts see J. Tait, *E[nglish] H[istorical] R[eview]*, xvi (1901), 110-115.

B

at the court of Henry II who were concerned about enabling the King to resume the *iura regis et regni* in general, and the royal castles in particular, which had been lost to baronial opponents during the 'anarchy' of Stephen's reign. The object was thus not to bridle the king, or to restrict *his* power of alienation, but to deprive his opponents of rights acquired by prescription at the Crown's expense during Stephen's reign. Freedom to alienate his patrimony, if he considered it desirable, was an important part of the prerogative of all English kings throughout medieval history.

There are a number of other facts impinging upon the concept of an English royal demesne in the medieval period which almost make one doubt whether it ever existed at all. Indeed, it is not too much to say that the careful researcher, seeking for documentary confirmation of Stubbs's general ideas, finds the whole historical concept of a medieval English royal landed estate crumbling away under his prying eyes. After the Domesday Survey, and until the later fifteenth century, there do not appear to be any surviving records which enable a statement to be compiled of its component parts and geographical extent or of its economic and financial value. There are now dozens of medieval pipe rolls in print and the medieval pipe roll, based on the annual accounts of the sheriffs of the shires, ought to provide such information, or at least give some indication of where it can be found. But all we can discover there are references to the sometime existence of partial lists of some royal manors tallaged, or of manors given away (the *terrae datae*) or of certain manors in hand at certain dates. The surviving records of the great inquiries of 1264 which produced the Hundred Rolls, and of the subsequent, similar inquiry of 1279 show that these inquiries were not inquiries into royal landholding or royal land revenues, but into the usurpation of liberties and franchises and into the misconduct of local officials. The survey of the kingdom in 1316, known as the *Nomina Villarum*, was compiled to facilitate the levying of soldiers for the Scottish wars and, although it applied to the whole kingdom, it cannot be used to pick out and identify a royal demesne. If one turns back to the pipe rolls and their subsidiary documents for an identification of any land revenues whatsoever which reached the Exchequer, one discovers that the identifiable items and amounts consisted entirely of the issues of lands which were only temporarily in the king's hands, accruing to him as a result of an escheat by failure of heirs, or by a forfeiture, by a vacancy in the case of an ecclesiastical tenant-in-chief, or during the minority or idiocy of a lay tenant. Moreover, all such lands, sooner rather than later, disappear from subsequent annual accounts. Indeed, the very terms 'royal demesne', crown lands or crown estates, in the sense in which Stubbs understood them, simply do not occur in the well-known and comprehensive twelfth-century reference book, the survey of exchequer practice entitled the *Dialogus de Scaccario*. The author of that treatise reserved the concept of 'crown lands' for those lands held directly of the king by his tenants-in-chief.[7] Yet the only modern historian who has attempted to write a history of the English royal demesne tells us the very opposite of this: that the concept of medieval royal demesne, essentially a feudal concept, comprised those estates which the king had not sub-infeudated.[8]

Although attempts have been made to estimate the theoretical potential value of the *terra regis* in Domesday Book, no one has yet succeeded in estimating the income which William I received from it. It is known that such income as reached the king from his lands came as part, but only part, of the sheriffs' farms. Those manors which he did not sub-infeudate were committed to the sheriffs for fixed sums. But when information about the total sheriffs' farms does at last appear in the isolated survival of a pipe roll for 1130, and then continuously year by year from 1155, the low total revealed is in startling contrast to the reputed potential value of William I's *terra regis*. This fact constituted the germ of Stubbs's idea of massive and wanton alienation of their substantial royal landed patrimony by our early kings, who were followed along the same path by almost all their successors on the throne who either did not care or could not help themselves. The total theoretical value of these sheriffs' farms, before any allowances or deductions were made, was about £10,000 during the reign of Henry II (1154–1189) and remained unchanged until the thirteenth century. But we must remember that besides the farms paid for royal manors this figure included the proceeds of the sheriffs' jurisdictional activities: the profits of hundred and shire courts, views of frankpledge, castle-ward, sheriff's aid and like payments. Moreover, it has been reliably calculated that in 1169–70 more than £4,500 of this had already to be permanently deducted from the total each year for the *terrae datae* alone, which were a financial write-off to the Exchequer, and by 1200 this deduction had risen to nearly £7,000.[9] Recently a distinguished English medieval historian has suggested that in fact even William I never did receive a huge land revenue on the scale of the Domesday valuation of 1086 and that all he had were shire farms already approaching the much

---

[7] *Dialogus de Scaccario*, ed. and trans. Charles Johnson, London, 1950, p. 96.
[8] R. S. Hoyt, *The Royal Demesne in English Constitutional History*, Ithaca, N.Y., 1950, p. 6.
[9] R. L. Poole, *The Exchequer in the Twelfth Century*, Oxford, 1912, p. 134; W. Parow, *Compotus Vicecomitis: Die Rechenschaftslegung des Sheriffs unter Heinrich II von England*, Berlin, 1906, pp. 27, 49; J. H. Ramsay, *A History of the Revenues of the Kings of England 1066-1399*, Oxford, 1925, i, 233.

lower scale of 1130 and subsequent dates.[10] These are some of the very perplexing problems in the way of writing any coherent, continuous history of a royal demesne in English government before 1461, if we persist in interpreting that earlier history in terms of government finance and constitutional opposition to the Crown, in the traditional and still generally accepted Stubbsian manner.

Paradoxically enough the only identifiable impact made on the records of central government by any concept of an English royal demesne in the early and high Middle Ages seems to have been in the records of taxation, its contribution to what modern historians designate the 'extraordinary' revenues of the Crown. There can be no doubt that kings of England and their advisers, at least from Henry II and probably earlier, whenever they wished to increase their royal revenues, concentrated almost all their energies and ingenuity on taxing their subjects. One of the brightest jewels in William I's English Crown was the geld which he inherited from his Anglo-Saxon predecessors. Scutage, a Norman tax levied in lieu of military service, was a valuable new additional tax from those holding land by military tenure. It appears to have been Henry I and his advisers who conceived the bright idea of levying a further special tax on the increasingly prosperous towns of his realm who held their land not by military service, but by burgage or socage tenure. To some extent in 1164–5 and generally throughout the realm in 1167–8, Henry II extended this further special tax from the towns to other lands which were not liable for scutage, i.e. to other lands held by socage or burgage tenure.[11] Such lands were all the manors then in the king's hands, including those which he had by escheat, through failure of heirs, or by forfeiture or during minority. These appear to have been the fiscal developments which first brought the concept of a royal demesne into the records of English government as consisting of areas liable to a special tax called tallage, which became one of the most valuable financial assets of the Angevin kings. Certain privileges accrued to those who paid it; indeed certain tenants on this 'royal demesne' began to develop a special form of tenure which lawyers, with their love of precedent, began to call 'tenure in ancient demesne' in the later twelfth and thirteenth century. They also began to establish its legal authenticity by reference back to the *terra regis* of Domesday. Even in the later twelfth and thirteenth centuries legal fact and historical fact could thus already be two quite different things. Tenure in ancient demesne thus became a legal concept inseparably attached to lands which had been part of the *terra regis* in Domesday Book,

[10] R. W. Southern, 'The Place of Henry I in English History', *Proceedings of the British Academy*, xlviii (1963), 164–9.

[11] C. Stephenson, *Borough and Town*, Cambridge, Mass., 1933, p. 163.

quite irrespective of whether the king still held them or not, or irrespective of who had held them in the meantime.[12]

Hence from the late twelfth to the early fourteenth century, when kings ultimately ceased to levy tallage, there was a royal demesne which was a fiscal concept identifiable as towns or manors liable to this tax. Although they might pass out of the king's hands, certain lands thus remained subject to a special fiscal liability to him unless the king chose to grant this liability away together with the grant of the land concerned. He could reserve his right to continue exacting tallage from such lands if he wished, even when he granted them away. On the other hand his new acquisitions of land did not in future become liable to tallage by the mere fact of passing under the king's direct control. This distinction is not clearly discernable in the records until 1307,[13] by which time the very idea of tallage was almost obsolete because it was by then being merged in the newer, much more remunerative and convenient system of national taxation levied through Parliament. From 1336, a royal demesne in England, in so far as it existed at all, was thus identifiable only as a separate section of the taxation roll which never varied in composition thereafter and was liable to pay the standard tax on movable property at the higher rate of one-tenth, when the shires in general paid at the rate of one-fifteenth.[14]

We must therefore beware of accepting, as explanations of our medieval history, rationalizations made of it by seventeenth and eighteenth-century politicians and adopted by respectable nineteenth-century constitutional historians. We must also view with scepticism any modern views of a medieval English 'royal demesne' as a royal landed estate existing continuously from 1066. The Norman Conquest of 1066 covered the whole of England, and the new kings proceeded to rule the country through one system of 'undifferentiated government'.[15] Logically if we are to speak of an English royal demesne from 1066 in the same sense as the Capetian *domaine* of the French kings, then the term should be applied to the whole realm of England. This is not to say that kings of England from 1066 did not possess and own any land which was not enfeoffed by military service to tenants-in-chief. But Domesday Book represents one point in time of a process of distribution and redistribution which was never ending.

[12] Hoyt, *The Royal Demesne*, pp. 192-207.
[13] Hoyt, 'Royal Demesne, Parliamentary Taxation and the Realm', *Speculum*, xxiii (1948), 65.
[14] For the taxation roll see J. F. Willard, *Parliamentary Taxes on Personal Property 1290 to 1334*, Cambridge, Mass., 1934, pp. 12-13, 71 and references given there.
[15] The phrase is Professor Hoyt's in *The Royal Demesne*, p. 102.

The continuous history of the crown lands or crown estate in England up to 1460 can only be written, if it can be written at all, as a history, not of royal finance, but of royal patronage. This reservoir of lands, constantly emptying as the king fulfilled his obligations to his own family, to the Church, to his servants and agents whom he chose to honour, reward, or bind to his service, was also being constantly replenished: by the operations of feudal law, by forfeiture of estates because of disloyalty towards the king which was ultimately to constitute the crime of treason, and, on occasion, by royal purchase. These royal lands and the income derived from them were thus only subject to residual and intermittent financial control by the Exchequer. This office always had the herculean task of identification and account in this respect; of seeing that the king received every penny that was due to him from whatever rents, farms and casual land revenues happened to be in his hands at any one time, and which had not been already disposed of in fees, wages or pensions. But the significance of the ever changing English royal landed patrimony, throughout most of the Middle Ages, lay primarily in the political, military and social functions it performed for the king through the agency of those of his subjects who enjoyed its revenues, rather than in its residual financial importance to him.

The medieval English Exchequer therefore was not a land revenue office or a central financial court or treasury of a royal demesne comparable to the French *chambre des comptes*. The Norman, Angevin and Plantagenet kings of England up to 1460 did not have any such office and do not appear to have felt the need for one. By contrast, when we turn to considering the organization of a crown landed estate between 1461 and 1536, we find that what we are describing was indeed a consolidated landed estate controlled from a central, royal land revenue office which was both treasury and financial court, operating from the king's Chamber. This is not to say that chamber finance was an entirely new phenomenon in the history of English government from 1461. Indeed, cogent arguments have recently been put forward for believing that the Chamber, not the Exchequer, was already normally the central and controlling financial organ of English government in the twelfth century.[16] But all those periods of earlier chamber financial activity before 1461 which have so far been reasonably well documented are revealed, with one brief exception, as drawing their revenues almost completely from the same proceeds of taxation as financed the medieval Exchequer. Recent investigations into the activities of Henry II's and John's Chamber have confirmed this, and the older accounts of Tout show it

---

[16] H. G. Richardson and G. O. Sayles, *The Governance of Medieval England from the Conquest to Magna Carta*, Edinburgh, 1963, p. 239.

to have been true for the reigns of Henry III and Edward I, most of Edward III's reign and for the reign of Richard II. The sole possible exception was in the last few years of the reign of Edward II, the very reign which Stubbs regarded as the worst example of wanton squandering of the royal demesne since that of Stephen.

From 1322 there was indeed a permanent reservation of some fifty units of land, the biggest one being the lordship of Burstwick in Holderness worth 1,000 marks a year and the smallest ones being single manor units, which were all administered direct from the king's Chamber. Besides the local farmers and bailiffs, a central staff of receivers, surveyors and auditors was built up to control, visit, audit and develop these estates to the king's maximum financial profit.[17] The experiment had only four brief years of orderly development before Edward II was deposed and his chamber estate was appropriated almost in its entirety by Queen Isabella for her personal use. Its partial revival from 1333 by the young Edward III proved to be on a smaller scale and again the chamber lands began to disappear, albeit this time more gradually, as the new royal family grew in number and as Edward III proved lavish in his generosity towards boon companions and helpers in his great enterprise, the conquest of France. Whether or not the advisers of Edward IV were aware of this earlier brief fourteenth-century precedent for a royal land revenue office in the Chamber is not known.

A quite new consolidation of English and Welsh estates in the hands of the English royal family began to emerge from the early thirteenth century with the shrinking of that wider 'family estate of the Plantagenets',[18] the continental Angevin Empire. It was from this point that large-scale seigniorial units of administration were first created which can still be identified in the books of the Tudor Court of General Surveyors. The first was the county of Cornwall (1227), later an earldom and then a duchy from the fourteenth century. Next came the county palatine and earldom of Chester (1246) to which the Statute of Wales (1284) added Flintshire, all declared to be inalienably settled on the king's eldest son from 1333, with remainder to his heirs as kings of England. The royal county and honour of Lancaster was augmented by the forfeited de Montfort lands in 1265 and by the forfeited Ferrers lands in the following year. Further increased by various royal gifts to John of Gaunt and then again by his son's Bohun marriage, this vast Lancastrian inheritance returned to the crown at the Lancastrian usurpation of 1399. The whole principality of Wales, which was united to England in 1284, was given

[17] T. F. Tout, *Chapters in the Administrative History of England*, ii. 314-60.
[18] J. Le Patourel, 'The Plantagenet Dominions', *History*, L (1965), 289-308.

intact to the king's eldest son by charter in 1301 and must thus be included in this 'family estate'. There is no doubt that these family aquisitions were acts of deliberate policy by Henry III and Edward I. Seven of the comital families of England found their lands reduced for the benefit of the royal family by Edward I, who manipulated the laws of inheritance to achieve his ends at the expense of collateral heirs.[19] Edward III was only continuing this process when he added to the existing patrimony of his eldest son (the principality of Wales and the earldom of Chester) the rich estates of the duchy of Cornwall, on the death of his brother John of Eltham without heirs of his body. What was probably the first undoubted reference to the broad acres of the crown estate in a claim for a reduction of parliamentary taxation came when the early death of the Black Prince put his son Richard of Bordeaux on the throne at the tender age of ten. The Commons in the young Richard II's Parliament refused to believe in the professed poverty of his government because, they said, they knew he had inherited all his father's lands.[20]

It was a second accident of history, the usurpation of 1399, which gave England a Lancastrian king whose accumulated landed patrimony was certainly the greatest of any English king since William I had had his *terra regis* set out in the Domesday Book in 1086. This usurpation produced a unique time of severe political and financial crisis for the English monarchy, and it happened that the new king, Henry IV, had no queen, nor any sons as yet old or reliable enough to be given large endowments of land. Thus, whenever he met his Parliaments in the first few years of his reign with demands for immediate financial assistance for his shaky throne, almost invariably they raised counter demands that he should first mobilize his own evidently huge and unique landed resources effectively in furtherance of his usurped duty to provide the realm with 'good and abundant governance'. In 1404 the alleged financial resources of the crown landed estate were clearly associated, probably for the first time, with the plea for government solvency, economy and respect for private property which fourteenth-century parliaments had from time to time expressed in the slogan 'the king should live of his own'.[21] The parliamentary knights in Henry IV's Parliaments were thus not clamouring for an ancient, outmoded and impracticable medieval constitutional ideal, as Stubbs would have us believe. They were continuing to condemn the traditional 'outrageous prises' of Henry IV's household purveyors which deprived them of their 'own', just as the Ordainers had similarly

---

[19] K. B. McFarlane, 'Had Edward I a "Policy" Towards the Earls?', *History*, L (1965), 145-59

[20] *Rot[uli] Parl[iamentorum]*, iii, 35 (no. 18).

[21] *ibid.*, iii, 547-9.

complained a hundred years previously; but they were now also drawing attention to the very unusual personal landed wealth of the new king and adapting old criticisms of government insolvency to new circumstances.

By 1404, English kings had in fact, time out of mind, financed the government of the realm by the exercise of their political right to command the goods and labour of their subjects and to tax their substance in direct and indirect taxation. They had called the Parliament of their realm into existence primarily to further this aim. New taxes designed to follow changes in the distribution of wealth among their subjects had repeatedly been devised to replace old and welltried, but declining ones. The fourteenth century had seen the heyday of an astonishing exploitation of national wealth for royal purposes through indirect taxes, notably the taxation of the wool trade. Now the very Parliaments which were pressing Henry IV to devote his allegedly substantial land revenues to the upkeep of his royal Household and other expenses were themselves being pressed to sanction yet a new tax, a graduated tax on incomes from land which was to be the origin of the later Tudor subsidy.

Fifteenth-century civil servants were just as ingenious as their predecessors in devising new taxes, but the Lancastrian period was also to be notable in the history of English government finance for the first attempt of a powerful public opinion, acting through the Commons in Parliament, to compel the king to develop a substantial and permanent crown landed estate able to make a permanent and reliable contribution towards government solvency. Henry IV himself was in fact able to shrug off the demands of his Commons once he had eliminated his rebels and opponents. His son, Henry V, managed to swamp criticism in the splendid surge of patriotic fervour which followed his conquest of France. But his infant successor, Henry VI, grew up to be by far the least able of all the kings of the Norman and Angevin line, a king who paralysed and confused the whole process of English government with a royal irresponsibility and inanity which had no precedent. The final losing stages of the Hundred Years War brought his government to complete, if temporary, financial and political bankruptcy. In 1450 his rebellious subjects murdered both the Treasurer of England and the king's chief minister, the duke of Suffolk; while his Parliaments of 1450 and 1451, backed by the authority of his most powerful subject, the duke of York, were able to compel him to revoke by solemn legislation all the grants of royal lands and revenues ever made by him, or in his name, since his accession in 1422.

The first five documents in this collection are designed to show the significance and importance which contemporaries attached to the efficient creation and maintenance of a substantial royal landed estate in the years immediately prior to 1455, the point at which some of the nobility of England finally decided that the kingdom could only be rescued on the battlefield from the consequences of Henry VI's kingship. The prominence of the crown estate in the struggles of the political arena round about 1450 was nevertheless, as previously in 1404, partly fortuitous. The infant Henry VI had been surrounded by an unusually numerous circle of near relatives who had absorbed almost all the landed resources of the monarchy in their personal endowments. Contemporaries did not normally object to this; indeed the Parliament of 1404 had urged Henry IV to endow his family more adequately. But by 1447 all Henry VI's relatives were dead, except for his young and alien queen and two half brothers who were minors. The two Lancastrian Queens dowager, Joan of Navarre and Catherine of Valois, had both died in 1437. His uncles Clarence, Bedford and Gloucester had died in 1421, 1435 and 1447 respectively. His great uncle Cardinal Henry Beaufort had also died in 1447. Between his coming of age in 1437 and 1449, Henry VI had alienated the spate of family lands, which thus came into his hands, outside the circle of the princes of the royal blood to an extent which was probably without any precedent in English history. In addition, almost the whole of the income from any royal lands which still remained in his hands was firmly in the grasp of members of his Household. A queen of England in the fifteenth century was considered to be entitled to an income of 10,000 marks from landed estate. When Queen Margaret reached England in 1445 there were virtually no lands available for her endowment.

Sir John Fortescue, the Lord Chief Justice of the King's Bench from 1442, and a member of the Council, was a devoted Lancastrian servant. Nevertheless, the sentiments of critics of Henry VI's policies in the 1440s were expressed at length in his *Governance of England* (Doc. 1). This work is alleged to have been finally presented to Edward IV sometime between 1471 and 1476, but numerous modifications and inconsistencies reveal that the text must by then have already passed through several recensions. The malaise of English government which it describes really fits only the 1440s. Fortescue's solution was a resumption of royal grants, the establishment of a substantial royal demesne, and an effective royal Council to control royal grants in the future. Should all this still prove insufficient then he felt it would be the duty of Parliament to sanction a new form of taxation on the model of the sales taxes or excise duties then current in France and Burgundy, which gave those rulers their financial strength, in order to enable the king to 'live of his own'. The undesirability of this latter course, if it could not be avoided, would be mitigated to some extent if the tax was enacted by consent in Parliament, a peculiarly happy and uniquely English device, according to Fortescue, and not arbitrarily imposed as it had been in those other two countries.

If, indeed, *faute de mieux*, the aged Lancastrian statesman did ultimately present this treatise to the Yorkist king, then Edward IV must have found it a compound of stale and misdirected advice by 1471. By that date, starting in 1450, there had already been at least six parliamentary acts of resumption enacted (e.g. Docs. 3, 9). Edward had long since instituted new policies towards the crown estates and the royal finances, along the lines desired by the earlier critics of Lancastrian rule (Docs. 6, 7, 8). As for the institution of an effective Council to control royal patronage, no king worthy of the name could submit to effective conciliar control and no Council could ever be a substitute for right-minded and effective kingship. An efficient Council depends on an effective, purposeful direction of affairs from the throne, and Fortescue's conciliar proposals, which were impracticable before the deposition of Henry VI, became superfluous with the accession of Edward IV.

In 1467 Edward IV personally addressed the Commons in Parliament on his plans to 'live of his own' (Doc. 8). What he meant by this will be discussed in the third section of this introduction, but the few Lancastrian documents at the beginning of this collection are important pointers to his policies. In the crisis of 1450 Henry VI's government was moved to sanction a detailed annual appropriation of specific items of revenue totalling over £11,000, much of it secured on resumed royal lands, to mitigate the burden which the maintenance of his Household imposed on his subjects (Doc. 4). After successfully sabotaging the first act of resumption in 1450, his government were also compelled by his next Parliament, who were supported by Richard duke of York, to allow an effective act of resumption which rendered void and resumed almost all grants of lands and revenues made by Henry since he came of age. The outcome to some extent justified Fortescue's hopes, but also confirmed his underlying fears. Government became rather less indigent thereby, as the receipt rolls of the Exchequer for 1451 and 1452 demonstrate, but the chief beneficiaries of the resumption were the queen, the king's two Tudor half-brothers and, subsequently, the infant Lancastrian prince of Wales, some of whose hereditary patrimony had been alienated by his father.

The revenues of a resumed royal demesne proved woefully insufficient to secure financial stability, but just before the king went mad in 1453 a grateful Parliament nevertheless gave him one of the largest grants of direct and indirect taxation of the later middle ages, although this was in traditional form and included no sales taxes. Document 5 illustrates how the Lancastrian sheriffs, the most important political and military agents of central government in the shires, the local executants of the king's commands without whom his writ could not run, and also the Exchequer's principal financial agents and sole debt collectors, were having to be excused their financial duties and released from all the age-old rigours of Exchequer accounting. Only by such concessions could men now be persuaded to serve in the vital tasks of preserving the elements of law and royal authority. These were some of the problems which the Yorkist usurpation of 1461 placed squarely on the shoulders of Edward IV. He was thus committed beforehand, by the events of 1450 and 1455, to certain policies and actions. In order to provide the 'good governance' for which the country clamoured he was committed to a policy of 'living of his own'. This policy was no centuries-old ideal of medieval government which it was becoming increasingly impossible to realize, but a comparatively new programme of political action which public opinion hoped to see achieved in the House of York.

The crown lands in Lancastrian and Early Tudor government: comparisons and contrasts

THE changes which the Yorkist kings and Henry VII made in the organization and functions of their landed resources reached their maximum impact by 1509, and began to decline in importance between 1509 and 1536 with a return to more traditional ways of augmenting revenues under the young Henry VIII and Cardinal Wolsey. The following three sections of the Introduction describe these changes chronologically between 1461 and 1536 from the documentary sources. This section is devoted to a comparative description of the nature, composition, extent and uses made of the crown lands before the onset of these changes and afterwards at the height of their effectiveness.

The terms 'crown lands' and 'royal demesne' are normally reserved by English historians to designate those royal lands which our medieval kings did not 'sub-infeudate', i.e. grant away to tenants-in-chief in return for some kind of military service. In historians' parlance they are thus fundamentally distinguished from that separate major category of lands held of the Crown by tenants-in-chief who held their lands in return for the incidents of feudal tenure, namely the provision of a customary amount of aid to the king, either in cash or in kind, on certain customary occasions, the payment of customary reliefs or entry fines when an heir took possession of his inheritance, and the royal enjoyment of the profits of the estate during the minority of the heir, which included the sale of the marriages of the widow and the wards.

But students of later-medieval England will find that the records of fourteenth and fifteenth-century government, whether written in Latin, Norman French or English, preserve little evidence of the current use of the term 'royal demesne' or any equivalent term in this special tenurial sense. When references were made to a royal landed estate in this period, either in the normal course of government business or in political controversy, it was only as part of wider concepts such as the king's livelihood, the king's patrimony, his hereditaments, the issues of his kingdom or 'his own'. Within such concepts were also comprehended those estates which had passed into the king's hands absolutely, through the death of a tenant-in-chief without any legal heir qualified to inherit other than the king, through forfeiture for treason until any rightful heir might recover them by due process of law or special royal favour, through absolute gift to the king, or through purchase by him. Equally considered to be part of 'his own' were all hereditary feudal incidents, all vacant ecclesiastical temporalities, all sheriffs' farms, all profits of justice, all fees exacted for government services such as the drafting, sealing and enrolling of documents, and all issues and profits which legally belonged to the king at any given moment of time, even the issues of indirect and direct taxation.

This was the result of several centuries of 'undifferentiated government' in England since 1066, in the course of which all royal resources were harnessed to royal needs at the king's discretion and convenience, subject only to the observation of the legal rights of his subjects in those spheres where they were able to enforce them. The income from landed estates which the Crown had at its disposal included feefarms or perpetual reserved rents, farms or fixed sums payable annually for a lease made for a term of years or for one or more lives (the farmer concerned being normally a middleman, not the actual tenant of the soil), and the actual rents, together with the casual revenues such as entry fines, woodsales and profits of courts, in cases where no intermediary farmer existed and where the Crown administered its lands and collected their issues through officials only, such as receivers, keepers or bailiffs. No distinction was made in the royal administration between lands held by the king absolutely and lands which came temporarily into his hands during minority of heirs, except that any bargain struck with a farmer or purchaser of wards' lands was for the duration of the minority only and subject to customary conventions to prevent disparagement of heirs or the waste of the lands concerned.

The income from landed estate at the king's disposal was normally preferred primarily for the maintenance of members of the royal family, secondarily for royal patronage, that is for the maintenance and reward of those royal servants and agents of government whom the king wished to reward or felt constrained to reward, and, finally, to make a residual contribution to the national finances. At no time during the later Middle Ages was the primary claim of the royal family upon the king's landed resources questioned, but their use for purposes of patronage was increasingly challenged at times of weak government and financial difficulties. At such times, for example in the earliest years of the fifteenth century and in the later 1440s, powerful agitation developed, centred on the Commons in Parliament, to ensure that such resources made an increased contribution to the national expenses, most notably to the maintenance of the king's Household, the power-house and show-piece of medieval government (Doc. 4).

The king's landed estate was not the mere attenuated demesne of William the Conqueror. As the reservoir of lands was depleted by the needs of the royal family and the demands of patronage, so it was replenished from many sources. The gradual, purposeful acquisition and consolidation of certain great complexes of estates to meet the needs of the English royal family from the early thirteenth century has already been mentioned. Lands granted to queens for life ultimately returned to the Crown and became available for disposal once more. During the thirteenth and fourteenth centuries the lands of the earldom of Chester, the principality of Wales and the duchy of Cornwall became the inalienable patrimony of the king's eldest son and heir, although a feckless king like Henry VI was able to make appreciable inroads even on these by his wanton distribution of royal patronage. Endowments made for royal uncles or younger sons, normally entailed on their legitimate heirs with remainder to the king, could be and were intended to be permanent alienations. Nevertheless spreading royal family trees were rare and such estates often returned ultimately to the Crown. The most outstanding example of the return of former royal lands to the Crown, however, resulted not from the accidents of birth and death but from the usurpation of Henry of Lancaster in 1399. This event brought in not only the huge estates of the duchy of Lancaster but also half the possessions of Henry's father-in-law Humphrey de Bohun earl of Essex, Hereford and Northampton which he held by right of his wife by courtesy of England during his life and which vested in his son Henry V on his death. The further similar usurpation of Edward IV in 1461 brought in the broad estates of the duchy of York and earldom of March which had not previously been in royal possession.

A brief consideration of specific examples of other types of acquisition from the thirteenth to the fifteenth centuries will illustrate the various ways by which the royal reservoir of lands was being constantly replenished. Sometimes landowners deemed it necessary to demise lands to the king so that they might have the undisturbed disposition of the rest of their estates, and in such cases the relative degrees of voluntary surrender or compulsion can now be very hard to determine. For example, in 1293 the dowager countess of Aumale,

Isabella de Redvers, appears to have alienated her birthright to Edward I for a mere pittance. Because the feoffees or trustees of Juliana de Leybourne countess of Huntingdon gave a remainder interest to the king when securing her life interest in 1362, many manors in Kent, Sussex and Hampshire became royal property at her death. One of the most valuable of later-medieval royal acquisitions was the county and lordship of Pembroke, with the lordships of Tenby, Cilgerran and Ystlwyf, which was settled on Edward III and his heirs in remainder by John Hastings earl of Pembroke when he married the king's daughter Margaret. All these lands came to the crown when Hastings's son was mortally wounded while practising for a royal tournament in 1389. The extensive lands of the earldom of Richmond, which had been held intermittently by the counts and dukes of Brittany since the early twelfth century, were apparently seized by Henry IV in 1399 and, after a quarter of a century in the hands of the Nevilles by his grant, came back once more into royal hands in 1425 to be held by the Lancastrians, Yorkists and Tudors.

Again the king might be given lands. In 1363 John de Cobham granted Edward III thirteen manors and later left the whole of his lands to the king out of affection for the Black Prince. The land of royal officials might be confiscated when they fell into debt or disgrace; lands could be forfeited for treason; kings could buy land. In 1327 Edward III paid 10,000 marks from a parliamentary grant to have the lands of Robert of Montalt settled in remainder on Queen Isabella, John of Eltham and his heirs and himself and his heirs respectively. Two years later the queen bought out the life interest of Robert's widow with a pension of £400 *per annum* and later compensated the collateral heir.[1] In 1418 Henry V bought the lordship of Chirk and Chirklands from his grandmother Joan de Bohun for 4,000 marks. By contrast Henry VI sold this considerable estate outright to Cardinal Beaufort twenty years later, an act which subsequently incurred the extreme censure of his Lord Chief Justice, Sir John Fortescue, in his *Governance of England* (Doc. 1).

The sixteenth-century dissolution of the monasteries was not the first occasion on which extensive church lands passed permanently into the hands of the Crown. The lands of the Temple were first confiscated in 1308. Although in theory they ultimately passed to the Hopitallers, in fact the Hospital of St John was forced to alienate some of them to the Crown, the best known of these being the valuable lordship of Burstwick in Holderness. Alien priory lands, the lands of religious houses owing allegiance to foreign abbeys, were first taken

---

[1] These lands were the manors and lordships of Mold, Hawarden, Lea, Bosley, Neston, Walton-on-Trent, Cheylesmore, Castle Rising, Snettisham, Kenninghall, Kessingland and Framsden.

into the king's hands from 1295 to 1303. While the English church profited and conventual priories were excluded from the final confiscation of 1414, a considerable amount of land was nevertheless placed at the king's disposal from this source for very long periods.

The king of England was 'the presumptive heir of the whole short-lived race of feudal tenantry',[2] and various statues, whether by accident or design, assisted the royal acquisition of land: *Quia Emptores* by multiplying the number of tenants-in-chief, *De Donis* by consolidating estates into a limited (normally tail male) succession, and *Mortmain*, which imposed a heavy embargo on alienations to the Church, useful to the king as a bargaining counter.[3] He could waive or give away his rights, but he could not be easily cheated. It is impossible to trace here in detail the chequered history of even a fraction of the lands which were crown lands in Lancastrian England. The history of the manor of Wadley and Wicklesham (Berks.) was perhaps not untypical of many smaller cases. In 1364 when Richard de Pembridge wished to entail this manor, said to be held in chief of the king, he gave the remainder to Edward III and his heirs. Eleven years later Pembridge's heirs failed, and it passed into royal hands. Later it was alienated to the Talbots but it came back yet again to the Crown. Henry V then bestowed it on the Erpinghams and, after yet another reversion to the Crown, on the Porters.

The history of the crown lands in the later Middle Ages is thus principally recorded, not in the records of the Exchequer, which enjoyed only a residual financial interest in them, but in the king's grants as enrolled in the records of Chancery on the Charter, Patent and Fine Rolls. No consolidated record of acquisitions exists, but the origins of lands granted out can be discovered piecemeal from the inquisitions *post mortem* and the miscellaneous inquisitions of the Chancery which recorded the routine processes of inquiry by which the king's rights to lands and property were discovered and established in law. But it happens that in 1450 and 1451 the Exchequer was called upon to carry out special inquiries through the sheriffs and escheators of the shires, the equivalent officers in the corporate towns, the chamberlains of North and South Wales, and the Warden of the Cinque Ports, into all royal grants made during Henry VI's reign which could possibly have occasioned any financial loss to the Crown. These inquiries rested on the authority of two parliamentary acts of resumption (Doc. 3) which initatied a long series of such acts of Parliament continuing throughout the period covered by these docu-

---

[2] Hubert Hall, *The Red Book of the Exchequer* (Rolls Series), iii. p. cccxi.
[3] This legislation of the late 13th century is discussed in T. F. T. Plucknett's book *The Legislation of Edward I* (Oxford, 1949).

ments.[4] The sheriffs and the other royal agents concerned held a series of inquisitions at which panels of jurors, selected for their local knowledge, made verbal depositions on the basis of which written returns were sent to the Exchequer where they were checked against the results of searches made in the central records and the results engrossed on parchment. These two acts were not concerned to resume grants of offices unless they had been newly created, or granted in perpetuity, or given increased remuneration since 1422. Only 19 examples of such offices were discovered by the returns made to the 1450 act, as opposed to 40 cases of annuities granted and 149 outright, comprehensive grants of lands, properties, privileges and franchises for life or in fee (freehold or entailed), some with reserved rents or farms, but many with no financial return secured for the Crown.[5] These grants ranged in size from huge lordships to single manors and to single houses in a London street. The returns made to the 1451 act, passed to supplement the 1450 act, produced details of 7 offices, 52 annuities and 151 outright comprehensive grants for life or in fee.[6]

A grant of an estate from the Crown might well include all the following: all fines, ransoms[7] and amercements of tenants, issues forfeit and things pertaining to the king from wastes of a year and a day[8] and from forfeitures and murders, chattels of felons, fugitives, outlaws and persons condemned, return and execution of writs, knights' fees, advowsons, wards, marriages, escheats, forests, chases, parks, woods, warrens, fairs, markets, waters, ways, fisheries, commons, assarts, wastes, purprestures, courts, views of frankpledge, hundreds, wapentakes, wreck, waif, royal fishes, liberties, royalties and free customs. The control and appointment of all officers on the estates concerned would also henceforth normally be a matter for the grantees concerned, and not the king.

As the jurors found in 1450 and 1451 it was often impossible to value the king's grants, and even where they did so the Exchequer, by

[4] The political significance and effectiveness of the Lancastrian acts is discussed in my article 'Acts of Resumption in the Lancastrian Parliaments, 1399-1456', *E.H.R.*, lxxiii (1958), 583-613.

[5] P[ublic] R[ecord] O[ffice], Exchequer, Pipe Office, Sheriffs' Accounts of Seizures, E. 379/175.

[6] P.R.O., Exchequer, Lord Treasurer's Remembrancer's Office, Escheators' Accounts, E. 357/41.

[7] Fines assessed in the royal courts according to a man's ability to pay without damaging his means of livelihood.

[8] Waste in this sense meant anything which did lasting damage to the freehold or inheritance; damage to houses, gardens, trees, etc. A year and a day was the maximum time within which a tenant had to be formally admitted to his tenancy. If a tenant committed a felony his land escheated to the king who had the right to waste it for a year and a day.

searching its records, produced some widely differing valuations in a number of cases, based on earlier extents by inquisition at higher rates, which it considered to be of superior validity. The surviving returns to these two acts of resumption do not quite cover the whole country.[9] Nevertheless there is no doubt that they did comprehend a major part of all the landed resources available to the Crown between 1422 and 1451 and, while it is impossible now to put a total financial value upon them, they do give powerful support to the views of the authors of the acts of resumption that the annual cash income which the king was receiving from crown lands on the eve of these acts was almost negligible (Doc. 3).

Throughout the later Middle Ages stable organizations of professional officers under the central control of receivers-general, chamberlains and stewards administered and controlled certain great royal fiefs which constituted the patrimony reserved for the king's eldest son. Also from time to time large complexes of estates were placed in the hands of professional receivers for other members of the royal family. But the rest of the crown lands were disposed of by petition to the king who made such grants as he deemed appropriate to the petitioners. Periods of maximum activity in this respect occurred whenever a queen died and her estate was broken up or when a powerful and well endowed royal uncle died without legitimate heirs of his body, like Humphrey duke of Gloucester in 1447. The disposal of this patronage was one of the most important of the king's prerogatives, the principal means by which able men were attracted to royal service and retained and rewarded for their loyalty and industry. At periods of strong and effective kingship, when other infinitely more productive sources of revenue were available to meet the financial needs of government, no serious criticism of this use of the crown lands was heard. Stubbs, who was struck both by the unusually lavish grants of one of the most successful of all medieval kings, Edward III, and by the lack of contemporary criticism of him in this respect, could only comment that the popular Edward III had thus made the nation accomplices in his imprudence. The material rewards for government service in the Council, in administration and justice, in military affairs and diplomacy could be very great, crowned with entry to the evolving English peerage or with elevation within its increasing number of ranks. Henry VI created nine baronies by letters patent between 1441 and 1449 and five earls, two marquises and five dukes within the same period. Permanent landed estates able to pro-

---

[9] There are no returns for the 1450 act for Cheshire, Durham, Lancashire, Leicestershire, Warwickshire, and North Wales. There are no returns for the 1451 act for Cheshire, Dover and the Cinque Ports, Durham, Lancashire, Norfolk, Suffolk and North Wales.

duce an income commensurate with his status and dignity were essential to a fifteenth-century royal servant, whether he was a humble king's esquire, a king's knight, or a duke; and his stake in the countryside, if not inherited or acquired by marriage, was most usually carved out of crown lands and endowments, the supply of which was being constantly replenished from the sources outlined above.

Unfortunately Henry VI dispensed his patronage with a lack of prudence, royal control or purpose unique among English kings. As one of his contemporaries, Abbot Wheathampstead of St Albans, who knew him well, put it, he was accustomed to ask not what does this man deserve, but what is it fitting for a king to give. His period of personal rule also culminated in a general collapse of government authority, in armed rebellion in the South Eastern counties, and in crushing military disasters in France. Alleged misuse of the king's patrimony enjoyed by 'guilty men' then became a central issue of politics as expounded in the preambles to the acts of resumption of 1450 and 1451 (Doc. 3).

Sir John Fortescue's *Governance of England* was in essence a plea to create an inalienable royal landed estate by a fundamental reversal of traditional policies. The purpose was to relieve the financial necessities of the Crown and to make the king a greater landowner than any of his subjects. In this way the king would cease to be undermighty and the problem of the overmighty subject would no longer exist (Doc. 1). An effective act of resumption was to be the first essential step; royal service was henceforth to be rewarded and paid for only by the fees and wages of office or by annuities. The king had hundreds of offices scattered all over the country on royal estates which, if properly disposed, could in themselves constitute an immense source of royal power and prestige. Grants of lands, if made at all, should be made only for terms of years or for life. The whole process was to be supervised by the royal Council, appointed and instructed under elaborate rules and precautions. The authors of the acts of resumption also thought along very similar lines. They, too, wanted an inalienable crown estate. They also wanted the process of initiating all grants of land and properties removed from the Signet Office and put under the control of a special committee of the Council. Their aim was to ensure that leases of crown lands were finalized in the Exchequer on the basis of competitive offers.

These plans for reform may seem superficially compelling. But they left out of consideration the personality and ability of the king who would have to preside over their execution, and they also showed no appreciation whatsoever of the dangers inherent in arbitrarily restricting the king's vital prerogative to alienate and dispose of his lands and properties at his supreme discretion. Nevertheless, both Fortescue and the authors of the Lancastrian acts of resumption had posed some fundamental problems of government which the Yorkist kings and Henry VII and their advisers had to face.

Before turning to a survey of the organization and functions of the crown lands in 1509, some estimate of the actual financial yield under Lancastrian rule of sources of royal revenue other than taxation, including the crown lands, is desirable for purposes of comparison. A less controversial and more normal period than the extreme crisis years of 1450 and 1451 ought perhaps to be selected, and in any case suitable information is only available for one particular year throughout the whole Lancastrian period. The Lancastrian Exchequer was in the habit of producing frequent, possibly annual, estimates of royal financial needs and resources for consideration by the Council and fragments of several of these do survive in the council minutes. But in 1433 one of them was engrossed in its entirety on the rolls of Parliament at the express demand of the Treasurer of England.[10] There is scope for much argument whether or not this was a typical year considering revenue and expenditure as a whole,[11] but it does seem to have been a fairly average year as regards the sources of revenue with which we are for the moment especially concerned. The reasons why Ralph lord Cromwell, the Treasurer, insisted on the production of this estimate in Parliament and on its full enrolment for his own protection were twofold. In the first place he was faced with an acute crisis of priority of assignment. That is the demands being made upon him from all sides for allocation of revenue sources to meet the government's obligations could not possibly all be met at once, and he required a firm council directive backed by the authority of Parliament as to who should be first paid and who should have to wait. Secondly, he realized that the only satisfactory solution to the acute shortage of cash would be the grant of a customary tenth and fifteenth in direct taxation by Parliament which would in itself be sufficient to balance revenue and expenditure for the moment and to make a contribution towards paying off the royal debts.[12] Giving Parliament the figures was thought to be the best method of driving this home.

Cromwell's statement did not include any direct taxation of which the last previous grant had been half a tenth and fifteenth in the previous year, presumably already entirely disposed of. Indirect taxation, averaged over the previous three years, was estimated to con-

---

[10] *Rot. Parl.*, iv, 432-9.
[11] This is discussed by J. L. Kirby in 'The Issues of the Lancastrian Exchequer and Lord Cromwell's Estimates of 1433', *Bulletin of the Institute of Historical Research*, xxiv (1951), 121-51.
[12] W. Stubbs, *Constitutional History of England*, iii, 121.

tribute £31,000 out of a gross total of £54,000 and £27,000 out of a net total of £36,000. Other revenues (gross £23,000, net £9,000)[13] included £938 gross and £903 net from the crown lands proper, that is from farms worth 40s or more. Exchequer custody of these was evidently inconsiderable in amount, and, to judge from the fact that they were almost entirely unassigned, had been of brief duration. Strictly speaking we ought to add the farms of lands worth less than 40s, but Cromwell gave these only in a composite total together with sheriffs' farms and fines of green wax (profits of the law courts) of £5,676 gross and £1,903 net, so that no separate estimate for these can be obtained from his figures. These items were petty forfeitures and escheats for which the sheriffs had to account; they are unlikely to have exceeded £500 gross at the very outside and were probably much less than this net. Feefarms or perpetual leases of towns and manors totalled £3,600 gross and £634 net. The Windsor estate had a gross revenue of £207, but it was already over-assigned by £72 *per annum*. Then there were the amounts given for the patrimony of the heir to the throne in the king's hands (North Wales, South Wales, Chester and the duchy of Cornwall) totalling £5,790 gross and £1,256 net; alien priories £277 gross and £205 net; escheats estimated at £500; farms of wards' lands £1,600 gross and £1,598 net and, finally, given separately, the farm of the duke of Norfolk's lands £1,333. Cromwell had obtained some figures for the duchy of Lancaster (£4,952 gross and £2,544 net) but he did not incorporate these in his totals because he had no authority or control over these revenues. Thus, if we also exclude the duchy of Lancaster, the gross total of all land revenues in 1433, including sheriffs' farms and profits of justice (green wax), whether received from royal officers, from feefarms, farms, escheats, alien priories, or wards' lands, probably came to about £20,000, but of this total some £11,750 was permanently tied up and paid out at source in fees, wages, annuities and costs of collection, leaving only some £8,250 at the disposal of the central government, or perhaps about £6,750 without the sheriffs' farms and profits of green wax. Indirect taxation alone provided more than four times as much.

Cromwell's separate mention of the duchy of Lancaster reminds us that the primary function of crown lands was to provide for the royal family. In 1433, for example, the Richmond lands were held in fee by the duke of Bedford and the Pembroke lands by the duke of Gloucester. If Henry V had died without issue, his wish had been that the duchy of Lancaster lands should also be divided between his two surviving brothers. The Lancastrian kings had retained their Lancastrian patrimony for family purposes as a separate corporate entity quite independent of the Exchequer. Apart from the two royal

[13] My figures to this point are given to the nearest £1,000.

uncles in 1433 and the widow of a third, the duchess of Clarence, there were two queens still alive, Queen Joan and Queen Catherine. Catherine was enjoying duchy of Lancaster revenues (£4,360 9s 7d net in 1432) and income from North Wales and the duchy of Cornwall. Henry IV had wished his Queen Joan to be provided for out of the duchy of Lancaster after his death, but this had not happened and she was mainly dependent on income from alien priory lands. The most substantial single ascertainable family charge on royal land revenues in 1433 was £6,000 a year produced by extensive portions of the Lancaster estates put into the hands of feoffees for the performance of Henry V's will. While the feoffees advanced loans for the conduct of the war from time to time these all had to be and were repaid.[14]

Henry V proved to be the last king who was able to find a solution for his financial difficulties solely in heavier taxation. His son's ministers found themselves conducting unsuccessful war under a royal master who lacked not only political acumen but also all the necessary attributes of successful kingship. From about 1433 they were increasingly pressed to release the whole of the income of the great royal duchies for the expenses of government. From 1450, following ten years of wilful dissipation of the royal patrimony by Henry VI, the demand for the creation of a substantial inalienable crown estate in the interest of good governance and financial solvency became a central issue of politics.

Against this survey of a traditional pattern of functions and organization of crown lands, which was under mounting pressure for radical change by the mid-fifteenth century, we can now consider the impact of fifty years of Yorkist and Tudor rule. Henry VII's acts of resumption in 1485 and 1487 provide a good half-way glimpse and starting point. The exemption clauses to his 1485 act, which was back-dated to cover royal grants since 1454, constitute a survey of over 650 separate royal offices in England and Wales within the king's grant, not including the offices of central government, that is appointments in the Council and its committees, in Parliament, the Judiciary, Exchequer, Chancery, Privy Seal Office and Household, and not including sheriffs and escheators of English counties or customers in the ports.[15] The fact that these hundreds of local offices are listed in

[14] Robert Somerville's comprehensive *History of the Duchy of Lancaster*, i (London, 1953), described this stage in its history as a 'period of dismemberment' under Henry V and Henry VI. Figures quoted here will be found on pp. 206 and 208

[15] These officers were constables, parkers, keepers, stewards, foresters, verderers, receivers, approvers, auditors, surveyors, porters, bailiffs, feodaries, etc.

the exemption clauses, without distinction being made between offices requiring actual exercise and sinecure appointments, does not detract from the importance of this information. That an act of resumption should now provide it illustrates the significance of extensive lists of royal offices with their fees and wages appearing in Richard III's signet office docket book,[16] and of the Croyland chronicler's observations on the great care with which Edward IV distributed the keeperships of castles, manors, forests and parks throughout the country among his trusted servants.[17]

Sir John Fortescue's general ideal of one man one office had hardly been achieved, or even his special exception to his general rule that officers of the central government might be allowed one local office only in addition to central appointment. The exemptions to the 1485 act show that some royal servants held groups of offices in certain localities while others held several offices simultaneously in widely separated parts of the kingdom. Again, members of the central Household were clearly not confined to one local office. Nevertheless both the 1485 and 1487 acts of resumption,[18] in contrast to the acts of 1450–1455, assumed the existence of an extensive crown estate, retained in hand and administered by salaried officers, where appointments to offices, whether sinecures or requiring actual exercise, were made directly by the king. This was the result of a quarter of a century of Yorkist rule. Undoubtedly Fortescue's proposal that the king 'should more so reward his servants with offices, as there shall be little need to give them much of his livelihood and his offices shall then be given to such as shall only serve himself' had been applied as royal policy under the Yorkist kings to considerable effect.[19]

For a comprehensive picture of the organization and financial yield of Henry VII's crown estate, enabling us to survey both its traditional and its new features, we have to wait until the opening years of the sixteenth century. The Lancastrian Exchequer in its two divisions of Upper Exchequer, or Exchequer of Account and Pleas, and Lower Exchequer, or Exchequer of Receipt, in theory controlled both the administration of crown lands and the disposition of their

---

[16] See below, p. 63.

[17] As printed in *Rerum Anglicarum Scriptorum Veterum*, ed. W. Fulman (Oxford, 1684), i, 562, or in the translation of H. T. Riley in *Ingulf's Chronicle with the Continuations* (Bohn's Library, 1854), p. 480.

[18] *Rot. Parl.*, vi, 336-84; 403-8.

[19] Chapter xvii of Fortescue's *Governance* (pp. 150-3 in Plummer's edition), in which occurs the often quoted reference to 'braggers and suitors to the king for to have his offices in their countries to themselves', should be read in this connection. Fortescue there estimated the total number of all offices available for distribution by a determined king as over 1,000, not including those on the patrimony of the prince of Wales.

revenues. The Lancastrian kings had no other accounting office, court or treasury of land revenues except for the independent organization of the duchy of Lancaster. There was no rival office of receipt or account to the Lancastrian Exchequer competing for what it controlled, yet exchequer control of land revenues was in fact slight because the royal system of granting away lands and properties through the sign manual and signet for life, in reversion, or in fee, normally deprived the Exchequer of its function of making any crown leases which were a good financial proposition. Only for a brief time during the impact of the resumption acts of 1450, 1451 and 1455 did competitive leasing at the Exchequer have any effect. This did happen briefly at that time because royal lands, for once, came on the market and there proved to be plenty of men willing to profit from the misfortunes of those dispossessed. There was a very keen demand for any land which came on to the mid-fifteenth century market, and leases of crown lands were worth having on almost any terms. All these factors and the temporary impact of the acts of resumption pointed towards the need for new machinery to administer royal estates.

As regards the collection and spending of such land revenues as the Lancastrian kings did enjoy, the Exchequer did not collect revenues for the major part, but assigned them by means of tallies of assignment or reward to the king's creditors or officials who then made their own arrangements to secure the cashing of their tallies. This process applied to all the revenues of the Crown and might be thought to be a fifteenth-century equivalent of modern bearer bonds, but crucial considerations peculiar to royal creditors or officials of that date were the doubtful degree of priority which they could obtain for their assignments and the very real possibility that these might not be honoured at all. The process of final account for land revenues devolved on the heads of the hard-working, frequently changing sheriffs who were the Exchequer's only debt collectors and servers of writs. They accounted to the auditors of the pipe on the Great Roll or pipe roll in response to a 'summons of the pipe' listing all the financial demands of the Exchequer, sent out to them each year. The only exceptions were any receivers-general or chamberlains of royal family lands temporarily in the king's hands, such as the receiver-general of the duchy of Cornwall and the chamberlains of North and South Wales and Chester who accounted to the foreign auditors of the Exchequer on the foreign account rolls of the Exchequer, a series of accounts subsidiary to the main series of annual pipe rolls.

By the end of Henry VII's reign this venerable system of financial control, receipt and audit had ceased to apply to the land revenues of the crown. Professional salaried officials now collected royal land revenues in cash and delivered them in person to the treasurer of the king's Chamber. They accounted annually before a separate board of auditors or surveyors of land revenues, the king's General Surveyors, who were in fact at one and the same time a committee of the royal Council and a royal revenue court.

The same process of cash receipt in the king's Chamber now also applied to well over four-fifths of all the revenues of England, whatever their source, which were also now spent by the Chamber as well as being received and stored there. The significance for the historian of the part played by land revenues in this new process of receipt and issue lies not merely in the substantial financial contribution which they made to it but also in the fact that changes which began in the collection of royal land revenues ultimately spread over the whole field of government finance, leading to the displacement of the Exchequer of Receipt by the Chamber as the king's principal treasury and of the Exchequer of Account by committees of the Council as the king's principal place of final account.

The new system of receipt and account by which Henry VII ultimately controlled all his revenues was a royal development of normal, large-scale, private, seigniorial estate management as it existed in 1461. Edward Plantagenet earl of March and duke of York began to transfer it from his comital and ducal estates to the royal finances at his accession in 1461; Richard Plantagenet duke of Gloucester who was also a considerable seigniorial and marcher lord at his accession in 1483, could appreciate what his brother had done and improved and extended it; Henry Tudor, in spite of his desire to appear as the heir of Lancaster and his initial reluctance to follow Yorkist precedents until they had been proved sound, ultimately followed along the paths laid down by Richard III. Seigniorial estate management with its roots in manorial practice was quite different from the royal exchequer system. It supplied cash to the lord's central treasury through a hierarchy of officials who were checked by perambulating and central auditors and supervised by a seigniorial council. In essential outline, leaving aside the numerous specialized appointments which might or might not be sinecures (stewards, seneschals, constables of castles, parkers, keepers, foresters, feodaries, etc.), the manor, the smallest economic unit, was controlled by a reeve or bailiff who looked after the lord's financial interests and collected his revenues. Money collected was transferred to the central treasury of the receiver of an honorial or territorial group of estates. Transfers of money were recorded by written indentures, not by tallies. The receiver then delivered cash to the central treasury of the earl or duke, to the earl's wardrobe, for example, in the earl of Lancaster's household in the early fourteenth century,[20] or to the duke's receiver-general in the same household by the end of the fourteenth century.[21] Here was the chief financial officer providing central control. We can also follow out the same system at work on the patrimony of Richard duke of York between 1411 and 1460.[22] Large amounts of money were thus moved about the roads of England in apparent safety and went unmolested throughout most of the later middle ages.

Auditors travelled around, singly or more usually in pairs, to audit the accounts of local officers during the autumn and early winter at various local centres. At a later date they would audit the account of the receiver-general himself. A central estates steward, seneschal or supervisor might provide parallel supervision and might also be the principal auditor himself. Thirdly, the activities of local officers were supervised by the lord's council, and a chancellor or equivalent officer would have charge of the lord's writing department.

Seigniorial accounts (in Latin), whether those of a manorial bailiff or reeve or of a receiver, were all made up *mutatis mutandis* on the basis of a charge (*recepta*) and discharge (*reprisa*). The charge began with any arrearage left over from the previous account, followed by rents and farms, profits of courts, proceeds of sales, etc. Against this was then set a discharge consisting of fees and wages, repairs and maintenance, etc. The account was then summed up to show either an arrearage of what was still considered to be due to the lord or a surplusage if the accounting officer had paid out more than he had been charged with. Next would follow the allowance of non-routine but authorized expenditure or allowances (*liberata*), including the amounts of cash paid over and costs of transportation to a superior officer and allowances for uncollectable debts, losses due to natural disasters, etc. Then a further arrearage or surplusage would be struck which would be carried over to the next account. If it was an arrearage it would appear as the first item in the next year's *recepta*, if it was a surplusage it would be allowed for in the next year's

---

[20] J. F. Baldwin, 'The Household Administration of Henry Lacy and Thomas of Lancaster', *E.H.R.*, xlii (1927), 180-200. This is really a misleading title for what is in fact a succinct account of seigniorial estate management by a historian well versed in the workings of central government. He also was at pains to point out the fundamental differences between royal and seigniorial financial administration.

[21] R. Somerville, *Duchy of Lancaster*, pp. 71-133 (chaps. v, vi, and vii) provides an account of the same organization described by Baldwin but some 100 years later.

[22] Joel T. Rosenthal, 'The Estates and Finances of Richard, Duke of York (1411-1460)', *Studies in Medieval and Renaissance History*, ed. W. M. Bowsky, University of Nebraska Press, Lincoln, USA, 1965, ii, 115-204.

liberata. A final balance was only struck with an individual officer when he relinquished his office, or with his heirs if he died in harness. His successor started with a clean sheet.

Richard duke of York had been most heavily dependent for his income on what he obtained from his estates through his receivers.[23] John Milwater's account as Edward IV's receiver from 1461 to 1463 covering March, Lancaster and royal lands, grouped together on a regional basis (Doc. 7), is an example of a superior receiver in the crucial stage of transfer from private to royal service, paying henceforth into the royal Household coffers instead of to the Plantagenet ducal or comital coffers. The royal coffers were for the moment presided over by a royal household cofferer, John Kendal, who had previously been the household treasurer and cofferer of the duke of York[24] and who was to be succeeded in this royal function from 1465 by a treasurer of the Chamber.

By the later years of Henry VII's reign the treasurer of the Chamber, John Heron, had become the principal receiver of the king's revenues and their principal spender. His receipt and issue books,[25] too voluminous to be included in this collection of documents, are a charge and discharge account of all cash received and cash issued by him. They were summed by terms and by years, and a final balance was only struck at Henry VII's death and before Heron was taken into the employment of Henry VIII. Heron then had a surplusage, which appears difficult to understand if one thinks of this as meaning that he had issued more than he had received. The explanation was that Henry VII himself also personally received money into his coffers which Heron did not include in his sums of receipts. The king himself entered these amounts separately in Heron's books from time to time and separately charged them to Heron. Nevertheless, if Heron subsequently paid out any of this money it was included in his discharge.

These Chamber accounts dealt only in cash and consist of entries made in chronological order of receipt and issue, not grouped according to source of receipt or purpose of issue. It is possible to use them to estimate the total annual revenue and expenditure of Henry VII's government if one remembers awkward little complications like the intervention of the king in the account and the fact that there were occasions when some items of revenue were entered twice in the account and included twice in the sums, for example where an issue of a sum of imprest to a royal officer was subsequently returned in

---

[23] Rosenthal, pp. 173, 193.

[24] Rosenthal, p. 179, for notice of John Kendal as treasurer and cofferer of York's household.

[25] See below, p. 68, note 4 and p. 70, note 7.

part to Heron unspent. As a development from the practices of seigniorial estate management these accounts are quite different from the so-called receipt and issue rolls of the Exchequer, the equivalent central financial record of Lancastrian times. These by contrast had become more of a legal record than a financial document, the main purpose of which was to record the king's obligations to his creditors and theirs to him.

Receivers with jurisdiction over seigniorial or regional groups of royal estates under Henry VII now paid their receipts directly to the treasurer of the Chamber. Their accounts, along with the accounts of subordinate officers, were audited by perambulating 'foreign' auditors. A central board of audit, the king's General Surveyors, really a committee of his Council, now maintained a consolidated annual summary of these accounts which enables the system to be described in detail at the time of its widest operation (Doc. 16). The treasurer of the Chamber now had his accounts audited only by the king himself, who also examined and minuted the consolidated summaries of receivers' accounts produced by the General Surveyors, probably at the same time. The General Surveyors also acted as a revenue court, supervising, maintaining, improving and adjudicating on all matters pertaining to the land revenues of the Crown (Doc. 17).

Almost all history, and especially the history of government, is a story of continuity, but the historian is naturally most concerned to identify change and explain the reasons for it. Really significant changes in the processes of government are exciting to discover and explain, but the historian cannot avoid qualms of conscience lest he should read into apparent administrative changes a scope and significance which would have been meaningless to contemporaries. Fortunately in this instance contemporaries argued out the relative merits of these two systems of estate management and their implications for the royal finances and recorded their conclusions in a council memorandum of 1484 (Doc. 14 [32]).

The General Surveyors' book of declarations of accounts for the year 1503-4 furnishes a comprehensive survey of the king's land revenues, with the exception of the duchy of Lancaster (Doc. 16). The lands are listed there under some forty named receivers each with one or more charges, as well as under other receivers not named. The groupings of the lands concerned are in the main familiar from Lancastrian times, with Yorkist and Tudor accretions added from those same various sources which had made up the Lancastrian crown estate. They are headed by the lands of Queen Elizabeth who had died in 1503. Two points require comment here. The net yield of the queen's lands was a little less than £3,000, which was a big reduction from the income of Lancastrian queens who could expect to receive up to 10,000 marks (£6,666 13s 4d) from their endowments. Secondly, as subsequent records show, Queen Elizabeth of York's lands were retained in hand intact under the control of a receiver and the General Surveyors until taken over by Henry VIII's Queen Catherine of Aragon and were not dispersed into grants and farms as had been Lancastrian practice. The whole of the patrimony of the heir to the throne (North and South Wales, Chester and Flint, duchy of Cornwall) is included. Prince Henry had been divested of his title to the lands of York and the lands of his great-uncle Bedford (died 1495) on succeeding to his brother Arthur in 1503. But this account and subsequent accounts show that the General Surveyors and the treasurer of the Chamber retained control of the issues of the new prince of Wales's lands for the king's use as well as the lands of the duchies of York and Bedford (Pembroke, Glamorgan, Abergavenny, etc.).

In effect therefore, with the exception of his mother, the countess of Richmond, Henry VII endowed no members of his family with royal lands in his latter years. Had he lived longer he would ultimately have had to divest himself of a very considerable portion of these lands with a consequent drop in his receipts. On the other hand it must be observed that in Lancastrian times similar periods when there had been a dearth of adult members of the royal family able to absorb lands, namely between 1399 and 1405, and during the personal rule of Henry VI, had not seen the king and the national revenues benefiting at all. These had been the very periods which had produced demands for acts of resumption. The existence of the General Surveyors and the chamber treasury now provided automatic and permanent means of ensuring that the national revenues did benefit from such situations, although such arrangements could not prevent a change of policy at the top from adversely affecting the financial yield of the crown estate, as the early years of Henry VIII's reign were to demonstrate.

Notable acquisitions inherited from the Yorkist period were the lands of the duchy of York and earldom of March, and the Neville inheritance (Warwick, Salisbury and Spencer lands) which had meantime passed through the hands of George duke of Clarence, Richard duke of Gloucester, and, subsequently, Richard III and his queen, Anne Neville. Mention of Neville and Clarence forfeitures draws attention to the sole new source of royal lands which had become available since Lancastrian times, acquisitions by act of attainder. During the fourteenth century, only fee simple (freehold) estates and his widow's dower were subject to forfeiture to the king when a man was convicted of treason. In 1398, at Richard II's behest, Parliament made entailed estates also subject to forfeiture, but public opinion was against this notion, and it was not enforced until the attainder of the Yorkists in 1459 began a period of statutory application of the penalties of treason to entailed lands by acts of attainder. In fact these penalties were not uniformly enforced even then, and individual attainders were subsequently repealed on many occasions, though not necessarily with full restoration of entailed lands. But the effect on the king's land revenues towards the end of Henry VII's reign was clearly very marked, considering the values of lands newly accruing to him under the attainers of 1495 to 1504 and listed below in the declaration of 1503-4: Sir William Stanley's, Lord Fitzwalter's, Edward Ashley's, the earl of Suffolk's, Lord Audley's, Sir William de la Pole's and Sir James Tyrell's.

To turn to the organization and administration of the royal lands under receivers in 1503-4; the units of management here were almost entirely those seigniorial groupings in which the lands concerned had passed into the king's hands. National grouping were, however, applied to certain categories. With one or two possible exceptions which had their own receivers, all wards' lands, together with vacant ecclesiastical temporalities, were grouped together in one declaration. In the following year this was made by William Lychfelde, styled receiver-general of wards' lands. There was also a consolidated return for wood sales made by Richard Empson, also styled receiver-general in this capacity in the following year's account. Two further consolidated returns were for farms and feefarms and for annuities or annual payments, each totalling about £1,000. These appear to have been the residue of what had been exchequer farms and feefarms in Lancastrian times, together with some similar items which had more recently fallen into the king. There certainly had been earlier attempts to organize such miscellaneous farms and feefarms under receivers responsible for groups of contiguous counties, with authority to seek out, levy, collect and receive all manner of rents and services due, to distrain for debts, to expel insolvent or bad tenants and to put in new ones. Receivers were appointed to eight such groups of counties in 1461, to seven in 1471 and to six or more in 1485 when they paid a total of £456 16s 4d into the Exchequer of Receipt during the Michaelmas term of that year.[26]

There is another complete book of declarations of all the king's lands made before the General Surveyors for the twelve-month period ending at Michaelmas 1505.[27] Payments to Heron made from current issues by receivers had now risen to nearly £32,000, apart from wards' lands. Within this total the declaration of farms and feefarms

---

[26] The appointments of the 1461 and 1471 groups were enrolled on the patent and fine rolls. The existence of the 1485 group is revealed by P.R.O., Special Collections, Ministers' Accounts, Addenda, S. C. 6/3545/88: 'Declarations of Several Receivers, Divers Counties, 1 Hen. VII'.

[27] P.R.O., Exchequer, Treasury of Receipt, Miscellaneous Books, E. 36/212.

had fallen to £514, but the declaration of annuities (annual payments) had risen to £1,254. The separate declaration for wards' lands now showed Heron receiving £5,422 8s 10¼d, also a considerable increase on the previous year, but including a sum of nearly £1,000 which the previous year's summary had shown as owed by the executors of the bishop of Durham (Doc. 16., p. 146). The burgeoning jurisdiction of the General Surveyors in 1504–5 now also included the accounts of Robert Southwell in his capacity as Chief Butler, as well as accounts for Calais and Guisnes, Berwick, Corbridge and Shilbottle which, together with accounts for the temporalities of the bishoprics of Durham and Chichester, were noted as still being in the hands of Hugh Molyneux.

The problems involved in estimating Henry VII's total annual revenues are complex. Nevertheless, the task is very much easier than for any earlier period of English history because of the existence of the treasurer of the Chamber's accounts and the principles on which they were compiled. The evidence seems to suggest that over the last five years of his reign, excluding the clerical and lay subsidies, they probably averaged not more than £113,000, out of which £42,000 came from land revenues. The amounts of land revenue identifiable in the chamber accounts for the three years 1502–5 average £40,286.[28] If we compare these figures for land revenues with Lord Cromwell's estimates of 1433 there appear to be some obvious explanations for the spectacular increase: Henry VII had almost no royal family to support, while the royal family in 1433 had been large and demanding, and Henry VII had simply acquired a great deal more land.

But there were other factors involved. It is difficult to demonstrate from specific units of estates common to the surveys of both the Lancastrian and early Tudor periods that superior organization and royal control was responsible for any significant increase, because of the lack of comparability in almost all the individual items involved, but it can be attempted for the duchy of Cornwall. In 1433, gross revenues for the duchy were stated to be £2,788 13s 3¾d. Fees, wages, annuities, reparations and necessary expenses amounted to £2,637 12s 6½d, leaving £151 9¼d for the king's use. The account which the duchy receiver-general, Richard Nanfan, rendered before the General Surveyors for 1503–4 began with an arrearage of £1,633 19s 2¾d and a current total charge of £4,172 16s 8⅝d. Reprises totalled only £601 6s 7½d, leaving £5,205 9s 3⅝d of which £1,479 15s 8¼d was arrearage and £3,725 13s 7⅜d current issues. Non-recurrent allocations or obligations not yet redeemed, including £324 4s 6¼d due from certain merchants of the stannaries and

---

[28] I have discussed these problems at length in my article 'Henry VII's Land Revenues and Chamber Finance', *E.H.R.*, lxxix (1964), 225-254.

£375 3s 1¼d from the deputy receiver-general, accounted for £921 3s 3⅛d of this, leaving £4,284 6s 0½d which had been delivered in cash to the treasurer of the Chamber for the king's use.[29]

If we turn to comparing total amounts of Lancastrian and early Tudor revenue the importance of changes in organization and management becomes even clearer. Between 1502 and 1505 Henry VII was receiving something like £40,000 *per annum* in cash in his Chamber from his land revenues and perhaps £105,000 in cash in his Chamber from all sources. Should these amounts be compared with the gross or net figures in the statement of 1433? They are not strictly comparable with either, though more nearly comparable with the net figures because the gross figures of about £54,000 for all revenues in 1433 and about £20,000 for land revenues both included fees, wages, annuities, reparations, costs of collection, etc. The total net revenues in 1433 were about £36,000 and the total net land revenues, on the most favourable estimation possible, about £8,250. But these net figures were in their turn only estimates of what the central Exchequer thought was still available for assignment in several hundred places scattered over the whole country in the shires, towns and ports of the land.[30] Further comparison is unnecessary when the fundamental differences between Lancastrian and early Tudor governmental finance are thus revealed. While it might possibly be maintained that the expenses of central government under the Lancastrians were much less than under Henry VII because so much was met by local assignment, it can hardly be denied that a substantial supply of ready cash available at the centre would have solved the 1433 crisis of assignment. Towards the end of his reign, Henry VII was receiving in cash in his Chamber nearly twice the gross total of all the revenues the Lancastrians had at their disposal even before local charges or costs were deducted, or any assignments made.

Such was the measure of the administrative and financial changes brought about by the new policies of the Yorkist kings and Henry VII, which were based on applying the financial methods of seigniorial estate management to the national finances. Although the contribution of land revenues to the national finances began to suffer a steep decline from 1509, the king's Chamber had within a few years further expanded the scale of its activities to embrace the receipt and issue of

---

[29] P.R.O., Exchequer, Treasury of Receipt, Miscellaneous Books, E. 36/213, fol. 9r (page 17).

[30] Including sheriffs and escheators, but not including customers, etc., concerned with levying indirect taxation at the ports, the Lancastrian Exchequer regularly listed on the roll which it prepared for the sheriffs' Michaelmas proffers well over 250 persons on behalf of whom it required an account, even if that account should show nothing due.

over £600,000 in cash for war expenses in one period of little more than twelve months.[31]

It may be objected that England had seen periods of royal chamber finance before, and that the chamber finance of the Yorkists and early Tudors was but a reversion to earlier, more primitive medieval patterns of English governmental finance. This collection of documents furnishes a different explanation of its origins and, with the exception of the brief period at the end of Edward II's reign, such modern studies of those earlier examples of chamber finance in English history as exist reveal important differences between them and what was happening from 1461 and 1509.[32] In any case, there is nothing to suggest that the Yorkist kings and Henry VII were antiquarian minded, while earlier chamber finance, because of its remoteness in time and its intimate, secretive nature, had left little evidence behind it to serve as precedents. Yet another school of thought sees the origins of Tudor cameral and conciliar finance in the royal duchy of Lancaster, but this view affords no explanation for the complete lack of impact by duchy methods on royal government and exchequer finance during the first sixty years of its history in the hands of the English crown under the Lancastrian kings. The story of Henry VII's achievements had its origins in the estates of the House of York and March and can in fact only be told from 1461 with the accession of the earl of March to the throne of England.

[31] See below, p. 86.
[32] Cf. above, pp. 22-23.

The Yorkist land revenue experiment

STUBBS'S generation, and several later generations of English historians, thought that the period of Lancastrian kingship saw a major constitutional experiment in English government. They believed that the Lancastrian branch of the English royal family had been nurtured in a tradition of opposition to arbitrary rule which could be traced back to the sainted Ordainer Thomas of Lancaster, cousin and opponent of Edward II. By contrast, therefore, the Yorkist kings were deemed to have reverted to more autocratic methods, abandoning what had become the goals of normal medieval constitutional government: rule with frequent parliaments through a Council of notables, according to a right course of law, by a king expected to 'live of his own'. Like Hallam before him Stubbs saw Edward IV manipulating parliamentary institutions in a reign which was the first in our history to see no enactment whatsoever which furthered the liberty and security of the subject.

This picture was more or less the reverse of the truth. After a few initial years of uncertainty the Lancastrians succeeded in re-establishing a strong, masterful and autocratic kingship under Henry V which was reminiscent of Edward III in his prime, but the personal character of his son and heir rendered impossible the maintenance of this remarkable achievement. The earlier prominence of the Council and of the Commons in Parliament for much of Henry IV's reign can now be seen as due to no policies or desires of that king himself. The subsequent pleas for 'good governance' during the final, personal rule of Henry VI, for the strengthening of the Council, for the due enforcement of law, and for solvency and economy, were the policies advocated not by royal ministers, but by exasperated government critics in parliaments, in popular pamphlets, in the manifestoes of rebellious subjects, and by the Yorkist faction among the nobility and gentry.

Edward earl of March was driven into assuming the Crown when his most prominent associate, the earl of Warwick, lost possession and control of the captive Henry VI by the second battle of St Albans in February 1461. He consolidated his immediate hold upon it with the financial backing of the city of London and with successful trial by battle at Towton. But it is not too much to say that he was already pledged to a tradition of Yorkist constitutional principles. His father Richard duke of York, when he first entered the political arena in 1450 on his return from Ireland without royal permission, had thrown his weight behind the Commons' demands for a strengthened Council, for household appropriations and for an effective act of resumption. The 1460 manifesto of the Yorkist lords had complained that Henry VI had no 'livelihood of the Crown of England whereof he may keep his honourable Household which causeth the spoiling of his said liegemen by the takers (purveyors) of his said Household'. This was followed by the request that 'it will please his good grace to live upon his own livelihood'.[1]

In 1467 Edward IV pledged himself in person before his Commons in Parliament to 'live of his own' (Doc. 8). The enrolment of this speech on the roll of the Parliament was followed immediately by an act of resumption (Doc. 9). This was a proffer of alliance between himself and his Commons to give effect to the policies of earlier parliamentary oppositions under the Lancastrians. There can be no doubt that Edward was personally identified with its success because his rebellious peers, Clarence, Warwick and George Neville, taunted him with unfulfilled promises on this score in their Calais manifesto of 1469.[2] It will be seen that his 1467 speech contained important reservations. Who was to judge what were 'great and urgent causes', necessitating financial assistance from his subjects, but Edward himself? Nevertheless, there are indications from 1461 of conscious efforts to remedy the deficiences of Lancastrian rule, of policies which required government solvency and economy, that is, relating current spending to total current income available from all sources.

To contemporaries, criticism of the expense of government was concentrated on the king's Household. If it lived off the land, was inflated in size and arbitrary and undisciplined as it moved about the countryside, then this was conspicuous waste. The medieval king's Household was his essential power-house of authority and action. Edward IV set new standards of solvency and efficiency in this respect which may not always have been maintained, but which were in evident contrast to the 'expensive inefficiency' and 'shabby indigency'

---

[1] *An English Chronicle*, ed. J. S. Davies, Camden Soc., 1856, pp. 86-7.
[2] Printed by J. O. Halliwell in the notes to his edition of *Warkworth's Chronicle*, Camden Soc., 1839, p. 51.

of Henry VI's court.³ The perennial complaints against household purveyance disappeared from the parliament rolls between 1461 and 1482. Dr Myers has described what was attempted by effective regulations, ordinances and discipline. Edward IV ultimately reduced Household running costs below those of Henry VII, let alone Henry VI, yet he managed to keep a splendid and impressive court. In the estimate of contemporary public opinion, a regular, lawful income for current Household expenses was highly desirable. From 1462 he ordered all exchequer farms and feefarms worth 40s or more to be removed from the jurisdiction of the sheriffs and reserved them for household expenses (Doc. 6), at the same time creating a new network of county receivers to administer them. These receivers were entirely financial agents, yet they were given authority to declare their accounts on oath at the Exchequer so that they could concentrate on collecting current issues and not be enmeshed in the paralytic web of exchequer debt demands and book-keeping (Doc. 12, a). From 1466 the lucrative profits of the Cornish tin and lead mines were similarly devoted to Household expenses.⁴ There is no doubt that Edward also used the revenues of the duchy of Lancaster for household expenses, although we cannot say to what extent because of the absence of duchy accounts for the earlier part of the reign.⁵

Parliaments now became less frequent but sat longer and transacted more business. Acts of resumption became instruments of government policy. They had been forced on a reluctant Lancastrian government in 1450 and 1451 mainly for financial reasons. The best informed of the Yorkist chroniclers similarly states that Edward IV was primarily moved by financial considerations in his policy of resumptions (Doc. 11). But the same chronicler also noticed elsewhere how carefully Edward disposed of the keeping of his castles, manors, parks and forests to trusted agents throughout his kingdom, ensuring thereby that he was well served in the localities. On the whole this latter was the more important function of Yorkist resumptions. The acts of 1465 and 1467 completed the endowment of the royal family; the act of 1473 was a necessary review of the disposition of crown lands and offices as affected by the brief restoration of Lancastrian rule in 1470. It also aimed at a peaceful curbing of the dangerously expanding power of the Duke of Clarence by a process which was now becoming almost a routine act of administration. However, in the case of Clarence, Edward failed, and a special Parliament and a separate act of attainder proved necessary in 1478 to bridle this most arrogant of over-mighty subjects.

[3] A. R. Myers, *The Household of Edward IV*, Manchester, 1959.
[4] C[alendar] of P[atent] R[olls] *1461-1467*, p. 519.
[5] R. Somerville, *History of the Duchy of Lancaster*, pp. 234-6.

But the impact of Edward's financial policies can best be measured neither in the Exchequer, nor in Parliament, but on the crown estates and in his Chamber. A quick count through the records of instruments issued under the great seal during Edward's reign reveals that over and above offices on the duchy of Lancaster estates he made nearly 100 separate appointments of receivers, surveyors and auditors to operate outside the Exchequer in the administration of royal land revenues. The Lancastrian method of disposing of crown estates had been the traditional one. By this method the fate of a manor, whether it was in the king's hands for a limited period or in absolute possession, was decided as a result of petitions to the king by well-informed, influential, would-be beneficiaries. Only when an estate had to be created and maintained for a member of the royal family were receivers, surveyors and special auditors employed. In theory the Treasurer of England and his exchequer staff had the duty of letting such manors at farm at the current market valuation, with their issues subject to exchequer assignment by tally, and the sheriffs were responsible for the final accounting according to the 'ancient course of the Exchequer'. But only in very exceptional circumstances, such as the immediate aftermath of the 1451 act of resumption, did this system operate in fact. The Exchequer always went through the complicated motions of account, but the amount of revenue derived from crown lands was normally a subsidiary consideration to the king. If a bargain was made by the king over the leasing of a manor, it was political and not financial. Of course the perquisites so obtained by those 'in the know', mainly the king's household men, were their rewards for services rendered or to come. But with a king as ineffective and irresponsible as Henry VI there appears to have been no element of bargaining at all in such transactions (Doc. 2). The disposal of crown lands and their revenues was an area of the royal prerogative where the Lancastrian Council as a body did not presume to interfere after 1437 when Henry VI came of age. By 1450 the degree to which Henry was both ill-served and impoverished by his largesse had become a national scandal.

The organization of extensive private estates in fifteenth-century England was quite different from the royal practice. It is sometimes alleged that large-scale private landowners were also normally able to exercise substantial rights of purveyance and taxation (tallage) over their tenants, comparable to royal fiscal rights over the whole kingdom, but we have little concrete evidence of this and, on the whole, it seems likely that dependence on such sources of taxation were the special privilege of royal finance alone. The large-scale private landowner was dependent for his income on his land agents. Several professional officers usually controlled his estates from the centre, under the supervision of a council if he was a man of real substance: a receiver-general, a surveyor and one or more auditors. Qualifications and training for all these three posts appear to have been the same, and their duties were largely interchangeable. Estate management at the highest level also appears to have run in certain families; for example, the Hetons in the service of the Stafford dukes of Buckingham, the Leventhorpes in duchy of Lancaster service, and the Sapcotes and the Kidwelly family in the employment of the Yorkist kings. The receiver or receiver-general supplied the lord with his cash. He had to be a man of some substance himself, 'of haviour of richesse', as Richard III's advisers put it in 1484 (Doc. 14 [32]), because he acted as a kind of banker to his lord. He collected the revenues from farmers, bailiffs and reeves, paid such officers, saw to the replenishment of stock, the making of leases, the eviction of bad tenants, the sale of woods, repairs of property, etc. He supplied money or goods to meet the lord's household expenses and paid his creditors. An essential part of his job was to journey wherever required with substantial sums of cash and, therefore, to anticipate requirements and to keep the necessary amounts in hand. The auditor was employed to control and supervise the receiver's activities by means of estate accounts drawn up and presented at regular intervals. He also had to be qualified to make a 'valor' or survey of estates. A man at the top of his profession, like the Yorkist auditor John Luthington, might well have several charges as an auditor and also be a receiver-general of substantial estates in a different part of the country. Likewise an auditor like John Eltonhead, who was employed in royal service by Edward IV for the duchy of Cornwall and earldom of Richmond estates, was also auditor for Lincoln's Inn and for various magnates.

This typical pattern of large-scale, private estate management has been best preserved for posterity in the splendid records of the duchy of Lancaster whose estates were kept intact and separate from the Exchequer by the Lancastrian kings. However, its methods were not allowed to permeate the Exchequer or the management of the rest of the royal lands, and the issues of the duchy, insofar as they were allowed to be used for government expenditure between 1399 and 1460, were disposed of and accounted for through the Exchequer. But immediately from 1461 we have records of a royal receiver's accounts, John Milewater's, who was at one and the same time a receiver of March lands, of duchy of Lancaster lands, of lands in the king's hands during minority, and of royal lands proper, all grouped together on a regional basis, and the relevant accounts were audited outside the Exchequer by John Luthington (Doc. 7). They reveal that Milewater took his instructions from the king for making payments, not by exchequer tally or writ, but by signet office letter, and that he paid the bulk of his receipts in cash direct to the king in his Chamber wherever he was bidden to deliver it (*ibid*). So we can see how Edward IV, when he wished to redeem jewelry and valuables pawned by his father to Sir John Fastolf, could not merely make Fastolf's executor, John Paston, an assignment of money on various exchequer feefarms, but could also back this up with an undertaking of repayment from his own coffers in the quite likely event of the Exchequer assignments being slow in realization, or being repudiated altogether.[6]

It has long been known that Edward IV took almost £14,000 a year on average from the Exchequer into his Chamber during the first eight years of his reign.[7] In addition some notable sources of revenue in the 1470s, his benevolences, his French pension and the profits of his trading activities (Doc. 11) made no impact on exchequer records. Likewise if we examine the surviving accounts of his household expenditure we find that whereas the Exchequer had been responsible for financing and accounting for the whole of this under Henry VI, by 1466–7 the treasurer of the Household was receiving as much if not more from the king's coffers in his Chamber.[8] This same treasurer of the Household, Sir John Fogge, was now required to hand over sums of money which reached him from other sources, probably by routine exchequer assignment, directly to the financial staff in the king's Chamber (Doc. 12, b). The year 1461 thus saw the beginnings of a process which by the end of Henry VII's reign was channelling over four-fifths of all royal revenues into the king's Chamber. Its origins lay in Edward IV's continuation and extension, when he seized the throne, of those methods of finance which had supplied him with his income as earl of March. He appointed a treasurer of the Chamber under the great seal during pleasure in 1465, the first of such appointments ever recorded.[9] Unfortunately we have no surviving Yorkist chamber accounts. Chamber finance was secret, and no doubt Edward's treasurer of the Chamber, Sir Thomas Vaughàn, accounted only to the king in person, as was the case with his successor under Richard III whose accounts were audited and authenticated solely by the king's signature (Doc. 13).

There are other kinds of documents, apart from Milewater's accounts, which show that Edward's Chamber created a new central office of land revenue. Every officer handling the king's money ultimately found himself summoned to the Exchequer whenever his

---

[6] *The Paston Letters*, ed. J. Gairdner, Edinburgh, 1910, ii 33-5 (no. 407).

[7] J. H. Ramsay, *Lancaster and York*, ii, 467.

[8] P.R.O., Exchequer, King's Remembrancer, Various Accounts, E. 101/411/11, 13, 14; 412/2 (treasurer of the Household, 1461-7).

[9] *C. of P.R. 1461-1467*, p. 459.

existence became known to it through its own records, through the records of the Chancery, extracts from which were regularly copied for it as a matter of routine, or through records ultimately deposited in its keeping for safe custody. This process might be slow. It took eight years for Sir John Fogge's payments into the chamber coffers between March and September 1461 to come to the knowledge of the Exchequer, but in 1469 they duly demanded an account of them (Doc. 12, b). Not until 1477 did the Exchequer discover that on February 5, 1467 the king had sold the keeping of certain lands to Sir John Howard for £200 paid into his Chamber (Doc. 12, f). When in 1482 it demanded an account from a certain receiver of the honour of Richmond for the period 1478–1482, and ordered the sheriff of Lincolnshire to seize his lands and goods as security, it transpired that accounts for those lands had been audited outside the Exchequer by John Luthington since December 4, 1461 (Doc. 12, j). Such exchequer activities were hardly productive of revenue for Edward IV, but they do preserve for posterity evidence of a Yorkist royal land revenue organization which functioned without any current exchequer help or official knowledge of its existence (Doc. 12, *passim*).

Among the estates newly placed in the control of receivers and special auditors at the beginning of the reign were the forfeited Richmond, Beaufort, Roos, Northumberland and Wiltshire lands. Similar appointments were made for duchy of York lands, and for the earldom of March lands in East Anglia, the Home Counties, Cambridge and Huntingdonshire. From 1462 to 1464, the temporalities of the bishopric of Durham were put in the hands of the treasurer and controller of the Household assisted by Thomas Colt and arrangements were made to audit their final accounts, not in the Exchequer, but before special auditors sent to Durham.[10] Wards' lands of sufficient importance were similarly treated. The estates of the Talbot earls of Shrewsbury were in Edward's hands for most of his reign because one minority followed closely on another. They were handled by a succession of royal receivers-general: Richard Fowler, John Milewater, Richard Croft, John Swift and Thomas Stidolff (Doc. 12, e and i). As Sir James Ramsay long since pointed out, the revenues of such estates are missing from exchequer accounts. In the case of the Talbot lands, the special auditors drew up final accounts at Hereford, Sheffield and elsewhere.

Similar arrangements were intended for the extensive lands which George duke of Clarence forfeited by his rebellion in alliance with the earl of Warwick in 1470 (Doc. 10). Of course, Edward, who was driven temporarily from his kingdom by this rebellion, could not implement them. After his decisive victories of Barnet and Tewkesbury,

[10] B. P. Wolffe, 'The Management of English Royal Estates under the Yorkist Kings', *E.H.R.*, lxxi (1956), 6 and references given there.

which finally put an end to all the hopes of would-be rebels, he tried hard to reach an accommodation with this dangerously ambitious and treacherous brother for several years. But the act of attainder which ultimately destroyed Clarence in 1478 was followed by a revival of the abortive arrangements of 1470 for the most efficient financial management of Clarence's 'Warwick, Salisbury and Spencer lands' for the benefit of the royal coffers (Doc. 12, h). In 1472, when Edward deprived the younger Neville brother, George archbishop of York, of the estates which he held by royal gift in Oxfordshire, he put in Richard Croft there as receiver and surveyor, exempting him from exchequer accounting (Doc. 12, c).

Not all the forfeited resumed or escheated lands which came under Edward IV's control were treated in this way. As explained above, Edward had obligations towards members of his family and pursued the traditional policy of endowing all his close relatives with substantial estates, being unlike his successors, Richard III and Henry VII, in this respect. He also had political and military needs which required the outright gift of some estates to key supporters. Some lands temporarily in his hands were sold for the duration of the royal control at his valuation (Doc. 11), for lump sums paid to him in his Chamber (Doc. 12, f and g). But it is quite clear that where arrangements for control by receivers and special auditors were made, the object was to avoid their dispersal by petition to courtiers or their friends and associates, to keep these lands from passing into the Exchequer farming pool and to ensure that their revenues were paid directly into the king's coffers in his Chamber, unless he had authorized disbursement elsewhere.

Edward IV thus required an efficient network of receivers of land revenues to feed his royal coffers. The revenues they collected were immune from routine dispersal by exchequer assignment. He did not relieve the Exchequer of its ultimate duty to secure accounts of all the king's revenues, and those special auditors who drew up final accounts outside the jurisdiction of the Treasurer of England and the Barons of the Exchequer still appear to have been bound to deposit those accounts, when they were no longer needed, in the Exchequer of Account, there to be retained of record (Doc. 12, j). But whenever any royal receiver, or a loyal subject who had made a personal bargain with the king for the purchase of a royal interest in land, was troubled by an exchequer writ or process of account, he received a royal acquittance in the form of a prohibition sent to the Exchequer. There was no question of exchequer officials being able to submit him to the normal, meticulous, slow and lengthy processes of examination and account according to the 'ancient course of the Exchequer'. The most that was then permitted to the exchequer officials was to receive a declaration of account from the person concerned, made on oath and assisted by the information which the writ of prohibition contained. Eleven examples of these usually lengthy writs of prohibition are printed here (Doc. 12). Some, such as the one for John Hayes, a receiver of 'Warwick, Salisbury and Spencer lands', are quite informative, showing that the signet clerks in the king's Chamber, who wrote them, were in fact recording summaries of accounts, in this case of Hayes's annual account (Doc. 12, h). One of these writs states that John Beaufitz, the receiver concerned, had been 'appointed and assigned' to 'account and reckon with us thereof in our Chamber afore certain persons by us thereto assigned' (Doc. 12, d). Here, in embryo, was the Tudor Court of General Surveyors. The tenacity and timelessness of the exchequer process, and the scrupulous, unhurried enrolling in full of every incoming letter there thus to some extent pierce the veil of secrecy surrounding Edward IV's Chamber finance. Nevertheless, even in these exchequer records the frequent appearance should be noted of such ambiguous, blanket phrases as: 'we thereof of our certain knowledge and mere motion will and straightly charge you'; 'that express mention of the certainty of the premises herein be not made'; 'any other matter whatsoever you to the contrary moving notwithstanding', etc.

Although these writs of prohibition reached the Exchequer as writs from the Privy Seal Office, the central clearing house for royal instruments, it is evident from their being dated at various royal palaces that they originated in the Signet Office which was as mobile as the king and located in the king's outer Chamber under the control of his Secretary. The Privy Seal Office merely copied the place and date of the original signet letter. In rare cases where the original signet office letter also survives, this can be conclusively demonstrated. Fortunately, for the reign of Richard III, an actual signet office docket or entry book survives, and this immediately sheds a new flood of light on the last, final years of Yorkist chamber activity. It is of course still possible from 1483 to pursue the same exchequer sources of information. For example, they reveal that Richard III removed the duchy of Cornwall estates entirely from exchequer control (Doc. 12, k). The position of the final accounting responsibility for the duchy estates under Edward IV is not clear, although he had set up a new local, professional board or council in 1461 to have all leases of twenty-one years or less made locally instead of in the Exchequer at Westminster, arrangements renewed in 1469 and confirmed by Richard in 1483.[11] The exchequer records continue to be useful for the reign of Henry VII, and, rather surprisingly, even for

[11] *C. of P.R. 1461-1467*, p. 201; *ibid., 1467-1477*, p. 197; *ibid., 1477-1485*, p. 461.

the early years of Henry VIII. Nevertheless, from 1483 the intermittent survival of actual chamber records makes possible a much fuller picture (Doc. 14).

The thirty-three entries printed here are selected to provide a survey of the work of Richard III's Chamber as a central land revenue office. Some of these entries almost justify its description as a court of law: certainly as a 'seigniorial' estate office covering towns, lordships and manors throughout the kingdom, all bound in a special relationship to a central organization in the king's Chamber. We can look forward to parallels in the early-Tudor courts of General Surveyors and Augmentations, but we cannot point to anything like it under earlier kings of England.

This selection of documents from Richard III's Signet Office thus demonstrates that usurpation of the throne did not necessarily mean a break in the continuity of government. Richard duke of Gloucester moved into the seat of royal power with his advisers, many of whom were his brother's servants, and extended and intensified the operations of his brother's cameral and conciliar land revenue office. In his Chamber Richard III received and gave acquittances for payments from receivers, from purchasers of wards' lands and for vacant ecclesiastical temporalities. Individual receivers of the duchy of Lancaster were dealt with direct in the same manner as other receivers (Doc. 14 [4, 5, 6, 11, 12, 13, 14, 20, 22]). Instructions went out to receivers to pay his debts, perhaps to a saddler or to a goldsmith, etc. (*ibid.* [2, 19]). Letters went out to local receivers, farmers and tenants on the lands of the rebels of the autumn of 1483, notifying them that certain ushers of the king's Chamber and other royal servants had been chosen to take possession there and enjoining their obedience (*ibid.* [3, 9, 16]). There are appointments of new receivers and auditors in the king's service, some taken on along with the lands which they had previously administered for their displaced masters (*ibid.* [7, 8, 9, 16, 18]). Remonstrances and royal threats went out to crown officers or tenants who were attempting to delay payments (*ibid.* [10]). There are peremptory demands for the appearance of royal receivers to render account before the king and his auditors (*ibid.* [15]).

Not all the instruments recorded were financial in intent. Orders went out to inhabitants of certain lordships in Kent to welcome a new steward as the king's representative and 'in no wise to presume to take clothing or be retained' with any other man (*ibid.* [17]). Some instruments copied into the register are surprising in their detail, and, at first sight, for their triviality; for example, the detailed instructions for the safe gathering of a hay crop at Warwick under the supervision of an esquire of the body who was also the constable of the castle there (*ibid.* [21]). One can only assume that an adequate supply of fodder at Warwick castle was particularly important to Richard at that time. Likewise the king was particularly concerned to see that local revenues were permanently available for the regular payment of forty soldiers garrisoning Beaumaris castle under their captain, an esquire of the body (*ibid.* [23]). There are many direct instructions to various receivers up and down the country, and again including those in charge of duchy of Lancaster lands, ordering them to pay for cattle and provisions purveyed for use of the royal Household (*ibid.* [26, 28]). The ineffectiveness, delays and injustices of earlier dependence on exchequer assignment by tally for this purpose had been one of the most widely resented practices of Lancastrian government. This was the kind of action by which a king could most patently demonstrate his intention to 'live of his own'.

Many of these entries thus demonstrate the central treasury of a crown estate in action and the advantages of having a nation-wide network of royal receivers and agents able to satisfy local creditors or to give local effect to royal policies. There also emerge glimpses of a 'seigniorial' court in action. A royal tenant in the remote North had a certain rent remitted by instruction sent to the receiver and auditor concerned because the king had deprived him of the use of some of his land by building a royal brickworks on it (Doc. 14 [24]). A commission was sent out to ensure a report of the facts in a dispute between royal tenants and the abbot of Fountains (*ibid.* [25]). Another commission was intended to secure the administrative reorganization and regrouping of certain royal boroughs and lordships (*ibid.* [27]). Instructions went out to local officers and tenants consequent on the Council's deliberation over the disputed possession of certain manors (*ibid.* [29]).

So far we have been describing the briefer, more routine documents. There are a number of much longer ones recording deliberations and decisions on high policy. One is a detailed annual assignment of £10,574 6s 8d, apportioned almost entirely on the king's land revenue receivers throughout the country, for the expenses and wages of the Household (Doc. 14 [33]). Another similar assignment totalling £1,344 was made for the upkeep of a royal household to be maintained at Sandal and elsewhere within the county of York (*ibid.* [30]). Richard III seems to have furnished his key officers and representatives with written statements of their duties and responsibilities as his agent and representative. The stewardship of the duchy of Lancaster castle and honour of Tutbury was indeed a key post, held successively since 1476 by William lord Hastings, and Henry duke of Buckingham, both of whom he had been forced to eliminate in the seizure and consolidation of his throne. When he appointed Buckingham's successor, Sir Marmaduke Constable, in 1484, he sent him detailed instructions on his relations with the inhabitants, also telling him what qualities and qualifications he required in the offices of bailiff, parker, lieutenant, bowbearer and receiver; who should be preferred in making leases, how the woods should be managed, etc. (Doc. 14 [31]).

Finally there is a 'remembrance' or survey of the whole system of land revenue accounting, based on the central authority of the king's Chamber and Council (*ibid.* [32]). It begins with criticisms of the delays and weakness of exchequer procedure, and with suggestions for its improvement; exchequer revenues are listed as the sheriffs' and escheators' issues, the feefarms of cities and boroughs, the proceeds of direct and indirect taxation and the revenues of Calais. For the rest the Exchequer was to be 'clearly dismissed and discharged with any meddling'. These were the land revenues of the principality of Wales, the duchies of Cornwall, York and Norfolk and the earldoms of Chester, March, Warwick and Salisbury, together with all forfeited lands and wards' lands, being those groups and classifications of estates which had come to be separately administered from the Chamber. This left only the duchy of Lancaster which was to preserve its accounting autonomy, and the lordships of Glamorgan and Abergavenny which were the personal property of Richard's queen, although other documents in this collection show that Richard in fact treated the queen's lands just the same as if they were his own.

The rest of this document extols the advantages of employing stewards, receivers and auditors, listing the desirable qualities to be looked for in the holders of each post and stressing the extra profit which ensued from their activities as opposed to the exchequer system of farming lands out for lump sums ('farms in certain'). For the first time we have here a statement of the calendar of the receivers' and auditors' year which hitherto could only be sketchily deduced from the dates of appearances in the Chamber as revealed by subsequent writs of prohibition to the Exchequer. The period for making up receivers' account by the auditors was from Michaelmas to Candlemas (February 2nd). Between Candlemas and Palm Sunday the accounts were to be submitted for examination 'afore such persons as the king's grace will thereto assign at London' to the end that 'his grace may be ascertained yearly of the whole revenues of all his livelihood, and what thereof is paid and what is owing and is whose default'. No surveys of land revenues are known to survive which can be identified as the endproduct of such a system for the reign of Richard III, but they would quite obviously have been almost identical with the one for 1503 to 1504 from which extracts are printed below (Doc. 16). The earliest known comparable annual survey of the exchequer side of the revenues which this 'remembrance' also calls for dates from the year

1505–6. This 'remembrance' itself is undated, but it entered between documents dated October 2 and 23, 1484.

Quite apart from the extensive diplomatic correspondence which this unique signet office register also contains, a class of business which the Signet Office had already been handling in Lancastrian times, the selection of documents now printed here still does not exhaust every type of entry in it. There are, for example, four separate lists of royal offices in England and Wales with the fees and wages attached to them. Taken together, these four lists suggest that the Yorkist kings had at least 800 offices worth altogether about £13,000 *per annum* at their disposal. Out of this total about 700 derived their income from crown lands, feefarms and sheriffs' farms, to a total of about £7,000 *per annum*.[12] Purposeful control of such patronage, widely distributed over the whole kingdom, was an important aid to political stability in Edward IV's last years, according to the Croyland Chronicle. It is doubtful whether any earlier kings had such statistical information available in their Chamber, but its appearance at this point is obviously in line with all the other aspects of the development of the Yorkist royal demesne which our documents describe.

Finally this signet office docket book contains a formidable list of royal grants of lands, which at first sight seems to contradict all the rest of the evidence.[13] Indeed it has been asserted that the appearance of this list in MS. Harley 433 neatly substantiates the well-known judgement of Sir Thomas More on Richard III, when he described him as gaining unsteadfast friendships with large gifts: that is, he was reduced to making a panicky, wholesale distribution of crown lands after Buckingham's rebellion. The lands concerned were valued at £13,500 *per annum* and were granted away for reserved rents totalling about £750. These grants certainly do show Richard III disposing of some lands to his supporters which had formerly belonged to the staunch Lancastrian families of de Vere and Courtenay and which he and his brother Clarence had held under Edward IV. They also reveal that he was similarly divesting himself of Rivers and Grey estates, thus increasing the circle of those who had a stake in opposing any future rebellions either in the Wydeville or Richmond cause. But the overwhelming majority of these royal grants represent a savage proscription of the rebels of 1483. He was in fact giving away very many of their lands, and very few of his own. The Croyland chronicler says that in 1484 and 1485 the whole South of England groaned under the 'plantation' of his Northern supporters, and this list of royal grants affords confirmation of the chronicler's observations rather

---

[12] B[ritish] M[useum], MS. Harley 433, ff. 310-6, 317-21, 322, 336-9.
[13] *ibid.*, ff. 282-289v.

than of More's judgement. Richard's grants of those royal lands in the list which had been in his brother Edward's possession at his death, or in his own hands as duke of Gloucester, may have been worth about £2,500 *per annum*. On the other hand there were some substantial, newly acquired, forfeited estates which he did not grant away (Doc. 14 [33]).

No comprehensive survey of royal income from the Yorkist landed estate can be compiled from this record. From valuations put upon the various complexes of estates during the Yorkist period which are known to have been in Richard III's hands, it seems likely that he had between £22,000 and £25,000 *per annum* available from this source, over and above the £7,000 *per annum* previously mentioned as earmarked for office holders. This sum must be taken to include the considerable local expenditure on garrison expenses, victuals for the royal Household, etc., of which this signet office book provides many examples. Before his rebellion, the duke of Buckingham also had a free hand to take land revenues in Wales and the West Country for the expenses of the regional government of which he was the head. Richard had put him into this high position of trust to replace the prince of Wales's council at Ludlow which had been destroyed by the usurpation. £1,346 *per annum* was also earmarked for the expenses of the separate household which Richard kept in existence in Yorkshire (Doc. 14 [30]).

The total also included such annuities and pensions as the king chose to settle on his relatives, friends and supporters. In Richard's case these were not extensive, the outstanding exception being the £1,000 *per annum* on the duchy of Cornwall granted to Thomas Howard to support the dignity of earl of Surrey during the lifetime of his father the duke of Norfolk and Earl Marshal. Richard had in effect eliminated the whole royal family. His own queen had no endowments beyond her own personal inheritance of Glamorgan and Abergavenny, exempted from the process of chamber accounting in one document in MS. Harley 433, but included in another (Doc. 14 [32, 15]). His son and heir did not live long enough to receive any endowment. William Herbert earl of Huntingdon, who married Richard's illegitimate daughter Katherine, was given £152 10s 10d *per annum* out of the revenues of the principality of Wales.

The greatest single item of central expenditure from Richard's land revenues was the assignment of over £10,000 *per annum* which he made on his receivers for the expenses and wages of his main Household (Doc. 14 [33]). This was more than double the amount Edward IV had earmarked for his Household from the same sources in 1482 and more than Henry VII could find in 1485. By 1489, when

Henry VII was beginning to endow his own royal family, this figure had shrunk again to £7,100 and by 1495 it was down to £6,000.[14]

The provision of a few substantial annuities to key men like the future victor of Flodden, whose service was required for his personal abilities not his broad acres, and the availability for local expenditure of ready cash in the hands of several score of reliable receivers at many places throughout the kingdom, were factors which enhanced rather than diminished the importance and significance of this Yorkist land revenue experiment. By destroying the cohesion of the House of York, by stooping to infanticide and by punitive measures of land confiscation which recalled the would-be tyrant Richard II, Richard III lost more political and military support than he gained. But he did not dissipate his brother Edward's crown estate. Edward IV before him had never bound himself to 'live of his own' solely on the issues of his crown lands, but it is clear from the records here printed that both he and his brother Richard III introduced a new dimension into English government finance with the development of a land revenue office in the royal Chamber. This was still intact in 1485 and we must now consider the effects of a second usurpation upon it, the usurpation of Henry of Richmond.

---

[14] These figures are arrived at by totalling the relevant items shown in the acts passed by parliament for Household expenses in these years and printed in the *Rotuli Parliamentorum*.

The Court of General Surveyors and Chamber finance under Henry VII

THE most striking characteristic of Henry Tudor's government in its early years was the new king's desire to conform to traditional methods. He was the heir of Lancaster, not the founder of a new dynasty. Wherever possible, his early legislation was drawn up on Lancastrian models and the processes of his government had to be demonstrably based on law and statute. Consequently, after the verdict of Bosworth Field on August 22, 1485, the central records of Signet Office and Chamber ceased and we are thrown back once more on the enrolments of the Exchequer to describe the functions of the crown lands in the workings of government.

Two classes of exchequer enrolments reveal the immediate financial impact of the Tudor usurpation of 1485. The receipt rolls of the Lower Exchequer, or Exchequer of Receipt, record that those numerous Yorkist receivers and farmers of land revenues who survived the revolution, or their replacements, began to pay in their receipts there and the Exchequer also began to make assignments by tally upon all such sources of land revenue as it considered to be available. Since the Yorkist period had been notable for the new consolidation and augmentation of such revenues described in the last chapter, the impact of these resources, suddenly diverted to the Exchequer when the process of chamber receipt and accounting ceased, was bound to be traceable there. Fortunately for our enquiry, the battle of Bosworth took place almost at the end of an exchequer year.

There are, however, several difficulties in the way of quoting figures. Late fifteenth and early sixteenth-century English government records did not classify revenues according to sources. Such information, insofar as it can be ascertained, is accidental to the purpose and methods of their compilation. Also the receipt rolls of the Exchequer, in spite of their name, are far from being a straightforward record of receipts of the king's revenues. Nevertheless a meaningful comparison between the receipt rolls for the last year of Richard III and the first year of Henry VII is possible. If we exclude from consideration in both cases the traditional items of exchequer accounting (sheriffs' farms, feefarms of towns and payments due from bailiffs of liberties) and the entirely fortuitous but individually substantial items of vacant ecclesiastical temporalities, the results of administrative change are revealed as follows. For Michaelmas Term 1484 and Easter Term 1485, cash receipts at the Exchequer from land revenues were under £700 and assignments made upon them a little over £1,800. For Michaelmas Term 1485 and Easter Term 1486, cash receipts were over £4,700 and assignments made on land revenues were over £7,000.

If we turn to the records of the Upper Exchequer, the Court of the Exchequer, or the Exchequer of Account, we find significant changes from 1485 in a series of account rolls called foreign accounts. By the Exchequer Ordinance of 1323 it had been laid down that where royal manors were in the hands of receivers and not farmers their accounts should be enrolled, not on the main annual pipe roll under the ultimate responsibility of the Exchequer's principal accountants, the sheriffs, but on 'foreign rolls', separate from the main annual account. Even before the Yorkist multiplication of receivers of land revenues, there had been brief, occasional, though unsustained employment of such receivers: for example, when a member of the royal family holding crown lands died without heirs other than the king, and their principal receiver was taken into exchequer service while the lands concerned were being dispersed. Thus Sir James Ramsay, who first observed the multiplication of Yorkist receivers of land revenues in permanent royal employment, duly remarked on the absence of their accounts from their proper, legal place, the 'foreign account' rolls. Under Richard III, even the accounts of the receiver-general of the duchy of Cornwall had disappeared from these rolls (Doc. 12, k). But with the accession of Henry VII, receivers' accounts began to reappear there and it is possible to trace on the foreign account rolls the Barons of the Exchequer recovering control of receivers' accounts during the first four regnal years of Henry VII. At the same time some of the surviving Yorkist receivers managed to secure continuing exemptions from exchequer accounting.

Both the first and second sessions of Henry VII's first Parliament passed acts of resumption.[1] The first declared him to be the heir of his uncle Henry VI and of his father Edmund Tudor. The second invited him to 'resume' into his hands all lands and possessions legally

---

[1] *Rot. Parl.*, vi, 270-3; 336-84.

belonging to Henry VI on October 2, 1455 or at any time since. There seems to have been some doubt still remaining after the passing of these acts, even when strengthened by the attainder of Richard III, whether Henry had acquired full legal title to the lands of the House of York. He certainly seized them all with the exception of the possessions of the dowager duchess of York, Cecily, and the somewhat reduced provision which he made for Edward IV's queen, who had lost everything under Richard III. But as late as 1495 two other acts were found necessary specifically to assert the king's legal title to all the lands of Richard III which he had held as duke of Gloucester and to all the lands which the House of York had originally acquired by grants of Edward III and Richard II to Edmund of Langley duke of York.[2] It proved impossible for Henry VII to acquire and retain estates quite as extensive as Richard III had held. Apart from making some amends to Elizabeth Wydeville, he had to provide for the new queen (though he did so only to the extent of £3,000 *per annum*); he made a substantial grant of royal lands to his mother, and of lands worth £2,000 *per annum* to his uncle Jasper Tudor. He also appears to have been under heavy obligations to Sir William Stanley. There were a number of Lancastrian supporters and victims of Richard III's savage proscriptions who had their lands restored. On the other hand, after the recent experiences of Richard III's reign the climate of opinion was against extensive attainders and confiscations. Henry did attaint a moderate number of Richard's supporters, but parliament was hostile to it. In the words of one member, Henry's bill 'sore was questioned with', while a contemporary chronicler confirms that it met with 'considerable censure' in the House of Commons.[3]

Henry of Richmond was a realist, for all his desire to act as the heir of Lancaster and to eschew the methods of Richard III. It is clear that by July 1487 his treasurer of the Chamber, Thomas Lovell, was receiving substantial sums of money into the king's coffers there. From this date we have a new kind of chamber record, books of receipts covering the years 1487 to 1495 and 1502 to 1505, after which date they have once again failed to survive. The three books extant for Henry VII's reign are examples of the treasurer of the Chamber's accounts, drawn up and audited by the king and authenticated by the king's signature only,[4] exactly as stipulated in Richard III's appointment of his treasurer and receiver of the Chamber in 1484 (Doc. 13). These books show that the first Tudor chamber treasurer

[2] *ibid.*, vi, 459-61.
[3] *Red Book of Colchester*, ed. W. Gurney Benham, Colchester, 1902; the Croyland chronicle, printed in *Rerum Anglicarum Scriptorum Veterum*. ed. W. Fulman, Oxford, 1684, i, 581.
[4] P.R.O., Exch. K. R. Various Accts., E. 101/413/2/1, 2, 3.

began to operate on the basis of the proceeds of Henry's first parliamentary subsidy, which was forwarded to the chamber coffers from the Exchequer, although by Easter 1493 there is evidence that collectors of tenths and fifteenths were delivering money directly into the king's own hands and receiving subsequent exoneration from account at the Exchequer. According to the chamber books, the first items of land revenue received there reached Lovell in July 1487. The first exoneration sent to the Exchequer for a receiver of land revenue who had paid cash to the Chamber was dated February 16, 1488. If we classify as land revenues all those items in the chamber accounts which can be identified as coming from receivers and farmers of estates and property, from the sheriffs' issues, from fee-farms, from bailiffs of liberties, from wardships, marriages and vacant temporalities, from fines for alienations and other feudal incidents, then these chamber books show that, over a two year period from 1487 to 1489, land revenues averaged £3,000 a year out of total annual receipts of £17,000. For the years 1492 to 1495 the comparable figures were £11,000 out of a total of £27,000 and for the years 1502 to 1505, £40,000 out of an annual total of £105,000.

Thus the increase in land revenues received from 1502 kept pace proportionately with the spectacular increase in the total chamber receipts from the same date. It is evident that, for the last six or seven years of his reign, Henry VII enjoyed land revenues on a scale previously unknown in English history, roughly of equal importance to the total yield of his other main source of revenue, indirect taxation, for the customs have been estimated to have averaged £40,132 *per annum* towards the end of his reign. The only year in the fifteenth century for which any comparable figures can be produced is 1433, when the Treasurer of England calculated that the customs were averaging £30,722 *per annum* and the total land revenues appear to have been something less than £8,265[5] (see above pages 37–38). 1433 seems to have been a reasonably typical year as regards land revenues for the Lancastrian period, except during the later personal rule of Henry VI when they were most probably reduced almost to nothing, but even this low figure of land revenues for 1433, unlike the total of £40,000 for 1502, did not represent cash received. It was only what the Exchequer considered ought to be available for assignment, a very different matter indeed.

By 1502 the chamber treasury was in effect financing the whole of the government of England. The Exchequer had been reduced once more to the comparatively minor position which it had occupied as a

---

[5] *Rot. Parl.*, iv, 433-8.

royal treasury during the later years of Yorkist rule. Towards the end of Henry VII's reign the Exchequer handled only some £12,600 in cash and assignments which did not pass through the Chamber. Its financial operations then covered little more than paying its own officers, and rewarding the sheriffs and the customers in the ports.[6]

Some obvious questions are posed by the availability of these figures for certain years of Henry VII's reign. How were these results achieved, and was it a gradual process of change covering the whole reign, or a sudden process affecting only the last few years? As regards the total scale of chamber financial operations, the survival of chamber issue books for the whole period from October 1495 to the end of the reign enables a partial answer to be given.[7] They suggest that it was the financial stresses of the Scottish campaign of 1496 to 1497 which first led Henry VII to control the major part of his government's financial operations from his Chamber and that the dominance which the Chamber then established as the central treasury of receipt and issue continued unbroken for the rest of the reign. But the knowledge of what money was spent in a particular year is no guide to when and from what sources it was received. The questions remain unanswered as to how and when Henry VII's Chamber became an office of receipt independent of the Exchequer and how it came about that land revenues could contribute the huge sum of £40,000 *per annum* in cash to its coffers.

Here we must fall back on exchequer records to answer the first question. According to an act of resumption passed in 1487,[8] it appears that the cautious Henry was then just beginning to reorganize his landed estate on the Yorkist pattern. A commission was set up in 1488 with authority under this act to review all appointments of receivers, auditors and farmers for the king's lands under the Treasurer, John lord Dynham, who had been Richard III's steward and surveyor of the duchy of Cornwall.[9] Its task, to quote the words of the act, was to arrest the decay into which 'the king's honours, manors, lands, tenements possessions and inheritances be greatly fallen, and further in decay shall daily fall, if remedy in this behalf be not provided....' The first definite evidence of a decisive reversion to the Yorkist practice of central control and audit of land revenues

---

[6] B. P. Wolffe, 'Henry VII's Land Revenues and Chamber Finance', *E.H.R.*, lxxix (1964), 250 and references given there.

[7] P.R.O., Exch. K.R. Various Accts., E. 101/414/6, 16, 415/3; B.M. Add. MS. 21480; P.R.O., Exch. Treasury of Receipt, Miscellaneous Books, E. 36/214. There is also the former MS. Phillipps 4104, now in the possession of The Robinson Trust, Pall Mall, London, an original chamber issue book running from Michaelmas 1502 to Michaelmas 1505.

[8] *Rot. Parl.*, vi, 403-8.

[9] *C. of P.R. 1485-1494*, p. 230.

in the Chamber is found in a writ to the Exchequer dated March 2, 1493. This informed the Exchequer that with effect from Michaelmas 1491 all their jurisdiction over the accounts of three of the king's principal receivers, Reginald Bray, Hugh Oldham and John Walsh, was annulled for ever, because the king had decided that their final accounts should be determined before himself and his Council and that their issues should be paid yearly into his own hands and nowhere else (Doc. 15). This meant, of course, that payment was to be made direct into his chamber coffers. Similar injunctions to the Exchequer for other receivers followed from time to time, though the cautious king seems to have authorized many of these only *ad hoc* to cover the specific years for which the Exchequer was then demanding account. He seems to have regarded the annoyance of exchequer demands as a salutary check on the good behaviour of his receivers, a process which was ultimately reinforced by the taking of substantial financial obligations in the Court of General Surveyors from receivers and others for the satisfactory performance of their duties (Doc. 17, *passim*).

Probably from Michaelmas 1491, all the principal receivers of land revenues, apart from the receiver general of the duchy of Lancaster, were once more rendering their final accounts before a committee of the king's Council in his Chamber. Besides the evidence of Bray's, Oldham's and Walsh's exoneration from exchequer accounting from this date there is a similar permanent exoneration back-dated to the same date and issued on March 4, 1497 for Richard Cholmeley, receiver and surveyor of lands in the North formerly held by Richard III when duke of Gloucester. Another document of February 20, 1505, containing a list of accountants whose accounts had been withdrawn from the jurisdiction of the Barons of the Exchequer to be heard '*coram consilio Regis*', but unfortunately containing few dates and in an imperfect state, does nevertheless reveal that in one case the accounts concerned dated back to January 12, 1492.[10]

For the year Michaelmas 1503 to Michaelmas 1504 it is possible to follow this process of cameral, conciliar audit in the case of Richard Nanfan, the receiver-general of the duchy of Cornwall.[11] The auditing committee then consisted of Roger Layburne bishop of Carlisle and Sir Robert Southwell. Nanfan had to be available in London for the three months of January, February, and March, together with his two foreign auditors, Robert Coorte and Thomas Hobson, with the accounts they had previously drawn up and the documents subsidiary to them. Nanfan himself produced fifteen indentures to prove that he had paid £4,284 6s 0½d from arrears and current issues to the treasurer

[10] P.R.O., Exch. K.R. Misc. Accts., E. 101/517/10.
[11] P.R.O. Special Collections, Ministers' Accts., S.C. 6/Hen. VII/1084.

of the Chamber for the king's coffers during the twelve months under review. Certain items allowed him by the foreign auditors were then reduced, and the king's councillors entered a summary of the account in a book containing summaries of all the accounts heard before them for that year (Doc. 16), which was then examined and signed on each page by the king himself. The king also picked out and marked for future easy reference each item of cash which John Heron was there stated to have received. From the extracts given below it will be seen that these sums amounted to £24,620 7s 8½d from current issues of receivers, plus £3,003 16s 8½d from wards' lands. To get a complete total for Heron's land revenue receipts during this twelve months' period we would have to add the items of arrears paid to him between Michaelmas 1503 and Michaelmas 1504, information which the book of summaries also records, as well as having to ascertain and add what he received independently from the duchy of Lancaster.

Further analysis of the content of this book of summaries of receivers' accounts for the year 1503–4 (Doc. 16) enables us partly to determine how and when the build up of land revenues received in the Chamber had occurred. It was the death of Prince Arthur in 1502 which brought the revenues of Wales, Chester and Flint, Cornwall and March to the royal coffers. The duke of Bedford's lands had been controlled by the Chamber since his death in 1495. The chamber revenue from the duchy of York lands had been augmented by the death of the dowager duchess in the same year and the queen's lands had come to the Chamber on her death in 1503. Apart from this striking wind-fall of royal family endowments which had benefited the Chamber, the book contains some very substantial additions which were the result of the acts of attainder and forfeiture passed between 1495 and 1504, notably Sir William Stanley's, the earl of Suffolk's, Lord Audley's, Sir William de la Pole's and Sir James Tyrell's.

Nevertheless, however highly we rate the accidental factors of royal births and deaths and of forfeitures in this process of land revenue augmentation under Henry VII, we know that when such happenings occurred before 1461, in the Lancastrian period, the results had been quite different. Following the usurpation of 1399, when the crown had received a considerable access of land and had no members of the royal family able to absorb it, there were six years or more of repeated parliamentary clamouring for acts of resumption to augment the financial resources of a near-bankrupt government. The ineptitude which Henry VI later displayed, in disposing of the flood of estates placed in his hands by royal deaths between 1437 and 1447, had been a major stimulus to public opinion and to Yorkist policy which concentrated demands for the king to 'live of his own' on the nature and extent of the crown landed estate. Henry VII in supplanting the Yorkists on the throne as the heir of Lancaster had nevertheless adopted and extended the scope of Yorkist land revenue organization.

Books of summaries or 'declarations' of the final accounts of some forty receivers, appearing annually before the king and his conciliar committee, some of them several times for separate charges, survive for the four years between 1502 and 1506. In addition these 'General Surveyors' heard the final accounts of a number of farmers of lands, of feefarms, reserved rents and of all wards' lands and vacant temporalities, the whole of which payments went into the chamber coffers (Doc. 16). But from Hilary Term 1505 to Trinity Term 1508 we have another most interesting and important docket book, in many ways similar to MS. Harley 433 of Richard III's reign and in others different and more sophisticated. This book (Doc. 17) records first instance court appearances before the bishop of Carlisle, Sir Robert Southwell, and one other, Henry Edyall, clerk, who joined them at Trinity Term 1508. Occasionally it also records decisions of the king's Council requiring action by them (Doc. 17 [12, 58]). It also records that Carlisle and Southwell in their turn determined cases which had begun in the prince's council or in the exchequer at Chester or themselves ordered appearances in those places (*ibid.* [17, 22, 26, 40, 61]). Throughout its pages this book is a record of court appearances and reappearances on appointed, specified days. The personnel of the court are repeatedly stated (*ibid.* [29, 39, 40, 46, 47, 48, 49, 52, 55, 57, 59, 61, 62]). Specific references to it as a court are frequent (*ibid.* [1, 3, 28, 33, 34, 38, 44, 46, 50, 56, 59, 62]). Meeting places referred to are 'at St John's' (*ibid.* [47]) and in the Prince's Chamber at Westminster (*ibid.* [59]). The units of land management referred to and the names of the receivers concerned are, of course, identical with those of the summaries or declarations of account (Doc. 16). Unlike the instruments of MS. Harley 433, which were the product of the Signet Office, appearances, information and action were obtained by Henry VII's General Surveyors by means of the privy seal (Doc. 17 [24, 27, 37, 46, 49, 55, 60, 62]). On one occasion a messenger, a pursuivant, was sent out with twenty-seven privy seals for the Warwick lands (*ibid.* [37]). Since the court was naturally concerned among many other matters with the improvement of leases (*ibid.* [35, 44]), putting new lessees in possession (*ibid.* [12, 58]) and making placards for woodsales (*ibid.* [42, 63, 64]), it follows that the great seal was at its disposal, presumably through the medium of the privy seal, as and when required.

There is one other important difference between this record and MS. Harley 433: its greater specialization. This docket book is the record of a court only and does not include receipts for the cash payments, which were made to Heron. Neither does it record the routine appearances of receivers. The separate treasurer of the Chamber's books and the General Surveyors' own summaries or 'declarations' of accounts now fulfilled these two separate functions. There is one apparent exception to this (Doc. 17 [7]), a single receipt given for a payment 'in our lodging at Stepney', but this may have been a copy of a receipt given by Heron. This docket book is thus concerned with the means by which Heron's supply of cash was maintained and increased. Payments were obtained for him (*ibid.* [32, 61]), inquiries held into sums due (*ibid.* [9, 20]), and investigations made into the king's rights and dues (*ibid.* [11, 27, 30, 50, 56]). One of these investigations required the appearance of the Mayor and Fellowship of the Calais Staple before the General Surveyors (*ibid.* [30]). Demands for accounts to be rendered were backed up by substantial penalties and powers of attachment (*ibid.* [25, 28, 49]). Likewise when ensuring the levying of sums due they had powers of attachment and imprisonment (*ibid.* [13, 21, 32, 34, 52, 53, 54]). Monetary penalties for non-appearance might be very heavy (*ibid.* [47]). The court had written evidence produced for its perusal (*ibid.* [4, 10]); it had evidence taken down on its instructions (*ibid.* [5, 6]); learned counsel appeared before it (*ibid.* [8]). It took many obligations from those on whom it sat in judgement: to perform certain tasks; as security for the efficient performance of their duties, as well as for payments undertaken (*ibid.* [10, 15, 16, 17, 18, 22, 26, 33, 38, 52, 57]). Apart from the mass of court entries which follow a sequence of law terms there is also a section consisting of some 125 obligations taken before the court and entered separately and consecutively in the book (from folio 46).

Other powers of the court included instituting commissions of inquiry (*ibid.* [43, 46]), making allowances to farmers (*ibid.* [2, 23]), adjudicating in disputes between tenants (*ibid.* [3, 4, 60, 62]) and ordering the production of a valor (*ibid.* [14]). It will be observed from the dates given in this book that, unlike the practice in the Exchequer Court, there were no long delays between one court appearance of a defendant and his next. Also this volume, for all its appearance of being a rough entry-book only, does reveal the final outcome of proceedings from time to time at the place in the volume where the first notice of the case appeared. To obtain similar information from contemporary exchequer records involves the searching of many parallel series of enrolments, often extending over many years, often without any final result. Here then, in the records of court appearances before Henry VII's General Surveyors of Land Revenues, lies a major part of the explanation for the augmentation of such revenues for which the opening years of the sixteenth century were remarkable. The young Henry VIII's Council, well attended by his judges, was to declare such courts, the 'by-courts', illegal, because, unlike the Exchequer Court, they were not 'courts of record' (Doc. 18). Nevertheless its not being a court of record during the last years of Henry VII had not prevented the Court of General Surveyors from being an effective court of land revenue.

The decline of the General Surveyors, 1509 to 1536

HENRY VIII began his reign with revenues enhanced far beyond what any of his predecessors had enjoyed, thanks to the deliberate, persistent priority of financial gain which his father had set upon his relations with his subjects. Lest resentment at the grim financial realism of the father should tarnish the bright promise of the new reign, the young king's Council now showed themselves inclined to bow to hostile public opinion and to sanction the continuation of Henry VII's financial methods only where these were manifestly grounded in the law of the land. In two meetings which were well attended by the king's legal advisers (the judges, sergeants-at-law, his solicitor and attorney) the royal Council commented adversely upon the standing and possible future of so-called 'by-courts' like the Council Learned and the General Surveyors and advised their abolition (Doc. 17).[1] With the chief judges present they also cancelled some of the financial bonds held for the king's use because they had been entered into by subjects who had been 'by the undue means of certain of the learned council of our said late father thereunto driven, contrary to law, reason and good conscience, to the manifest charge and peril of the soul of our said late father'.[2] Empson and Dudley, in their Council Learned, bore the brunt of public resentment and suffered the direst consequences. But the General Surveyors were also seriously affected because they too were a 'by-court', owing their existence to no statute or legal instrument under the great seal and thus enjoying no legal recognition as an accepted court of law. No longer backed by personal royal favour and participation in their activities, they were curbed and restricted by the cautious policies now to be followed.

[1] I owe my knowledge of these minutes to Mr J. P. Cooper's transcription of the substance of them in the *Historical Journal*, ii, 1959, pp. 121-2. I am also greatly indebted to Mr Cooper for lending me his photostats of Ellesmere MS. 2655.

[2] L[etters] & P[apers] Hen. VIII, i (new ed.), 448 (4).

In the Chamber John Heron was for the moment recognized for what he really was by the conferment of the new title of General Receiver of the king's revenues in the first Parliament of the new reign. His acquittances and receipts were given the full force of law by this act of Parliament, with the king's subjects for their part acquiring the statutory right to sue him or any successor in that office in the king's courts of law for recovery of any sums unlawfully obtained or withheld from them (Doc. 19). The General Surveyors, on the other hand, with effect from June 1510, were made subject to the full rigours, delays and restrictions of the Court of the Exchequer and deprived of the use of the privy seal (Doc. 20). Sir Robert Southwell was appointed an extra auditor of the Exchequer with pre-eminence over the other five auditors, having as his charge the audit of the account of all accountants who had previously rendered their accounts before the General Surveyors. He took the prescribed oath of office on July 16, 1510 (Doc. 20, p. 170). He was to have the assistance of Bartholomew Westby, one of the Barons of the Exchequer, in the work of audit, and the Barons of the Exchequer were to order appearances before him and to swear the accountants.

It is clear that Southwell was henceforth to do his work equipped only with the normal powers of an exchequer auditor, according to the normal processes of the Court of the Exchequer. The only exception was that Heron's warrants now had full legal authority and were to be accepted by him without any prior authorization in the Exchequer (Doc. 20). As well as losing his independent means of summoning accountants before him, Southwell was now deprived of his discretionary powes of allowance when hearing accounts: 'so that all ... charges, neither ordinary nor whereof letters patent or special warrant may appear unto the said Sir Robert, be allowed not only by his discretion and advice of the said Bartholomew Westby ...' (*ibid.*). Gaps in exchequer records, consequent on the 'extra-curial' practices of the previous reign, were to be filled up by suitable declarations made in the Exchequer Court by the king's attorney, John Erneley. Southwell's charge was re-defined by letters patent dated July 6, 1511, and it will be noted that this included wards' lands, butlerage, vacant temporalities, Calais, the Staple, the Wardrobe and the Hanaper (Doc. 20, p. 171). He had, in effect, become the principal foreign auditor of the Exchequer. It appears, from a survey or valor which he made sometime after Michaelmas 1511, that his total charge for the first full Exchequer year under the new arrangements (Michaelmas 1510 to Michaelmas 1511) fell by over £20,000 from the level of 1508 to 1509 (Doc. 22 [1]). The principal reason for this was, of course, the removal of the hand of Henry VII, as another of Southwell's valors, made sometime after Michaelmas 1515, clearly demonstrates (*ibid.*

[3]). But the explanation put forward by the frustrated royal administrators, once they began to recover their influence in the Council of the new reign over the initial predominance of the lawyers, was the administrative ineffectiveness of the Exchequer.

The first evidence that their arguments had begun to prevail over their colleagues in the Council is contained in the long and complicated Statute 3 Henry VIII cap. 23 which was enacted in the parliamentary session of February 4 to March 30, 1512 (Doc. 21). It begins with a detailed justification of Henry VII's cameral and conciliar financial arrangements which had made the General Surveyors and the treasurer of the Chamber independent of the Exchequer, but continued with an exposition of the failure, vexation and trouble which had resulted from the Exchequer's efforts to make its recovery of control effective since the death of Henry VII. The king's wish was now declared to be to revert to the receiving and accounting processes of his father's time, and this statute ultimately explained how this was to be done. The first significant change was to authorize Southwell and Westby to 'survey and approve' all items contained in the charge of February 6, 1511 by direct authority of their own seal or seals. This gave them the power to issue necessary commissions of inquiry, orders for inquisitions to be held, or for valors to be made, etc., without which their central task of effective royal estate management was proving impossible. Two examples of such instruments under their seal, one issued from the Prince's Council Chamber on February 15, 1514, and another of 1525, are given below (Doc. 23 [23, 24]). Next the General Surveyors recovered their power to move the privy seal for purposes of summoning accountants before them, together with powers to take oaths and to make allowances on their own authority. Equipped with these basic powers for the first time by statute, their charge was now further extended to include surveillance of the account of the receiver-general of the duchy of Lancaster, subject to the final authority of the king and his Council.

But it is important to realize that there were still certain powers which they had not recovered. Throughout these early years of Henry VIII's reign, there was a cautious brake of legal safeguards for the rights of the subject applied to their activities, which had not been used before 1509. For example, their recovery of power to use the privy seal was now limited by a prohibition against the inclusion of any monetary penalty in their writs. Although Southwell and Westby, as General Surveyors, now had the power to receive suits and complaints by bill against any accountant appearing before them, such suits were to be heard and determined in the Court of the Exchequer before the Barons of the Exchequer. No provision was made in this act for the renewed annual compilation of the books of summaries of final accounts, as heard before them, which had become routine practice during the last seven years of Henry VII's reign. Neither did the General Surveyors recover their former power to take recognizances for due performance of an office or for the payments of debts. Their partially recovered powers were to lapse on November 30, 1512, thus making their continuance subject to parliamentary authority. This same statute also reviewed the position of John Heron in the Chamber. He reverted to his title of the previous reign, treasurer of the Chamber, and provision was now made for auditing his accounts only in the Chamber and not in the Exchequer. No mention of where or how he was to account had been contained in the earlier statute of 1 Henry VIII cap. 3 (Doc. 19) which had in any case lapsed with the meeting of this new parliament. Finally a committee was set up to deal with any 'ambiguity or doubt' which might later be found in this act, consisting of the Chancellor of England, the steward of the Household, the Keeper of the Privy Seal and the two Chief Justices, or any three of them.

The subsequent history of this legislation of 1536 does not suggest any renewal of the prime concern for financial profit which had marked the history of Henry VII's revenue courts. Changes made to Statute 3 Henry VIII cap. 23 appear to have now become matters of clarification of ambiguities, further safeguards for the rights of the subject, or the removal of certain obstacles to smooth administration. Before the act expired on November 30, 1512 its life was extended to the meeting of the next Parliament. At the same time Southwell and his fellow surveyors were required to draw up and deposit in the Exchequer a book of all recoverable debts within their charge due to Henry VII at Michaelmas 1508. They were also warned to observe the customs of the manors concerned when approving copyhold lands in the king's hands by reason of wardship or vacation, and not to make woodsales amounting to waste of such lands. A writ of *scire facias* returnable at the Exchequer was declared to be a method of appeal against their decisions in certain circumstances, while on the other side the Chancery and Privy Seal Office were ordered to afford the General Surveyors the same facilities for the issuing of necessary writs for proceedings in other courts as were already enjoyed by the Barons of the Exchequer, the king's escheators and other such royal officers.[3]

When this legislation next came up for renewal in the Parliament of 1515 it was prolonged to Lady Day 1516, with the addition of the following exemplifications and extensions of the powers of the General Surveyors which appear to bear the stamp of Chancellor Wolsey's clear

---

[3] Stat. 4 Hen. VIII cap. 18, 'For Sir Robert Southwell' (*Statutes of the Realm*, iii 68-73), passed in the session of parliament held from Nov. 4-December 20, 1512.

legal and administrative mind and went some further way towards restoring their old powers. The Surveyors now recovered their power to include a monetary penalty in their writs, though only to the sum of £100, but their writs were now once again backed by the old powers of attachment, imprisonment and power to fix bail which they had enjoyed under Henry VII. A timetable for receivers' accounting before them was now laid down, to be completed by January 13th each year, and arrears to be paid in annually by March 20th. All receivers were to find sufficient sureties to guarantee the fulfilment of this timetable before a certain date, otherwise their patents of appointment were to be automatically void. This recalled the routine monetary obligations and recognizances imposed by the General Surveyors on Henry VII's receivers. The General Surveyors were now also given power to move the great seal directly, without the mediation of the privy seal, for all leases made by them for terms of twenty-one years or less. The king was declared to have the power to appoint a committee of the Council to review their activities as and when he wished and a new schedule of the charge was prepared. It is possible that this charge was somewhat more extensive than before, because it now included the accounts of the keeper or farmer of the king's Exchanges in London, but one cannot be certain of this because the surviving 1511 list of their charge is mutilated and not entirely decipherable. Finally by this new act, the treasurer of the Chamber, hitherto accountable to the king in person only, was now made accountable alternatively 'before such as his Grace shall thereunto limit and appoint'.[4]

This act was replaced by another in good time before its expiry, with effect from January 1, 1516 and to endure until the morrow of the last day of the next parliament. This restored to the General Surveyors power to take, receive, record and discharge recognizances for debts within their charge. On the other hand it gave a right of traverse in the Exchequer Court to anyone charged with refusal to accept a writ from them or with failure to appear before them. It also laid down that their summonses under the privy seal must allow sufficient time for convenient appearance before them, otherwise no penalty for non-appearance could be incurred; it further ordered the printing of the act for sale and laid down an oath of loyalty and impartiality to be sworn by the General Surveyors in Chancery before the Chancellor.[5]

Seven years later, with the assembly of the next Parliament in 1523, a further measure was enacted to continue their powers until the

---

[4] Stat. 6 Hen. VIII cap. 24, 'The Act concerning the King's General Surveyors' (*Statutes*, iii 145-52), passed in the session of Parliament held from February 5 to April 5, 1515.

[5] Stat. 7 Hen. VIII cap 7, 'The King's Revenues' (*Statutes*, iii 182-96), which was passed in the session of Parliament held from Nov. 12-Dec. 22, 1515.

day following the dissolution of the subsequent Parliament. This contained no changes of substance except that the General Surveyors were now burdened with the additional but financially unproductive charge of auditing the expenditure of prests received by individuals from the king and any further additions which might be made to their charge were henceforth to be confined to certain specified catagories of accounts.[6] A new administrative restriction was imposed upon their activities from April 15, 1536, the year in which their statutory existence was made perpetual, when it was enacted that all their instruments must first pass through the signet office, unless the instruments concerned were for leases of land worth £6 13s 4d *per annum* or less, because the activities of such courts as the General Surveyors were depriving the signet office clerks of their fees. This measure cannot have been a discriminatory one directed against the General Surveyors alone for it also specifically stated that it was to apply also to the new Court of Augmentations founded in the same year.[7] Finally a short statute of 1536 at last gave Henry VIII's General Surveyors a permanent existence instead of the periodic survival extended from one parliament to the next which they had hitherto enjoyed, but it made no further material alteration of any of their powers.[8]

This story from exchequer records and statutes of abrupt decline from 1509 followed by gradual, partial restoration is confirmed and amplified by a docket book of the General Surveyors for the years 1514–1537 (Doc. 23). Unlike their docket book for Henry VII's reign, the Henry VIII volume includes regular annual entries of the receipt of views of receivers' accounts as delivered to the General Surveyors by the foreign auditors concerned in the Hilary Terms (*ibid.* [1]). These were on paper and were then handed back to the foreign auditors to be used in engrossing final versions of the receivers' accounts on parchment for delivery to the Exchequer (*ibid.* [2]). In the following Trinity Term these parchment engrossments were handed over to the

---

[6] Stat. 14 and 15 Hen. VIII cap. 15, 'An Act for the King's General Surveyors' (*Statutes*, iii 219-20). Additions to their charge were henceforth to consist of 'only such manors, tenements and other hereditaments which hereafter shall come to the king by purchase, escheat, attainder, or of such lands and tenements as shall be recovered to the king's use for payment of his debts, and of and for prests of such sums of money as hereafter by the king's commandment shall be delivered to any manner of person or persons for any of his foreign affairs, business and expenses'.

[7] Stat. 27 Hen. VIII cap. 11, 'An Act concerning Clerks of the Signet and Privy Seal' (*Statutes*, iii, 542-4), 1535-6. The primary purpose of the act was to get the signet clerks their fees when the use of the signet was evaded, rather than compel the use of the signet. The restriction does not, in fact, seem to have been applied to the Court of Augmentations.

[8] Stat. 27 Hen. VIII cap. 62, 'An Act concerning the General Surveyors of our Sovereign Lord the King' (*Statutes*, iii 631-2).

General Surveyors, who passed them on to the Exchequer, again entering a record of this action in their docket book (*ibid.* [3]). As stated in the docket book, this was the procedure required of them by Statute 3 Henry VIII cap. 23 (1512). Before the death of Henry VII, when they had themselves been the final accounting authority, they had compiled their own book of summaries of declarations of all the receivers' accounts each year, which was then inspected and audited by the king himself (Doc. 16). The very fact that this later docket book, extending to 1537, only began formal entries by terms from 1514, and contained a mere thirty-four undated entries before that date, confirms that the General Surveyors only recovered some of their separate identity as a court following the statute of 1512. But it was still a more formal, restricted existence than it had been up to 1509, as indicated, for example, by the use of Latin to record court appearances which under Henry VII had been entered in English, as well as by the new meticulous recording in the new book of each routine appearance of accountants before them. This had been quite unnecessary under Henry VII because of the annual book of summaries of final accounts which was regularly compiled and then retained in the court.

The act of 1512 also restored their right to hold regular court sessions in order to hear cases brought before them by privy seal writ, and a selection of these from 1517 is given below (Doc. 23 [4–18, 21]). The sums of money concerned were generally lower than they had been before 1509, and the book contains no proliferation of obligations entered into before the court or of recognizances taken by it, as had been the case before 1509. Not only was it now subject to the control of a series of parliamentary statutes, but the court now also followed the superior ruling of Star Chamber in cases concerning important people or tricky points of law and equity (*ibid.* [19, 20]). On the other hand, it appears to have been able to call upon the signet for a summons before it of an important nobleman like the earl of Northumberland (*ibid.* [22]). Nevertheless, the most striking contrast between the pre-1509 court and the post-1512 court is in the volume of business. The docket book for Henry VII's reign extends to 65 double folios for three years. The book for Henry VIII's reign covers twenty-three years in 90 double folios. Furthermore, as already mentioned, the Henry VII book, unlike the Henry VIII book, does not take up space with formal entries recording the routine appearances of accountants.

The comparative clarity and abundance of information, available for the latter years of Henry VII's reign, about his total income and its sources and, most specifically, about the contributions made to this total by the revenues controlled by the General Surveyors, cannot be matched for the period 1509 to 1536. In the first place we do not have any of the treasurer of the Chamber's receipt books, with the exception of a loan account for September 29, 1522 to April 1, 1523.⁹ The chamber issue books which do survive do not reveal sources of revenue, though they do, of course, give some indication of total expenditure. Secondly the General Surveyors no longer now produced consolidated annual summaries of accounts, and a note in their docket book explains why. In fulfilment of statutory instruction they now held views of accounts, returned the documents concerned to the respective foreign auditors for engrossment on parchment, and then merely acted as agents for the Exchequer in accepting these engrossments of individual receivers' accounts when completed, noting the fact of receipt in their record and then forwarding them to the Exchequer (Doc. 23 [2]).

However, certain *ad hoc* surveys of their charge and of its disposal were required at two points in time which appear to have coincided with the preparation of the statutes of 1512 and 1515 respectively, each of which increased their powers. We have one survey of their activities which gives figures for the three years 1508–9, 1509–10 and 1510–11 (Doc. 22 [1]); another for one whole year ending at Michaelmas 1515 (*ibid.* [2]), and a third designed to demonstrate that there was £24,719 17s 8⅛d less *per annum* reaching the king's coffers from the revenues under their surveillance at Michaelmas 1515 than there had been in the last year of Henry VII's reign (*ibid.* [3]). The first survey reveals that the General Surveyors suffered a decrease of over £20,000 *per annum* in the total of rents, farms and other issues controlled by them between 1508 and 1511. In spite of this Heron's declining receipts were drastically augmented in the third and final year of this survey, but entirely at the expense of fees, wages and other similar allocations hitherto paid from these revenues. The second survey for the year ending Michaelmas 1515 shows that the total charge had risen again by then, although it was still some £5,000 *per annum* less than it had been for 1508–9. However, this total charge now included the whole of the revenues of the duchy of Lancaster which was first included in the General Surveyors' charge by Statute 3 Henry VIII cap. 23 (1512), while fees, wages and other similar allocations in 1515 were once again back to the 1509–10 figure. Cash payments to the Household and Wardrobe at £9,099 7s 6½d in 1515 showed a very big increase, while the remainder of cash paid to the king's coffers showed a very big drop at £16,367 13s 6d. The differences in the financing of the Household and in accounting for the revenues of the duchy of Lancaster can be regarded simply as variations in book-keeping practice for the purposes of comparison

⁹ P.R.O., Exchequer, Treasury of Receipt, Miscellaneous Books, E36/221.

with the figures which we have for the latter years of Henry VII's reign:

Land Revenues

1503-4		1514-15
£24,620 7s 8½d	Receivers of land revenues excluding wards' lands	
£3,003 16s 8½d	Wards' lands	£25,468 11s 0½d
c. £9,250[10]	Duchy of Lancaster	
£36,874 4s 5d	Total	£25,468 11s 0½d

But the third survey is a contemporary document stating that £26,719 17s 8⅛d less *per annum* was reaching the king's coffers in 1515 than had been in 1509, of which £5,404 9s 5¾d was due not to diminution of receipts of land revenues in England and Wales, but to increased payments made from them to the Household and Wardrobe. A further £4,058 4s 1d of this decrease was due to loss of revenues or extra charges incurred at Calais, items not included in the Henry VII figures, so that some £9,500 ought to be deducted to get a valid comparison between 1504 and 1515 for land revenues in England and Wales. The first calculation gives a decrease of £11,405 13s 4½d *per annum* between 1503-4 and 1514-15, the second (contemporary) one a decrease of £15,256 14s 1⅜d *per annum* between 1509 and 1515. According to the contemporary survey, these decreases were due to lands being given away by the king without any reserved rents (£7,500); extra fees, wages and annuities granted (£3,000); restorations by act of Parliament (£2,500); annual payments due from various lands but remitted by the king (£1,000); lands freed out of the king's hands to lawful heirs (£400); diminutions of farms in England and Wales (£400), and lands recovered from the king by various persons (£200). With the removal of the old king's personal drive and control, the crown lands had thus become a rapidly wasting financial asset between 1509 and 1515. It has been asserted that from 1515 Wolsey so increased the efficiency of the General Surveyors and so effectively filled the place left vacant by the death of Henry VII, that land revenues were subsequently raised to even greater value than they had been before 1509. But Professor Dietz, the author of this view, only cites as evidence the passing of an act of resumption (Statute 6 Henry VIII cap. 25) and the forfeiture of the duke of Buckingham's lands. It is true that the resumption of the General Surveyors' activities

---

[10] R. Somerville, *History of the Duchy of Lancaster*, i, 275.

as a court (Doc. 23) seems to have depended to a very great extent on the further partial restoration of powers which they were given by statute in 1515 and 1516, but their docket book to 1537 still reveals a much reduced field and scale of operations compared with the previous reign even after these changes. Moreover, the act of resumption passed at this time did not apply to grants of land; only to certain classes of annuities and offices. This important fact was not noticed by Dietz or by those who have adopted his views.[11] It may perhaps be reasonable to suppose that some brake was now applied by Wolsey to spiralling grants of annuities and sinecure offices, although we have been given no specific evidence to show that this was in fact so. The only definite evidence we have of any augmentation of land revenues after 1515 and before the dissolution of the monasteries is what came from Buckingham's forfeiture in 1520. According to the accounts of the receiver-general of these lands, which the General Surveyors regularly forwarded to the Exchequer, his average annual total charge seems to have been about £2,000 and the treasurer of the Chamber received rather more or less than £1,500 *per annum* from him.[12]

The statutory restrictions imposed upon Henry VIII's General Surveyors and the lack of personal interest and involvement in their affairs shown by the king himself thus produced a significant downward trend in the financial importance of the new royal revenue courts which had been established by his father. Henry VIII's personal disinclination to participate in and support the work of the revenue courts was also approved of by public opinion. Nevertheless, at Michaelmas 1515 the royal cash income from land still seems to have been about £25,000 *per annum*, compared with £40,000 or more *per annum* at the death of Henry VII, and this income was now once more administered and controlled by a separate royal land revenue office. Royal policies dating back to 1461 and designed to enable the king to 'live of his own' had thus added a permanent new dimension to English government finance, second in importance only to the annual yield of indirect taxation.

The decline in land revenues from the peak of Henry VII's last years occurred on the eve of 'the first large and sustained fall in the purchasing power of money of which we have any record'.[13] It also

---

[11] F. C. Dietz, *English Government Finance 1485-1558*, 2nd ed. London, 1964, p. 99. cf. K. Pickthorn, *Early Tudor Government, Henry VIII*, p. 55, 'many grants of lands ... were resumed'. The *Journal of the House of Lords*, for all its imperfections, correctly designates the measure as 'billa Resumptionis Officiariorum et Annuitatum' (i, 41).

[12] P.R.O., Special Collections, Ministers' Accounts, S.C. 6/Henry VIII/5853, 5854, 5861 (i.e. for 12-13, 14-15 and 24-25 Henry VIII).

[13] E. Victor Morgan, *The Study of Prices and the Value of Money* (Hist. Assoc. Helps for Students of History, no. 53, 1952), p. 19.

coincided with the period of by far the greatest expenditure of cash resources by an English king ever recorded to that date. Because the Chamber was now the national treasury and because no chamber receipt books are extant, the source of the fortune expended by Henry VIII and Wolsey on foreign adventures must remain a matter for speculation. Between April 1512 and June 1513 an initial amount of over £600,000 was paid out by the treasurer of the Chamber for war expenses.[14] This study of the General Surveyors demonstrates that the land revenue courts of the early Tudor kings, at least before 1536, could hardly have provided a major portion of such sums for war expenditure, either from current resources or from accumulated reserves. The belief that it was drawn from a cash fortune left by Henry VII dies hard. There is one solitary near-contemporary English reference to savings in ready money left to Henry VIII by his father,[15] but the legend of an inherited 'mighty treasure' squandered dates from 1529, from the disgrace of the royal minister who was then alleged to have squandered it.[16]

There is a possibility that Henry VIII did inherit jewels and plate up to a value of £300,000 from his father,[17] and there is no doubt that Wolsey had the chamber receipt books of Henry VII's reign searched to provide evidence of cash salted away for the future, because on January 23, 1513 Heron was ordered to surrender £10,000 in various coins 'particularly entered in your book of receipts by the hands of our most dearest father and of blessed memory Henry the VII', to pay for the retaining of soldiers in Flanders.[18] Some £8,600 of this can indeed be traced as entered in Henry VII's own hand in the chamber receipt book which ended at October 1, 1505,[19] the remaining £1,400 being recorded in a later book not now extant. But this is the only evidence we have of cash inherited and spent, and when Heron had closed his chamber accounts for the old reign his own payments out had exceeded the total charge alleged against him by over £9,000.[20]

[14] P.R.O., Exchequer, Treasury of Receipt, Miscellaneous Books, E36/215.
[15] In 1516, quoted by Professor R. B. Wernham in *Before the Armada*, p. 412, from C. Sturge, *Tunstal*, p. 39, where it is quoted from the *Letters and Papers*, Hen. VIII, ii, 2331.
[16] *L & P*, IV, pp. 2549, 2550, 2556 and cf. *Venetian Calendar*, IV, 694 (p. 298 dated 1531), where 6 millions in gold (about £1,300,000 according to Dietz), ready money, left to Henry VIII by his father is reported spent on the wars by Falier, the Venetian ambassador, who had been in England from 1528 to 1531 and who had heard it 'from a trustworthy person'.
[17] See my paper 'Henry VII's Land Revenues and Chamber Finance' in *E.H.R.*, lxxix, 253-4.
[18] B. M. Add. MS. 21481, fols, 347-348v.
[19] P.R.O., Exch. K.R., Various Accts., E101/413/2/3, fols. 1-3r.
[20] P.R.O., Exch. Tres. of Receipt, Misc. Books, E36/214, fol. 167v.

Neither is there any evidence that Henry VIII received any substantial repayments for 'loans' made by his father. The oldest meaning of this word is a gift or grant from a superior. In the royal accounts of the early Tudor period the word was also frequently used to mean sums of imprest. Again it is very doubtful whether any repayments was expected when Henry VII 'loaned' £226,000 or more to the indigent Habsburgs as an instrument of foreign policy; at least there is no evidence before 1530 of any repayment. Henry VII only took security for his payments to the Habsburgs in one case, a *fleur de lis* of gold and precious stones valued at £10,000, on January 8, 1509, and significantly the history of this pledge is not hard to trace. For example, Francis I was made responsible for redeeming it by the treaty of August 1529, twenty years later.[21]

There remains the much more likely possibility that Wolsey's tremendous war expenditure was financed from taxation, signifying that from the accession of Henry VIII emphasis on augmentation of royal revenues was switched back to where it had traditionally been before 1461. The money did not, of course, come from specific grants by Parliament or Convocation. Apart from some £33,500 for the 'poll-tax' of 1512–13[22] only three tenths and fifteenths had previously been granted (say £90,000). Clerical subsidies may possibly have averaged £9,000 *per annum* over the previous four years.[23] But the wording of one particular clause of the subsidy act of the parliamentary session of November to December 1512 should be noted. In it the king declared himself 'willing also the great estates, peers and nobles of this realm, towards the payment of that greater sum in such easy manner to be charged, that the same estates, peers and nobles shall have benevolent courage to charge themself in their preparation, for them and their retinues or companies towards and for the said defences...'[24] Certainly the Lady Margaret Pole was prevailed upon by Wolsey to offer the king 5,000 marks 'of her benevolent mind and free will offered and graunted to our said sovereign lord towards the charge of his wars', and paid over the first £1,000 to him on May 25, 1513.[25] There is a note of 1512 in Wolsey's hand 'how money is to be got to the extent of £640,000 a year, including the charges of the

---

[21] *L & P*, IV, 5515, 5881, 6231; *ibid.*, V, 1505.
[22] P.R.O., Exch. L.T.R., Enrolled Subsidies, E359/38. The gross yield before collectors' and commissioners' fees of 2d per £1 had been deducted was £33,449.
[23] See J. J. Scarisbrick, 'Clerical Taxation in England, 1485 to 1547', *Journal of Ecclesiastical History*, x (1960), 50.
[24] *Statutes*, iii 75.
[25] B. M. MS. Cotton Titus B, iv, fol. 116 (receipt given by Master Thomas Wolsey, the king's almoner).

army in Guienne and the defence of the kingdom against Scotland'.[26]

On January 12, 1513 reference was made to 'England raising unheard of contributions to sustain the war', with the English exclaiming against the tax gatherers but arming by sea and land.[27] The nearest contemporary chronicler speaks only of taxation for the wars.[28] Two independent reports to Venice in December 1512 and January 1513 each reported taxes of £600,000 laid upon the land and provided by Parliament for the king's expedition to France.[29] Taxation in the form of benevolences or forced loans, or both, seems the most likely source for this previously unheard of magnitude of expenditure. The levying of forced loans might be made easier by promises of repayment, but later Parliaments might be prevailed upon to release the king from his obligations. The imperfect *Journals of the House of Lords* reveal that Parliament was much concerned in 1515 with more than one bill concerning the paying of the king's debts.[30] Later Parliaments remitted his debts by statute on two occasions.[31] Good will towards Henry VIII's personal foreign adventure was higher on this first occasion than ever it was later. Benevolences and forced loans by this date were accounted for in the Chamber. Significantly the earliest surviving chamber receipt book for Henry VIII's reign is an account of the receipt of £216,078 17s ½d received there by loan between September 29, 1522 and April 1, 1523.[32]

The decline in the fortunes of the General Surveyors, Henry VIII's reversion to that less personal involvement of the king in financial policies which had been normal before 1461, and the revival of the ancient, traditional English emphasis on revenue exploitation and augmentation by means of taxation thus all coincided in the period between the rise and fall of Thomas Wolsey as the king's first minister. How far the subsequent rise of Thomas Cromwell and the expropriation of the revenues of the English Church marked a return to the great land revenue experiment of 1461 to 1509, as a reaction from Wolsey's more traditional and failing policies, is a most interesting further speculation, but one falling outside the chronological limits of this study.

---

[26] *L & P*, i (new ed.), 1412.

[27] *ibid.*, i (new ed.), 1564.

[28] *The Anglica Historia of Polydore Vergil*, ed. Denys Hay (Camden Soc.), p. 163 (1510) and p. 199 (1513).

[29] *L & P*, i (new ed.), 1512, 1578.

[30] *Journals of the House of Lords*, pp. 26, 27, 28, 33, 34, 35, 36. Even if one of these measures was concerned with the payment of debts owed to the king, it does not necessarily follow that they all were.

[31] Stat. 21 Hen. VIII cap. 24 (1529) and Stat. 35 Hen. VIII cap. 12 (1543).

[32] P.R.O., Exch., Treasury of Receipt, Miscellaneous Books, E36/221.

DOCUMENTS

1. Sir John Fortescue on the financing of government in the mid-fifteenth century

FROM *The Governance of England,* ed. C. Plummer, Oxford, 1885, pp. 133–6.

Wherefore me thinketh, that if the king might have his livelihood for the sustenance of his estate in great lordships, manors, fee-farms, and such other demesnes, his people not charged, he should keep to him wholly their hearts, exceed in lordships all the lords of his realm, and there should none of them grow to be like unto him, which thing is most to be feared of all the world. For then within few years there should not remain lordships in his realm, but which they might grow so great. Nor they might grow such by marriages, but if the king willed it. For to him fall all the great marriages of his land, which he may dispose as he lists. And by descent there is not like to fall greater heritage to any man than to the king. For to him be cousins the most and greatest lords of the realm. And by escheats there may not so much land fall to any man as to the king, by cause that no man hath so many tenants as he; and also no man may have the escheats of treason but himself. And by purchase, if this be done, there shall no man so well increase his livelihood as the king. For there shall none of his tenants alienate livelihood without his licence, wherein he may best prefer himself. Nor there shall no livelihood be kept so whole as the king's, considering that he may not honestly sell his land as other men do; and also his selling would be the hurt of all his realm. Such was the selling of Chirk and Chirklands whereof never man saw a precedent, and God defend that any man see more such hereafter. For selling of a king's livelihood is properly called delapidation of his crown, and therefore is of great infamy. Now we have found undoubtedly, what manner revenues is best for the endowment of the Crown. But since it is said before, that the king hath not at this day sufficient thereto, it is most convenient that we now search, how his highness may have sufficient of such revenues, which we found now best therefor.

2. New lessees acquire the royal lordship of Berkhamstead from Henry VI, 1447

A warrant for the Great Seal, Public Record Office, Chancery, C/81/1370/50.

To the right reverend father in God and right trusty and right well-beloved the Archbishop of Canterbury, our Chancellor of England.

Right reverend father in God, right trusty and well-beloved we greet you heartily well and signify unto you that we, understanding now late that our cousin John duke of Exeter was either dead or in point to die and not fully ascertained how it was with him, showed our grace unto our trusty and well-beloved knight Sir Edmund Hungerford, one of our carvers, and Gilbert Par, one of the squires of our body, in granting unto them by a bill signed with our own hand the lordship and castle of Berkhamstead to farm as in the said bill it appeareth more at large. And for as much as we be now credibly informed that the said our cousin is passed out of this uncertain life to God's mercy we send unto you by our said squire the said bill closed within these. Whereupon we pray you affectuously[1] and also charge you to do make without any delay our letters patent in due and effectual form like as in the said bill it is desired and that ye fail not so to do as our great trust is in you. Given under our signet at our monastery of Osney, the 5 day of August.

3. The First Act of Resumption, 1450

FROM *Rotuli Parliamentorum*, v. 183–4.

Pray the Commons in this your present Parliament assembled to consider, that where your Chancellor of your realm of England, your Treasurer of England, and many other lords of your Council, by your high commandment, to your said Commons at your Parliament held last at Westminster showed and declared the estate of this your realm; which was, that ye were indetted in £372,000 which is great and grievous, and that your livelihood in yearly value was but £5,000. And for as much as this £5,000 to your high and notable estate to be

---

[1] Obsolete word meaning earnestly, with earnest feeling and desire.

kept, and to pay your said debts will not suffer it, therefore that your high estate might be relieved. And furthermore it was declared that your expenses necessary to your Household, without all other ordinary charges, come to £23,000 yearly, the which exceedeth every year in expenses necessary over your livelihood, £19,000. Also please it your Highness to consider, that the Commons of your said realm be as well willed to their poor power to the relieving of your Highness, as ever were people to any king of your progenitors, that ever reigned in your said realm of England; but your said Commons have been so impoverished, what by taking of victuals to your Household, and other things in your said realm, and nought paid for; and the quinzime by your said Commons before this time so often granted, and by the grant of tonnage and poundage, and by the grant of the subsidy upon the wools, and other grants to your Highness; and for lack of execution of justice, that your poor Commons be full nigh destroyed; and if it should continue longer in such great charge, it could not in any wise be had or borne.

Wherefore please it your Highness the premises graciously to consider, and that ye, by the advice and assent of your Lords Spiritual and Temporal, and by authority of this your present Parliament, for the conservation of your high estate, and in comfort and ease of your poor Commons, would take, resume, seize, and retain in your hands and possession, all honours, castles, lordships, towns, townships, manors, lands, tenements, wastes, rents, reversion, fees, feefarms and services, with all their appurtenances, in England, Wales, and in the Marches thereof, Ireland, Guisnes, Calais, and in the Marches thereof, the which ye have granted by your letters patent or otherwise, since the first day of your reign; and all honours, castles, lordships, towns, townships, manors, lands, tenements, wastes, rents, reversions, fees, feefarms, and services, with all their appurtenances, the which were of the duchy of Lancaster, and passed from you by your grant or grants; and ye to have, hold and receive all the premises in and of like estate, as ye had them at the time of such grants made by you of them. And that all letters patent or grants, by you, or by other person or persons at your request or desire, made to any person or persons of the premises or any of them in that that is of any of the premises, be void and of no force...

4. Appropriations for household expenses, 1450

FROM The Memoranda Rolls of the King's Remembrancer, Public Record Office, Exchequer, K.R., E.159/227, 'Communia', Mich. M.17.

De Tenore cuiusdem Actus pro hospicio Regis.   For as much as the king our sovereign lord by the humble supplications made to his highness by his Commons in this his present Parliament hath conceived and understood that his poor liege people of this his realm by full long time hath been grievously charged with continual taking of their goods and chattels for the dispenses of his honourable Household whereof they have not been sufficiently contented nor paid to their great impoverishing, he therefore of his noble grace of great tenderness and affection which he hath to the release and succour of his said poor people in this behalf will ordaineth and establisheth by the advice and assent of the Lords Spiritual and Temporal and his Commons by authority of this his said Parliament that all several sums of money hereafter ensuing in writing assigned limited and annoted be yearly taken received and applied for the payment and contenting of the said dispenses by assignment severally to be made by the Treasurer of this his realm for the time being of the farmers or occupiers of the manors, lands, tenements, farms, feefarms, customs and other things hereafter following ... Sum total of this schedule: £11,002 6s 1d. And that the receiver general of the duchy of Lancaster for the time being shall pay to the treasurer of the king's Household for the time being by indenture to be made between them all such sums of money as shall grow of the remains of the said duchy over the queen's endowment, fees, wages, reparations, costs and expenses necessary as shall appear due upon the said receiver's account. And the said account to be showed yearly to the steward, treasurer and controller of the king's Household for the time being. And that the said treasurer of Household thereof account in the king's Exchequer, this act of the appointment for the Household to commence and take effect the 7 day of May next ensuing after the beginning of this present parliament and to endure by 7 years next following ...

[By writ of great seal to the Treasurer and Barons of the Exchequer, dated at Westminster 20 October 29 Henry VI.]

5. A sheriff allowed to 'declare' his account, 1451

FROM The Memoranda Rolls of the King's Remembrancer, Public Record Office, Exchequer, K.R., E.159/228, *'Brevia directa baronibus'*, Hilary m.18.

Henry by the grace of God, king of England, etc., to the Treasurer and Barons of our Exchequer, greeting. How it be that our well beloved William Mountfort, knight, named to be sheriff of our counties of Warwickshire and Leicestershire for this year hath for divers causes refused to take upon him the said charge; yet nevertheless to eschew all inconveniences that might follow by non-execution of our laws as in returning of writs, gathering up of issues and otherwise the said William hath granted to occupy the said office of sheriff of our said shires and to do all his devoir and diligence for to arear[1] and gather all duties and profits coming of the said counties that ought to be raised by virtue of the said office of sheriff from Michaelmas last past unto Michaelmas next coming, so that he be not charged in his account with the whole extent of the said shires, but only of that that he with his true diligence may arear and gather, and of all the remnant clearly to be discharged, by his oath or by the oath of his deputy for him accounting upon his said account. And we, considering how far this year is past will therefore and for other causes and considerations such as move us and by the advice of our Council charge you that in the account that the said William is or shall be to yield before you in our said Exchequer by cause of his said office for the time abovesaid ye ne charge him with the whole extent of the said shires, that is to say of these two farms called *de remanencia firme comitatus post terras datas, de firma pro proficuo comitatus* and also of these particular profits called *de vetero incremento comitatus, de auxilio vicecomitis, francumplegium, certi fines, amerciamenta*, issues and profits, nor of none other thing by him to be raised in the said shires save only of such parcels as he with his true diligence may arear and gather, and of all the remnant ye discharge him utterly and clearly by his oath or by the oath of his deputy sufficient for him accounting upon his said account, and thereof him, his heirs, and executors make be discharged and acquitted against us, our heirs, and executors in our said Exchequer for evermore. Given under our privy seal at Westminster the 7th day of June the year of our reign 29.

---

[1] Obsolete word meaning to raise, levy.

6. Edward IV appropriates all exchequer farms and feefarms worth 40s or more to household expenses, 1462

FROM The Memoranda Rolls of the King's Remembrancer, Public Record Office, Exchequer, K.R., E.159/238, 'Brevia directa baronibus', Hilary, m.23d., the second of two membrances so numbered.

Edward by the grace of God, king of England and of France and lord of Ireland to the Treasurer and Barons of our Exchequer, greeting. For as much as we have assigned all manner of farms and feefarms to the yearly value of 40s and above running in the annual roll of our Exchequer as well of cities and boroughs, lands and tenements as of ulnage unto the expenses of our Household. And we willing the said farms to be applied to our said Household and to none other use, for certain considerations us moving will and charge you that ye put not in execution the said farms in the summons of the pipe which ye send at this time unto the sheriffs of our several shires of England. But the said farms out of the said summons ye omit, anything you moving to the contrary notwithstanding. Given under our privy seal at our city of London the 19 day of February the first year of our reign.

7. John Milewater's Account, 1461 to 1463

Ministers' and Receivers' Accounts, Public Record Office, Special Collections, S.C. 6/1305/15.

Office of John Milewater receiver-general of various lands of the lord king	Account[1] of John Milewater, receiver general of various castles, lordships, manors and lands of the lord king Edward the Fourth, both of the earldom of March and of the duchy of Lancaster and the Crown, and also of various castles lordships and lands which were of Humphrey duke of Buckingham and John duke of Norfolk now being in the king's own hands by reason of the minority of the heirs of the said dukes, that is to say from the feast of St Michael in the first year of the aforesaid King Edward the Fourth to the same feast of Michael in the third year of the same king, that is for two whole years.
Arrears	None because this is the first account of the said receiver in this office.
Denbigh	But he has accounted for the receipt of £79 0s 5d received of David Middilton receiver there for the aforesaid time Sum £79 0s 5d
Montgomery, Kerry and Cedewain	And of £58 16s 5d received of Howell ap Jevan Lloyd receiver there for the aforesaid time Sum £58 16s 5d
Radnor and Maelienydd	And of £149 9s 9d received of Rees ap David ap Howell Veyne receiver there for the aforesaid time. Sum £149 9s 9d
Wigmore with the county of Hereford	And of £30 14s 4d received of John Hebyn receiver there for the aforesaid time Sum £30 14s 4d

[1] In Latin.

Of the county of Shropshire   Nothing

Builth   And of £56 received of Walter ap
                              David ap Howell receiver there for the
                              aforesaid time
                                        Sum £56

Clifford, Glasbury,   And of £37 received of Thomas ap
Winforton, Ewyas   Rosser and Philip ap Griffith Lloyd
and Dorstone   receivers there for the aforesaid time
                                        Sum £37

Usk and Caerleon   And of £121 11s 8d received of
                              Trahairon ap Jevan ap Menrek
                              receiver there for the aforesaid time
                                        Sum £121 11s 8d

Narberth   And of £25 received of John Doune
                              receiver there for the aforesaid time
                                        Sum £25

Of the earldom of March as far as this.

Brecon   And of £144 4s received of Thomas ap
                              Rosser Vaughan receiver there for the
                              aforesaid time
                                        Sum £144 4s

Talgarth   And of £6 received of the aforesaid
                              Thomas ap Rosser Vaughan receiver
                              there for the aforesaid time
              lately of
              the duke
              of
Hay   Buckingham   And of £11 13s 4d received of the
                              same Thomas ap Rosser Vaughan
                              receiver there for the aforesaid time
                                        Sum £11 13s 4d

Newport and   And of £200 received of William lord
Gwynllwg   Herbert farmer there for the aforesaid
                              time And he is also charged with £50
                              received of the said lord for Michael-
                              mas term before the beginning of this
                              account
                                        Sum £250

Haverfordwest of the Crown		And of £100 received of the said lord Herbert farmer there for the aforesaid time
		Sum £100
Swansea, Kilvey and Gower lately of the duke of Norfolk		And of £66 13s 4d received of the aforesaid William lord Herbert farmer there for the aforesaid time
		Sum £66 13s 4d
Monmouth with members	⎫	And of £275 9s 7d received of Hugh Huntley receiver there for the aforesaid time
		Sum £275 9s 7d
Kidwelly	of the duchy of Lancaster	and of £40 received of Henry Doune receiver there for the aforesaid time
		Sum £40
Ogmore	⎭	And of £64 received of John Stradlynge receiver there for the aforesaid time
		Sum £64
Forest of Dean of the Crown		And of 100s received of Robert Hiotte receiver there for the aforesaid time
		Sum 100s

    Sum Total of the Receipt   £1520 12s 10d

Fees

He accounts therefrom in the fee of Thomas Colt, chancellor of the earldom of March, for one year falling within the time of this account at £20 *per annum*, for £20 by acquittance. And in the fee of the aforesaid receiver reckoned both for his fee and for his expenses for the time of this account at £60 *per annum*, for £120.
    Sum £140

Payments by warrants of the lord king

And for a payment to James Friis, by a letter of warrant of the lord king dated at Greenwich the 5th day of January in the first year of the same

king, of £18 18s 8d by acquittance. And for a payment to Thomas Herbert, esquire, by a letter of warrant of the lord king dated in the palace of Westminster the 16th day of the month of October in the 2nd year of the aforesaid king, of £44 by acquittance. And for a payment to William lord Herbert by a letter of warrant of the same king dated at Durham the 17th day of December in the second year of the the said king of £400 by acquittance. And for a payment to the same lord by another letter of warrant of the said lord king dated at Pontefract the 17th day of November in the third year of the aforesaid king, that is to say in the price of 80 beeves delivered for the use of the Household of the said lord king, of £66 13s 4d by acquittance. And for a payment of William Benet by a letter of warrant of the lord king dated at the palace of Westminster the 5th day of March in the third year of the same king, of £30 15s 1d
   Sum £560 7s 1d

Deliveries of cash to the coffers of the lord king	And in cash delivered to the coffers of the lord king of the charge of the aforesaid John Milewater, receiver-general, now accounting, £820, of part of his abovesaid receipts for the time of this account by 3 acquittances of which the first acquittance dated at the castle of Fotheringay the 16th day of August in the second year of the said king contains £478 13s 4d, the 2nd dated at the palace of Westminster the 24th day of May in the 3rd year of the same king contains £208 and the 3rd dated at Coventry the 3rd day of

September in the third year of the same king contains £133 6s 8d
Sum £820

Sum of all outlays and deliveries £1520 7s 1d And he is charged with 5s 9d.

8. The King's Speech to Parliament, 1467

FROM *Rotuli Parliamentorum*, v. 572.

John Say, and ye Sirs, coming to this my Court of Parliament for the Commons of this my land. The cause why I have called and summoned this my present Parliament is, that I purpose to live upon mine own, and not to charge my subjects but in great and urgent causes, concerning more the weal of themselves, and also the defence of them and of this my realm, rather than mine own pleasure, as here to fore by Commons of this land hath been done and borne unto my progenitors in time of need; wherein I trust that ye Sirs, and all the Commons of this my land will be as tender and kind unto me in such cases, as heretofore any Commons have been to any of my said progenitors. And for the good will, kindness, and true hearts that ye have borne, continued and showed unto me at all times here to fore, I thank you as heartily as I can, as so I trust ye will continue in time coming; for the which by the grace of God, I shall be to you as good and gracious king, and reign as right wisely upon you, as ever did any of my progenitors upon Commons of this my realm in days past; and shall also, in time of need, apply my person for the weal and defence of you, and of this my realm, not sparing my body nor life for any jeopardy that might happen to the same.

9. Edward IV's Act of Resumption, 1467

FROM *Rotuli Parliamentorum*, v. 572.

For divers causes and considerations concerning the honour, estate and property of the king, and also of the common weal, defence, surety and welfare of the realm, and his subjects of the same, it is ordained, enacted and established, by the advice and assent of the Lords Spiritual and Temporal, and Commons, in this present Parliament assembled, and by authority of the same; that the king, from the feast of Easter last past, have, take, seize, hold and enjoy all honours, castles, lordships, towns, townships, manors, lands, tenements, wastes, forests, chase, rents, annuities, farms, feefarms, reversions, services, issues, profits and commodities which he was seized and possessed on the 4th day of March, the first year of his reign, or any time after, by reason of the Crown of England, the duchy of Cornwall, principality of Wales, and earldom of Chester, or any of them in England, Ireland, Wales and Marches thereof, Guisnes, Calais and Marches thereof, or that appertained or belonged to him the same 4th day or any time since, as parcel of his duchy of Lancaster, or by the forfeiture of Henry the Sixth, late in deed and not in right king of England, on any person attainted since the said 4th day of March, by authority of any Parliament holden since the said 4th day, or otherwise attainted by the course of the common law of this land, and passed from the king under any of his seals, to any person or persons, in fee simple, fee tail, term of life, or term of years. And that the king from the said feast of Easter, here, hold and enjoy every of the premises, in like estate as he had them the said 4th day of March, or any time after....

10. Arrangements made for the management of the duke of Clarence's forfeited lands, 1470

Council and Privy Seal Records, Public Record Office Exchequer, Treasury of Receipt, E.28/91/5.

Edward by the grace of God, king of England and France and lord of Ireland, to all manner [of] men as well our stewards, receivers, bailiffs, reeves, farmers and all our other liege people, sendeth greeting. For as much as we have committed, limited and appointed our right trusty and well beloved Walter Blount lord Mountjoy, Master Richard Martin, Henry Ferrers and John Hewik our auditors to direct, guide, oversee, examine and approve for our most avail and profit all such livelihood as late was George the duke of Clarence and now belongeth to us in the counties of Stafford, Derby, Leicester and Northumberland and to make levy to our use as well of all the arearage that late belonged to the said George duke of Clarence as of all the revenues and profits of the same livelihood and also to guide rule and establish all manner [of] officers, ministers, farmers and tenants and all other such particulars of the same to our most avail and profit after their discretion and all manner of defaults and reparations, costs and expenses necessary and behoveful by them to be assigned, limited and appointed and to every one of them; we will and charge you that unto the said Walter Blount lord Mountjoy, Master Richard Martin, Henry Ferrers and John Hewik our auditors jointly and severally you will be helping, obeying, assisting, favouring and supporting, in that you can and may, all such matters as you or any of them in our behalf shall seem expedient, behoveful and necessary for our weal, etc.[1]

11. Edward IV's financial policies from 1475

FROM The Croyland Chronicle.

Consequently the lord king returned to England with honourable conditions of peace secured. At least, the chief officers of the royal army so regarded them, although nothing is so irreproachable or seemly that it cannot be made out to be bad by evil talk. Indeed some began to condemn the peace at once and received suitable punishment for their presumption. Others, as soon as they were back home, took to pillage and robbery, so that no road in England was safe for merchants or pilgrims.

Thus the lord king was compelled to perambulate the country together with his judges, sparing no-one; even his own servants received no less than a hanging if they were detected in theft or murder. Such vigorous justice, universally carried out, put a stop to common acts of robbery for a long time to come. To be sure if this prudent prince had not vigorously nipped such evils in the bud the number of people complaining about the wasteful management of the wealth of the kingdom, with so much treasure scraped from every man's coffers and so uselessly consumed, would have increased to a point where no-one could tell which of the king's councillors' heads were safe; and especially would this have been true of those who had been induced by the French king's friendship or gifts to advocate the peace-making described above.

There is no doubt that the king felt the perplexity of this situation deep in his heart and he was not unacquainted with the condition of his people, how easily they could be drawn into insurrections and desire for change if they should find a captain. Seeing therefore that things had now come to this pass, so that he dared not from now on demand subsidies from the English people in his necessity, and also realizing (as indeed was very true) that the French expedition had come to nothing in so brief a time for lack of money, he bent all his thoughts towards gathering together a treasure worthy of his royal

---

[1] A Treasurer's Bill for a letter under the privy seal addressed to the Keeper of the Privy Seal, bearing the signature of John Tiptoft earl of Worcester, the Treasurer, and dated sometime between July 10 and October 30, 1470. I am indebted to Dr Robin Jeffs for bringing this document to my notice and for help with the dating.

estate from his own substance and by his own industry. Summoning a Parliament to this end he resumed almost all the royal patrimony, no matter to whom it had previously been granted, and applied the whole of it in support of the charges on the Crown. He appointed surveyors of the customs in every port of the kingdom, the most prying of men, and, by all accounts, excessively hard on the merchants. The king himself procured merchants ships, loaded them with the finest wool, cloths, tin and other commodities of the kingdom and, just like any man living by trade, exchanged merchandise for merchandise through his factors among the Italians and the Greeks. He would only part with the revenues of vacant prelacies, which according to Magna Carta cannot be sold, for sums which he had determined on, and on no other terms. He scrutinized the registers and rolls of the Chancery and exacted heavy fines from those heirs whom he found to have intruded themselves without due process of law, as recompense for the issues which they had enjoyed in the meantime. These were his acquisitive devices, and other similar ones more numerous than can be conceived of by a man not skilled in such matters. In addition there was the annual tribute of ten thousand pounds due from the French and frequent ecclesiastical tenths from which prelates and clergy could not excuse themselves. Within a few years he had made himself into a most opulent prince, so that none of his predecessors could have equalled him in collecting vessels of gold and silver, tapestries and precious ornaments for his palaces and churches, in building castles, colleges and other fine places and in acquiring new lands and possessions.[1]

[1] Translated from the Latin text of the Croyland Chronicle which now only survives in the printed version edited by W. Fulman in *Rerum Anglicarum Scriptorum Veterum*, i, 559. Oxford, 1684.

12. A selection of Yorkist writs to the Barons of the Exchequer restricting or annulling their control over the accounts of receivers of land revenues and informing them how certain sums of money had been disposed of and accounted for elsewhere

FROM the Memoranda Rolls of the King's Remembrancer.

(a) For Thomas Palmer. Edward by the grace of God, king of England and of France and lord of Ireland, to the Treasurer and Barons of our Exchequer, greeting. Where we by our letters patent under our great seal bearing date at Westminster the 26 day of February the first year of our reign ordained our well-beloved Thomas Palmer receiver and approver of all our castles, manors, lordships, lands and tenements, feefarms and mills with all the appurtenances in our counties of Warwick, Leicester, Northampton and Rutland, to have, occupy and exercise the said offices by him or his deputy sufficient as long as it pleaseth us, to perceive yearly for the exercising of the offices aforesaid by his own hands of the issues and profits of the castles, manors, lordships, lands and tenements aforesaid coming of fees and wages accustomed as in our letters patent more plainly appeareth; and how be it that after the date of our said letters patent we by our other several letters patent have granted to other divers persons great part of the said castles, lordships, manors, lands and tenements, feefarms and mills and they by force thereof have taken and received the issues and profits thereof so that the said Thomas Palmer meddled not of the receipt of any issues or profits of the same; and also the said Thomas Palmer divers others and many sums of money growing of divers others of the said castles, lordships, manors, lands and tenements, feefarms and mills resting in our hands ungranted could not levy arear nor gather notwithstanding he hath done all his true and faithful diligence for the arearing and gathering of the same; yet the said Thomas Palmer feareth him lest he in the account by him to be yelden in our Exchequer of his said offices he should be charged as well of all offices and profits of the said castles, lordships, manors, lands and tenements, feefarms and mills by us granted, as of the said sums of money not yet levied, to his great and importable charge without our grace special be showed to him on this behalf. We not willing him in any wise to be charged unto us of any sums of money other than such as he hath levied by force of his said offices, of our grace especial, certain science and mere motion will and charge you that ye account with the said Thomas at our said Exchequer as well of such sums of money the which he will charge him with as received of the issues and profits and revenues of the castles, manors, lordships, lands and tenements feefarms and mills or any of them here afore, as of all manner [of] reparations of all the same sums of money by him paid in or for the same castles, manors, lordships, lands and tenements and mills and of the parks, pales and lodges of the same or any of them and of all wages, fees and rewards of officers within the same, or any part thereof, for the time of that account by him paid by his oath; and that ye ne charge the said Thomas Palmer in his account of his said office to us yielden or to be yielden of any other or more sums of money than of such of the which the said Thomas will charge him by his oath; and that of all such sums of money the which the same Thomas will or shall allege upon that account by him not to have been levied nor to have been leviable of anything of the premises ye him utterly discharge and acquit against us and our heirs for ever; and that ye surcease of all manner of processes, executions, and demands made or to be made for us in any wise against him for any such sums of money by him upon that account alleged not to have been levied nor leviable; and that of the issues, profits and revenues aforesaid in that account ye allow, acquit and discharge the same Thomas Palmer as well of the same sums of money by him to be submitted in that account to be paid upon the same reparations of and for the said wages, fees and rewards, as of 40 marks for the labour, business and expenses of the said Thomas Palmer had upon the receipt of such sums of money as he in that account shall charge him with; that express mention of the certainty of the said letters patent or grants, accounts, sums of money, receipts or any other things concerning the premises herein be not had or made, or any statute or provision or restraint to the contrary had and made, or any other matter you in any wise moving notwithstanding. Given under our privy seal at our castle of Fotheringhay the 6th day of August the third year of our reign [1463].

(P.R.O. Exchequer, K. R. Memoranda Rolls, *'brevia directa baronibus'*, E.159/240, Mich., 3 Ed. IV m.22.)

(b) For John Fogge. Edward by the grace of God, king of England and France and lord of Ireland, to the Treasurer and Barons of our Exchequer, greeting. For as much as our trusty and well-beloved knight John Fogge, late treasurer of our

Household, received to our use and by our commandment betwixt the 4 day of March the first year of our reign and the last day of September the next following of sundry persons certain sums of money amounting in all to £799, the which sum of £799 the same late treasurer delivered within the same time into our Chamber, as well by his own hands as by the hands of the comptroller and cofferer of our said House and others to our own hands by our special commandment, as we have in our certain knowledge; whereof our said late treasurer cannot have allowance afore you without our warrant. We, having consideration to the premises, will and charge straightly that in the account the which our said late treasurer is in yielding afore you in our said Exchequer of his said office by the time abovesaid ye make plain allowance unto the same our late treasurer of the foresaid sum of £799 as money by him delivered unto our hands; and that ye as well the same our late treasurer, his heirs and executors, as all other thereof, against us acquit and discharge for ever, any cause or matter you moving to the contrary notwithstanding. Given under our privy seal at our palace of Westminster the 24th day of April the 9th year of our reign [1469].

(*ibid*. E159/246, '*brevia*', Easter, 9 Ed. IV, m.4.)

(c) For Richard Croft and others. Edward by the grace of God, king of England and of France and lord of Ireland, to the Treasurer and Barons of our Exchequer, greeting. Where George archbishop of York and late bishop of Exeter was our farmer of the manors of Woodstock, Hanborough, Wootton, Stonesfield, with all members and hamlets and other profits, commodities and with their appurtenances in the county of Oxford and of the hundred of Wootton in the said shire of Oxford, and that for certain considerations us specially moving [we] now late have commanded by mouth unto our trusty and well-beloved Richard Croft, squire, to attend the guiding of the said manors and to oversee and to be approver and our receiver of the said manors and hundred with all their appurtenances, and appointed him to pay all manner fees, wages and rewards as well of the steward, parker and all other officers within our said manor of Woodstock and of masons, carpenters, daubers, labourers and of all others feed or hired to do any service to us in the said manors or hundred and any part thereof, from the feast of Easter the 11th year of our reign hitherto; and also we, understanding that the same Richard Croft by that time hath borne and paid great charges of sums of money by him paid in the premises and willing him thereof to be recompensed, will and straightly charge you that ye account with the said Richard Croft of the issues, profits and revenues of the said manors and hundred from the feast of Easter in the 11th year of our reign hitherto; and that upon the same account ye allow, requite and discharge the said Richard of all such sums of money which by the oath upon that account of the said Richard is or shall be alleged to have been paid, delivered or expended by him upon reparations of the premises or any part thereof at any time since the feast of Easter in the 11th year of our reign hitherto, or for wages, fees or rewards of stewards of the said manors of Woodstock or for any other officers, servants, ministers or labourers within the said manors, hundred, or any of them, from the said feast of Easter hitherto, and of all sums of money by the said Richard Croft paid or delivered upon wages or hires of carpenters, masons, labourers, parkers of the said manor of Woodstock, park of Cornbury, lodges of the same, reparations and enclosures of the same parks and repairing of the mills and houses of the same manors whatsoever they be, and also other necessary costs and expenses; and by the said Richard Croft from the said feast of Easter in the 11th year of our reign hitherto within the said manors and hundred done, of the issues, profits, farms and revenues of the same manors and hundred coming, from the said feast of Easter hitherto; and where also by our letters patent now late have made and ordained the said Richard Croft to be approver and receiver of our said manors and hundred with the appurtenances, and to have and occupy that office as long as he should bear him well in the same, yielding account thereof yearly to us afore Thomas Aleyn whom we have assigned our auditor in that behalf at our said manor of Woodstock from time to time to be yielden and in no other place, as in our said letters patent it is contained more at large. We will and charge you that at any time hereafter ye ne call nor demand nor do any process to be made our of our Exchequer to the said Richard Croft for to do yield his account of the issues and profits of the said manors and hundred or any part thereof for any time hereafter; and also that ye ne award nor do make any process out of our said Exchequer against the said Archbishop for account to us by him to be yielden of the issues and profits of the said manors and hundred with their appurtenances or any part thereof, or for any farm demanded or to be demanded of the said Archbishop for any of the premises from the feast of Easter in the said 11th year hitherto or for any time hereafter to come, or any arearages thereof, but of all the accounts and farms and arearges ye discharge the said Archbishop and also surcease for ever of all process, executions and demands made or to be made or had for us against the said Archbishop or Richard Croft or any of them, for or in the premises. That express mention of the contrary of the premises or any of them or any thing them concerning herein be not had or made, or any act, statute, ordinance, provision or restraint or any other matter whatsoever you moving notwithstanding. Given under our privy seal at our palace of Westminster the 14th day of November the 12 year of our reign [1472].

(*ibid.* E.159/250, '*brevia*', Mich., 13 Ed. IV m. 4.)

(d) For John Beaufitz. Edward by the grace of God, king of England and of France and lord of Ireland, to the Treasurer and Barons of our Exchequer, greeting. Where process is made out of our Exchequer against John Beaufitz, receiver of the castles, lordships, manors, lands and tenements which late were Alice lady Lovell, Daincourt and Gray, now dead, being in our hands as well by the death of the same lady as by the nonage of Francis lord Lovell, cousin and heir of the same lady, to yield account of all castles, lordships, manors, lands and tenements aforesaid, that is to say from the 10th day of February in the 13 year of our reign hitherto, as in our Exchequer more plainly it appeareth. We certainly understanding that we, by our letters patent bearing date the 30 day of July in the 14th year of our reign, have granted unto Garard Canizian of London, merchant, the keeping of all the said castles, lordships, manors, lands and tenements and all issues profits, farms and revenues of the same to be perceived and had to the foresaid Garard, his executors and assigns, from the feast of Easter then last past unto the full age of the said Francis and unto the time the said Francis may have livery of the same in due manner after the course of our Chancery, without any peachment of us or of our heirs, as in the same letters patent is contained more at large, by force of which grant the said Gerard hath had and perceived all issues, profits and revenues of all the castles, lordships, manors, lands and tenements from the said feast of Easter hitherto. We also considering that as for any issues and profits of the said castles, manors, lands and tenements coming from the said 5th day of February unto the said feast of Easter have appointed and assigned the said John Beaufitz to account and reckon with us thereof in our Chamber afore certain persons by us thereto assigned. We thereof of our certain knowledge and mere motion will and straightly charge you that ye surcease for evermore of the said processes and all other processes and executions made or to be made for us against the said John Beaufitz for the said account or any other account to us to be yielden therein, for any time past or to come, and that ye him of all the same accounts and processes and every thing thereof hold and make quit and discharged against us for ever. That express mention of the certainty of the premises herein be not made, or that it appear not to you by matter of record in our said Exchequer the same John Beaufitz to have accounted with us in our said Chamber or any other matter or cause you moving notwithstanding. Given under our privy seal at our palace of Westminster the 17th day of February the 14th year of our reign [1475].

(*ibid.* E.159/251, '*brevia*', 14 Ed. IV m. 10.)

(e) For Thomas Stidolff. Edward by the grace of God king of England and of France and lord of Ireland, to the Treasurer and Barons of our Exchequer, greeting. Where we by our letters patent bearing date the 19 day of October in the 13th year of our reign gave and granted to Thomas Stidolff the office of steward of and receiver of the manor of Shrivenham with appurtenances in our county of Berkshire, the manor of Swindon and Broughton with appurtenances in our county of Wiltshire and the manor of Lydney in our county of Gloucester, they being in our hands by reason of the nonage of George Talbot earl of Shrewsbury, son and heir of John late earl of Shrewsbury, to have and occupy the said offices by the same Thomas as long as it may please us, with wages, fees to the same offices of old time due and accustomed as in the same letters patent is contained more at large. Whereupon process is made out of our said Exchequer against the said Thomas Stidolff to yield us account of the said manors from the said 19th day of October hitherto. Certainly understanding that we by our letters patent bearing date the 14 day of September in the 13th year of our reign gave to Richard Greneway the office of auditor of all the same manors with appurtenances, the which were of the said John late earl of Shrewsbury, to have and occupy the same office during the nonage of the said George, as long as the same manors should abide in our hands; and that the same Thomas Stidolff hath accounted of the issues and profits of all the same afore the same auditor for the time past and hath satisfied all duties thereof to us appertaining in certain form by us therein appointed; will and straightly charge you that ye surcease for evermore of all processes, executions, suits and demands made or to be made or had for us against the same Thomas for that account or for any time past of the premises or any of them to us to be yielden for any time past; and that the same Thomas of all the said accounts and every of them ye utterly acquit and discharge against us for ever. That express mention of the certainty of the premises or any of them herein be not had or made, or any statute, provision or restraint, or any other matter whatsoever, you in any wise to the contrary moving notwithstanding. Given under our privy seal at our palace of Greenwich the 18 day of February the 16th year of our reign [1477].

(*ibid.* E.159/254, '*brevia*', Easter, 17 Ed. IV, m. 1.)

[Easter m. 2 contains a like discharge *mutatis mutandis* for Richard Croft, knight, as receiver of the lordships of Goodrich, Irchenfield, Corfham, Blackmere and all other lands of the same late earl in Heref. and Salop. accounting before the same auditor, appointed by letters patent dated 1 October, 13 Ed. IV.]

(f) For the lord Howard. Edward by the grace of God, king of England and of France and lord of Ireland, to the Treasurer and Barons of our Exchequer, greeting. Where there is demanded to our use of John Howard, knight, and Margaret his wife £200 upon him charged, of the issues of the manor of Hereford in Hoo, the manor of Haldall and Serikkes in East Dereham, the manors of Kirkeham and Wilkokes in Little Fransham, the manor of Brokhall in Dersingham, and of the third part of the manor of Great Fransham, with the appurtenances, in the county of Norfolk, of the which Walter George, esquire, now dead, and Mary his wife, were seized in their demesne as of fee, for that that we the 5th day of February the 6th year of our reign, for £200 by the same John to us paid, granted to the same John and Margaret his wife the keeping of all the manors, lands and tenements, rents and such, with the appurtenances, the which were of the said Walter and Mary, to have from the time of the death of the said Walter till the full age of the heir of the said Walter and Mary, or as long as it should happen them to remain in our hands, as in our said Exchequer more plainly it may appear. We having certain knowledge that the said £200 were paid and delivered to our hands in our Chamber, of our grace especial, certain science and mere motion pardon, remit and release unto the said John Howard the said £200 and every part thereof, and all actions, executions, suits and demands what we have or may have against him therefore; and will and charge you that ye utterly acquit and discharge against us for ever the said John Howard of the said £200 and every part thereof, and surcease for evermore of all processes, examinations, suits and demands made or to be made for us against him for the said £200 or any part thereof. That express mention of the certainty of the said grant or any other of the premises herein be not fully had or made, or any statute, act, ordinance, provision, restraint, or any other matter whatever you to the contrary moving notwithstanding. Given under our privy seal at our city of London the 18 day of May the 17 year of our reign [1477].

(*ibid.* E.159/254, '*brevia*', Mich., 17 Ed. IV, m. 17.)

(g) For the abbot and convent of Chertsey. Edward by the grace of God, king of England and of France and lord of Ireland, to the Treasurer and Barons of our Exchequer, greeting. Where there is demanded to our use at our said Exchequer of the prior and convent of Chertsey 50 marks for the keeping of the temporalities of the same abbey, being void by the death of John Maye, Bachelor of Divinity, late abbot there, from the second day of October in the 19 year of our reign, unto the 5th day of December then next following, at the which 5th day we restored the temporalities of the said abbey unto Thomas Pigot, now abbot of the same abbey. We, having certain knowledge that the prior of the said abbey paid and delivered to our own person in our Chamber the said 50 marks, and not willing the said now abbot nor the prior or convent of the said place nor any of them to be troubled or vexed for the said 50 marks, of our grace especial, certain science and mere motion pardon, remit and release unto the said now abbot and to the prior and convent of the same place all actions, executions, suits and demands which we have or may have against them, or any of them, for the said 50 marks or any part thereof; and will and charge you that ye surcease for ever of all processes, actions, executions, suits and demands made or to be made for us against them, or any of them, for the said 50 marks or any part thereof; and that ye them and every of them of the said 50 marks and any part thereof utterly acquit and discharge against us for ever. That express mention of the certainty of the premises herein be not had or made, or any statute, act, ordinance, provision or restraint whatsoever heretofore had or made, or any other matter whatsoever you to the contrary moving notwithstanding. Given under our privy seal at our manor of Greenwich the 24th day of June the 20 year of our reign [1480].

(*ibid.* E.159/257, '*brevia*', Trinity, 20 Ed. IV, m. 5.)

(h) For John Hayes. Edward by grace of God, king of England and of France and lord of Ireland, to the Treasurer and Barons of our Exchequer, greeting. Where John Hayes, our receiver of our manor and lordship of Tiverton and of all other lordships, manors, lands and tenements in our counties of Cornwall, Devon, Somerset, Dorset, Wiltshire and Southampton, called Devonshire lands and Wiltshire lands, the which came unto our hands by the forfeiture of George late duke of Clarence, and of all manors, lordships, lands and tenements in our counties of Cornwall, Devon, Somerset, Dorset, Wiltshire and Southampton, called Salisbury lands and Spencer lands, the which by reason of the nonage of Edward, son and heir of the said late duke, came unto our hands, is accountable unto us at our said Exchequer of the issues and profits of the said manors, lordships, lands and tenements, from the feast of Saint Michael the Archangel in the

19th year of our reign, unto the feast of Saint Michael the Archangel then next ensuing. We will and charge you that ye acount with him thereof at our said Exchequer for that time and in that account ye ne charge him of or with any other sums of money than only of such sums whereof he by his oath shall charge himself therein; and of all the remnant thereof him utterly acquit and discharge against us; and also we, considering that the same John Hayes hath paid and delivered unto our own person in our Chamber at divers times £653 6s 8d of the issues and profits of the said manors, lordships, lands and tenements, and also by our commandment to him given by our mouth hath paid of the issues and profits of the said manors, lordships, lands and tenements unto Thomas Cutfold, scholar, 40s; and also to the keepers of the shrine of Saint Osmund at Salisbury and at the tomb of Bishop Lacy at Exeter for the finding of two lamps and a taper of wax continually burning £6 11s 4d; and also the same John hath borne by reason of the said office charges and costs amounting to the sum of £25 10s in riding and going in business divers times unto the said manors, lordships, lands and tenements about the gathering of the issues and profits of the same, as we certainly know; and also we willing the same John to have and retain in his own hands of the issues and profits of the same manors, lordships, lands and tenements the sum of £20 for his reward for his labour and business in approving for us the profits and avails of the premises and otherwise, by our especial commandment given to him by our mouth, all which sums amounteth in all unto the sum of £707 8s; and that the same John Hayes, in his account of the premises be fully allowed of the same sum, of our grace especial, certain science and mere motion will and charge you that in the account or accounts the which the same John Hayes is in yielding or shall yield or make unto us at our said Exchequer of the premises or any of them ye allow and utterly acquit and discharge against us forever the same John Hayes of £707 8s of such sums of money where he is or shall be unto us charged or chargeable upon such his account, and will and charge you that ye surcease for evermore of all processes, actions, executions, suits and demands made or to be made for us against the same John for the same sum of £707 8s or any part thereof. That express mention of the certainty of the premises herein be not fully had or made, or any statute, act, ordinance, provision or restraint, or any matter whatsoever you to the contrary moving notwithstanding. Given under our privy seal at our Tower of London the 3rd day of December the 20 year of our reign [1480].

(*ibid.* E.159/257, '*brevia*', Hilary, 20 Ed. IV, m. 3d., the second of two membrances so numbered)

(i) For John Swyft. Edward by the grace of God, king of England and of France and lord of Ireland, to the Treasurer and Barons of our Exchequer, greeting. Where process is made out of our said Exchequer against John Swyft, receiver of our lordships of Hallamshire and Worksop, with the appurtenances in the county of York and in the county of Nottingham, the which came unto our hands by reason of the nonage of George earl of Shrewsbury, for to yield unto us account of all his receipts unto us in his said office appertaining, that is to say from the second day of June in the 14th year of our reign hitherto, whereof he unto us hath not accounted, as in our said Exchequer more plainly it may appear. We considering that we by our letters patent bearing date the 14th day of September in the 13th year of our reign gave and granted unto Richard Grenewey the office of auditor of all castles, lordships, manors, lands and tenements, the which late were of our dear cousin John earl of Shrewsbury, the which castles, lordships, manors, lands and tenements by the death of the same late earl and by reason of the nonage of the said George as son and heir of the same late earl came unto our hands, of the which castles, lordships, manors, lands and tenements the said lordships of Hallamshire and Worksop, with the appurtenances, be parcel, to have and to occupy the same office unto the said Richard by him as long as he should bear him well therein, during the nonage of the said George, as long time as the said castles, lordships, manors, lands and tenements should remain in our hands, as in the same letters patent more plainly it is expressed; and by force of the same letters patent the said Richard Grenewey occupied and had and yet occupieth and hath the said office of auditor as we certainly know; and also we considering that the said John Swift [sic] hath accounted of the issues and profits of the said lordships of Hallamshire and Worksop coming, from the said second day of June hitherto, afore the said Richard Grenewey as auditor of the same lordships, at the castle of Sheffield in the said county of York, and that we be answered of the issues and profits thereof for that time as we certainly know; and we not willing the said John Swyft in any wise to be charged or chargeable against us for to yield any account afore you our said Barons of or for the said issues and profits for any past or any part thereof, of our grace especial, certain science and mere motion will and charge you that ye surcease for evermore of the said process and of all other processes, actions, executions, suits and demands made or to be made for us against the said John Swyft for the said account or any part thereof and that ye the same John Swyft of that account and process, and of every thing thereof, utterly acquit and discharge against us for ever. That express mention of the certainty of the premises herein be not fully had or made, or any statute, act, ordinance, provision or restraint, or any other matter whatsoever you to the contrary moving notwithstanding. Given under our privy seal at our Tower of London the second day of February the 21 year of our reign [1482].

(*ibid.* E.159/258, '*brevia*', Hilary, 21 Ed. IV, m. 1d.)

(j) For Richard Welby. Edward by the grace of God, king of England and of France and lord of Ireland, to the Treasurer and Barons of our Exchequer, greeting. Where process is made out of our said Exchequer by attachment against Richard Welby, our general receiver of all lordships, manors, lands and tenements the which be parcel of the honour of Richmond in the county of Lincoln called Richmondsfee; and also of the said [sic] castle, manor and lordship of Somerton in the said county, being in our hands by force of an act of Parliament, for to yield unto us account of the issues and profits and revenues of all the said lordships, manors, lands and tenements, castles, lordships, and manors, that is to say, from the second day of March in the 17th year of our reign unto the feast of Saint Michael in the 21st year of our said reign; and to answer unto us of a contempt by him made unto us for non yielding that account, by force of the which process Robert Tailboys, knight, late sheriff of our said county of Lincoln, took of the goods and chattels of the said Richard Welby unto the value of 26s 8d; and also the same late sheriff, by force of the same process the 28 day of September in the 21 year of our reign, hath taken of the lands and tenements of the said Richard, in the name of distress, into our hands three meses and 12 acres of land with the appurtenances in Milton, as in our said Exchequer more plainly it may appear. We, considering that we by our letters patent bearing date the 4th day of December in the first year of our reign gave and granted to John Lathington the office of auditor of all our castles, lordships, manors and tenements, honours and shire of Richmond, to be had unto him for term of his life. And that the same Richard Welby hath accounted afore the said John Luthington [sic] as auditor of the same lordships, manors, lands and tenements, castles, manors and lordships of all issues and profits thereof coming, from the said second day of March in the said 17th year unto the said feast of Saint Michael in the said 21st year of our reign; and that the same Richard Welby hath satisfied and contented unto us all sums of money due unto us of the said lordships, manors, lands and tenements, castles, manors and lordships whereof he was receiver, for and by the same time, as we certainly know, of our grace especial, certain science and mere motion pardon, remit and release unto the same Richard Welby the said contempt of all processes, actions, executions, suits and demands, the which we have or in any wise may have against him for the same contempt; and will and charge you that ye surcease for evermore of the said process and of all other processes, made or to be made for us, against the same Richard Welby for the said contempt and account, or any of them, and utterly acquit and discharge against us for evermore the said Richard Welby of the said contempt and account; and also utterly acquit and discharge against us for ever the said Robert Tailboys of the said 26s 8d and of all sums of money due or belonging unto us of the said three meses and 12 acres of land with the appurtenances from the time of the seizure thereof hitherto; and also will and charge you that ye cause to be restored unto the said Richard the said three meses and 12 acres of land with the appurtenances and cause our hands and possessions thereof to be utterly amoved and surcease for evermore of all processes, actions, executions, suits and demands made or to be made for us against the said Robert Tailboys for any account of the issues and profits of the said three meses and 12 acres of land with the appurtenances and for all accounts therefor unto us to be yielden. Provided always that the account taken before the said auditor of the premises unto the said feast of Saint Michael in the said 21st year of our reign be delivered in to our said Exchequer and by you our said Barons to be surveyed and that of right by those accounts should appertain unto us that we may be truly answered as reason will. That express mention of the certainty of the premises herein be not fully had or made, or any matter whatsoever you to the contrary moving notwithstanding. Given under our privy seal at our Tower of London the 26 day of October the 22 year of our reign [1482].

(*ibid.* E.159/259, 'brevia', Mich., 22 Ed. IV, m. 6.)

(k) For John Sapcote. Richard by the grace of God, king of England and of France and lord of Ireland, to the Treasurer and Barons of our Exchequer, greeting. Where process now late was made out of our said Exchequer by distress to distrain John Sapcote, squire, late receiver-general of our duchy of Cornwall by virtue of letters patent made to him by Edward Bastard late called King Edward the Vth the 21 day of May in the first year of his usurped reign, that is to say, from the 21 day of May unto the 18 day of July in the first year of our reign, to yield unto us account for that time, by virtue of the which letters patent the said John Sapcote never restrained nor took any issues or profits of the said duchy; and that we by our letters patent bearing date the same 18 day of July in the first year of our reign gave and granted to the [said] John Sapcote, squire, the office of general receiver of our said duchy of Cornwall, with the portage of money pertaining and belonging to the same office, to have and occupy the same office, with the said portage, by him or his sufficient deputy, as long as it should please us, with all other profits, commodities and increases to the same office with the said portage of old time due and accustomed, perceiving yearly thereof in and for the exercise of the said office, fees, wages and all other profits of old time due and accustomed and for the said portage, that is to say, of every hundred pounds carried and paid by warrant twenty shillings of the issues, profits and revenues of the same duchy coming or growing, by his own hands at the terms of Easter and Saint Michael the Archangel by even portions, as in the same letters patent it is contained more at large; by force of which letters patent the said John Sapcote hath had and occupied the same office of general receiver of our said duchy with the said portage of money from the said 18 day of July hitherto. We considering that the said John Sapcote for the account of the said office of receiver is charged afore Thomas Aleyn and Robert Coorte, auditors assigned by us, not willing the said John Sapcote in any wise to be vexed or troubled for any account or accounts thereof to us to be yielden by reason of any grant of the said letters patent to him in manner and form aforesaid made afore you our said Barons, of our certain knowledge and mere motion will and charge you that ye surcease for evermore of all processes, executions and demands, the which we have or may have or had or made against the said John Sapcote for the said account or accounts to be yielden, and that ye the said John Sapcote of the said account and accounts, processes, executions and demands, and of every thing of the premises, utterly acquit and discharge against us for ever. That express mention of the certainty of the said account or accounts, processes or any or any [sic] other thing concerning the premises herein be not had, or any statute, act, ordinance, provision or restraint, or any other matter you in any wise to the contrary moving notwithstanding. Given etc. [sic]. And these our letters shall be your warrant and sufficient discharge. Given under our privy seal at our palace of Westminster the 25 day of February the first year of our reign [1484].

(*ibid.* E.159/260, '*brevia*', Hilary, 1 Ric. III, m. 14d.)

13. Richard III appoints his treasurer of the Chamber to account personally to him only and to receive his acquittance by the sign manual (translation of Latin original)

FROM The Patent Roll, Public Record Office, Chancery, C.66/556, m. 21, no. 138.

The King. To all to whom [the present letters may come], greeting. Know that we, many times considering the fidelity, circumspection and industry of our well-beloved councillor and chaplain Edmund Chaderton, have created, ordained and constituted the said Edmund treasurer and receiver of our Chamber, to have and occupy the said office to the aforesaid Edmund during our pleasure, with the fees and wages due and accustomed to the said office, providing always that the said Edmund shall faithfully render faithful account or reckoning to ourselves only and to no other from time to time as shall duly be required; both of all and singular his receipts paid and delivered by our officers or ministers or by any other persons whatsoever to the said Edmund to our use, and which from time to time in future shall be paid and delivered, as of all payments and allowances whatsoever in any way paid and allowed from his same receipts at our commandment, by word of mouth or otherwise, to ourselves or to any other persons. And that he and his executors shall faithfully answer to us for all that which pertains to us, and shall justly be found to pertain to us, on the same account or reckoning, or the same accounts or reckonings. And that he and his executors shall be exonerated and quit of all such manner of account and reckoning or accounts and reckonings as aforesaid by him made and rendered and from time to time in future to be made and rendered, signed and to be signed by our sign manual, towards our heirs and our executors from time to time, and be every one of them exonerated and quit in perpetuity. Any statute, act, ordinance or provision made, ordained, or in any way provided to the contrary notwithstanding. In [witness] of which [we have caused these our letters patent to be made]. Witness the King at Nottingham the 26 day of April. By writ of privy seal and of [the aforesaid] date.

14. The King's lands, their revenues, officers, tenants, etc., as controlled through the Signet Office in the king's Chamber, 1483-1485

FROM British Museum MS. Harley 433, a signet office docket book.

fol. 107   Certain things that pass by the signet from the 4th day of July the first year of the reign of King Richard the IIIrd.

fol. 116v.
Evesham
An especial
acquittance

[1.] Be it known that we Richard by the grace of God, king of England and of France and lord of Ireland, have received this day here of our right well-beloved in God, John, abbot of our monastery of Evesham, an hundred and forty pounds of money to us due for the temporalities of the said monastery being in our hands by reason of the last vacation of the same and hold us fully paid and content in that behalf and the said abbot and his successors acquit thereof and utterly discharged against us and our heirs hereafter for evermore by these presents signed with our hand. Given, etc.,[1] the 21st day of September *Anno primo*.

fol. 117
Miles
Grenebanke

[2.] Richard, etc., to our trusty and well beloved squire for our body Geoffrey Franke, receiver of our lordship of Middleham, greeting. Whereas we be indebted unto our well-beloved Miles Grenebanke of our city of York, saddler, for certain stuffs to our use and behove of that his occupation in the same of £11 12s 2d as we certainly know. We, willing his contentation thereof as right requireth charge you that of such money as now resteth in your hands or next and first shall come to the same by reason of your said office ye pay and content unto the said Miles the said sum of £11 12s 2d, taking of him thereof his letters of acquitance, the which and these signed with our hand we will shall be unto you sufficient warrant and discharge therein against us. And that by the same ye shall have due allowance thereof before the auditors in your account. Given, etc., the 23rd day of September *Anno primo*.

---

[1] 'etc.' throughout is as it appears in the original.

fol. 121v.
Thomas
Fowler

[3.] To the receivers, farmers, tenants and all other occupiers and ministers of the castles, lordships, manors, lands and tenements within our counties of Bucks. and Beds. which late belonged unto our rebels and traitors Henry late duke of Buckingham, Thomas late marquis of Dorset, Sir William Norreys, Sir William Stoner, Sir Thomas Seintleger, Sir Richard Enderby, Sir John Don, Sir Thomas Dalamare, Sir Roger Tokotts, Sir Richard Beauchamp of Seinteourbant, knights, Walter Hungerford and John Cheny, squires, and to every of them, greeting. We let you wit that for the confidence and trust that we have in our full trusty squire Thomas Fowler, gentleman usher of our Chamber, we have ordained and assigned him to seize for us and in our name to enter into all the said castles, lordships, manors, lands and tenements and the revenues of the same to receive and levy to our use and behove. And in likewise to seize for us and in our name all manner of goods and chattels belonging unto any of our said rebels and traitors in whosesoever hands they may be found within our counties foresaid. Wherefore we straightly charge and command you, all and every of you, that ye content and pay all such rents and duties as be now growen and hereafter shall be due and grow of the issues and revenues of all the castles, lordships, manors, lands and tenements foresaid unto our said squire without delay as ye and every of you will eschew our grievous displeasure at your peril. Commanding over this our officers, true liegemen and subjects to be unto our said squire in the executing of this our commandment helping, aiding and assisting at all times as the case shall require. Given, etc., at Salisbury the 3rd day of November.

fol. 123
John
Sapcotte

[4.] Be it known that we, Richard by the grace of God, king of England etc., have received this present day of our trusty squire for our body John Sapcote, receiver-general of our duchy of Cornwall, for part of his receipt of the issues and revenues of the same our duchy for the year ending at Michaelmas last past by the hands of our right trusty servant John Kendale our secretary the sum of £200 of ready

122   THE CROWN LANDS

money, and in six obligations of our customs of tin within our county of Cornwall aforesaid containing the sum of £236, of which we knowledge our self content and paid and the said John Sapcote thereof to be acquitted and discharged and also to have due allowance of the same at our audit of our said duchy by virtue of these presents. Given etc. the 22 day of November *Anno primo Ricardi tercii.*

fol. 124 [5.] Be it remembered that we, Richard, etc., have re-
Nicholas ceived of our trusty servant Nicholas Spicer,[1] one of
Spicer   our receivers, the sum of £483 10s, that is to wit of our customs of Bristol £160 5s, of the revenues of our lordship of Glamorgan and Morganok £168 0s 6d, of our lordship of Abergavenny £80 7s, of the lordship of Bedminster £40, of Tedirton £8, of Edingworth 100s, of Thornbury 113s 4d, of the manor of Haresfield and Eastington £6 11s 1d and of Bonerston (or Boverston) £9 13s, of which sum or sums we knowledge us to be contented and paid and the said Nicholas thereof acquitted and clearly discharged. Given, etc., at London the 29 day of November *Anno primo.*

fol. 124v. [6.] Be it remembered that we Richard by the grace of God, etc., have received this day of our well-beloved William Herle, one of our receivers of the revenues of our Crown in the South parts by the hand of our fully trusty and well-beloved secretary the sum of £174 5s of the same revenues due unto us at Michaelmas last past, of which sum we hold us contented and paid and the said William thereof acquitted and discharged for ever. Given, etc., at London the last day of November *Anno primo.*

fol. 126   [7.] Robert Browne hath authority and power by the king's letters to hear and finally determine as auditor for this time only accounts of all the lands, manors and lordships belonging to the late marquis of Dorset of the which he hath been auditor aforetimes, for all such duties as was growen to at the feast of Michaelmas last past.

[8.] William Croke hath authority by the king's letters

[1] gentleman usher of the Chamber.

to take the accounts of all lands and lordships belonging to the late Marquis Dorset and Sir Thomas Seintleger within the counties of York, Cumberland, Chester, Derby, Rutland, Essex, Surrey, Wilts., Warws., Northants., Leicester and Wales of the which he was auditor before, for all things due and growen at Michaelmas last past.

fol. 129
Heys

[9.] A commission to John Heys for the receiving of the revenues of all the lands and tenements within the counties of Devon, Cornwall, Somerset, Dorset, Wiltshire and Hampshire called Devonshire lands, Warwick lands and Spencer lands and also of the lordship of Dartington and all other lands in the counties of Devon and Somerset which late appertained unto Sir Thomas Seintleger, knight.

Scrop

A letter to the lord Scrop and our commissioners of Devon and Cornwall for deliverance of all such money in their hands levied of the lands and goods of the king's rebels in the said counties to John Heys.

Hays

A like letter to the commissioners of Somerset and Dorset. A letter to Sir John Symond, priest, receiver of the bishopric of Exeter, of the temporalities to pay to John Hays such money as he hath received. A letter to Master William Wagette, canon of Exeter, for the delivery books of Seintleger lands to the said John.
A like letter to one Croke late auditor of the said Seintleger.

fol. 135
for Wales

[10.] Richard etc., to all and singular our officers, farmers, tenants and inhabitants of our lordship of Builth in Wales, greeting. And where labour hath been made unto us on your behalf to grant unto you a respite of the payment of such duties as be by you due unto us and ought to have been paid at Saint Catherine's day last past. We let you wit that our full mind is as against this your labour that ye in all diligence and goodly haste upon the sight of these without delay do content and pay unto us your said duties, and so from time to time, according to the old wages of our said lordships. As ye intend to stand in the favour of our grace and avoid the contrary. Doing you to wit that many of your lawful desires hereafter, ye

124 THE CROWN LANDS

doing your duties, shall have us your good and gracious sovereign lord. Given, etc., the 18 day of December *Anno primo*.

fol. 136
John
Bredefeld

[11.] Be it known that we Richard by the grace of God, king, etc., have received this present day of our well-beloved John Bredefelde, receiver of our duchy of Lancaster in our counties of Essex, Hertford, Middlesex and Surrey, by the hands of our trusty and well-beloved clerk and chaplain Master Edmund Chatterton the sum of a hundred forty and eight pounds of which sum of £148 we knowledge ourself fully content and paid and the said John his heirs and executors thereof to be acquitted and discharged by these presents. Given, etc., the 20th day of December *Anno primo*.

Martyn
Hawte

[12.] A like bill for Martyn Hawte, one of the receivers of the county of Northampton, for the contentation of £53 delivered the same day to the said Master Chatterton of like date.

John
Agarde

[13.] Memorandum that John Agard, receiver of the honour of Tutbury, hath delivered to the king by the hands of Sir Edmund Chatterton the sum of £102 the 23 day of December *Anno primo*.

John
Isham

[14.] Item that John Isham, receiver of the duchy of Lancaster within the counties of Huntingdon and Northampton, hath delivered the same day to the same Master Chatterton £30 the same day and year.

fols. 138v.
– 139.
Letters for
Receivers

[15.] To Thomas Frebody, receiver of our lands late purchased by the king Edward the IVth our brother. Well beloved we greet you well. And where it was so that we by our other letters heretofore to you directed, commanding you by the same to bring unto us all such money as then was due unto us by reason of your office. Which ye have not so done to our great marvel. Nevertheless yet eftsoons[1] we will and also straightly charge you that ye, incontinent upon the sight of these our letters by us to you now sent, all excuses and delays laid apart for the accom-

---

[1] Obsolete word meaning a second time, again.

plishment of this our second commandment, ye be with us in your proper person in all goodly haste, bringing with you all such sums of money as be now due unto us by reason of your said office. And also to make your account in that behalf before such our auditors as thereunto shall be assigned. Not failing hereof as ye will answer unto us at your peril. Given under our signet at our palace of Westminster the 6 day of January *Anno primo*.

A like letter to John Hayes, receiver
" John Penler, receiver of the lands late belonging to the duchess of Norfolk
" Richard Welby, receiver of the honour of Richmond
" William Harle, late receiver to Dame Elizabeth Grey
" Thomas Holbech, late receiver to Dame Elizabeth Grey
" Richard Grenway one of the king's receivers
" Thomas Fowler, receiver of the manor of Bushey
" John Luthington, receiver of the lands late belonging to the duke of Clarence
" John Bardfeld, receiver to Dame Elizabeth Grey
" John Issham, late receiver to the same Dame Elizabeth
" Robert Court, late receiver to Dame Elizabeth Grey
" John Woderowe, receiver of Wakefield
" Oliver Sutton, receiver of Wiltshire lands
" John Harecourt, receiver of the lands late belonging to the duke of Clarence
" Nicholas Spicer, receiver of Abergavenny and other places
" Martyn Hawte, receiver to Dame Elizabeth Grey

fol. 139

	David Midilton, receiver of Denbigh in Wales
,,	Thomas Totothe, receiver of the honour of Richmond
,,	Richard Croft, receiver of the earldom of March

A like letter to... [incomplete. Followed immediately, without any space left, by the entry of an order dated 6 January, 1 Ric. III appointing John Broun minister, guider and ruler of the king's bears and apes]

fol. 143v. [16.] John Kendale to enter and take possession for the king in the castle and lordship of Alington. And the rent of the same to levy to the king's behove.

fol. 144
Sir Marmaduke
Constable

[17.] Richard, etc., to the inhabitants of our honour and lowe[1] of Tonbridge and the lordships of Penshurst, Brasted, Hadlow and Yalding in our county of Kent and to every of them, greeting. Forasmuch as we, upon the special trust and confidence that we have in our trusty and right well-beloved knight for our body Sir Marmaduke Constable and for other causes us moving, have deputed and ordained him to make his abode among you and to have the rule within our honour of [sic] lowe and the lordships foresaid. We therefore will and straightly charge that ye nor any of you in no wise presume to take clothing or be retained with any man, person or persons whatsoever he or they be but that ye be ready to attend wholly upon our said knight at all times that ye by him shall be commanded to do us service. Not failing hereof as ye will avoid our great displeasure and the penalty that hereupon may ensue. Given, etc., the 22 day of January *Anno primo*.

fol. 144v.
Marden
Robert
Brakenber

[18.] Richard, etc., to all officers farmers and tenants and all other occupiers of our lordships of Milton and Marden within our county of Kent, greeting. We let you wit that we trusting in the truth, sadness and discretion of our trusty and well-beloved squire for

---

[1] lowe or low, obsolete forms of lough, meaning lake, loch, river or water.

our body Robert Brankenber have ordained and assigned him to receive for us and in our name all the issues, profits and revenues of our said lordships done and growen at the feast of St Michael the Archangel and the same so received to bring to us. Wherefor we will and command you and every of you that unto our said servant, or such as he shall depute and assign under him, ye do deliver and pay all such rents, farms and duties such as ye and every of you ought to have due by reason of your farms or tenures at the said feast. Charging you furthermore that unto our said servant or his deputies in duly executing this our commandment ye be attending, helping and assisting in all things as unto you appertaineth. Given, etc., the 25 day of January *Anno primo*.

fol. 148
Edmund
Shaw

[19.] Richard, etc., to our well-beloved John Isham, receiver of our lands in the counties of Northampton and Huntingdon, parcel of our duchy of Lancaster, greeting. We will and straightly charge you in all goodly haste possible, after the sight hereof, ye do content and pay of the revenues of your office to us due at Michaelmas last past to our right well beloved knight Sir Edmund Shaw of London, merchant, the sum of 200 marks sterling for certain New Year's gifts by us of him bought against the feast of Christmas in the 22 year of the reign of our brother king Edward the IVth. And these our letters shall be unto you upon your account to be yielden before our auditors sufficient warrant and discharge in that behalf. Given under our signet at Westminster the 5th day of February *Anno primo*.

fol. 176
Robert
Coort

[20.] Be it known that we Richard by the grace of God, king of England and lord of Ireland, have received the second day of June the first year of our reign by the hands of Master Edmund Chaderton, treasurer of our Chamber of Robert Coort, receiver of our duchy of Lancaster and the earldom of Hertford in the South parts of this our realm, one hundred and forty pounds sterling of the issues and revenues coming and growing of his said receipt of this present year. Given under our signet at our castle of Pontefract the day and year aforesaid.

128 THE CROWN LANDS

fol. 178v.
John
Hugford

[21.] Richard, etc., to our trusty and well-beloved servant John Agard, one of our receivers of the earldom of Warwick, greeting. We let you wit that we have commanded our servant Robert Clerk to do mow, make and in, in all haste possible, all our meadows at Warwick by the oversight of our full trusty squire for our body John Hugford, constable of our castle of our castle [sic] of Warwick and steward of our lordship there. The cost and charge of which business will amount to 10 marks or thereabouts, by estimation as we be informed, the which sum we have appointed the same Robert to have by your hands, willing and charging you therefore to deliver unto him the same without any manner delay or excuse to the contrary, so that from lack or sloth thereof no hurt grow unto us in this behalf, as we trust you and as ye will answer. And in as much as the certainty of the said charge cannot as yet be fully understood, we will that at the next account to be yielden at Warwick ye examine groundly the parcels of the said charge as your wisdom shall think best, and in case the said Robert be found in surplusage that ye then of your receipt content unto him the same. And in semblable wise if any thing remain unbestowed of the said 10 marks ye to demand and receive again of him the sum to our use as it appertaineth. And these our letters, with the said parcels to this attached, shall be your sufficient warrant in this behalf at your next account before our auditors to be yielden. Given, etc., the 20th day of June *Anno primo*.

fol. 179

[22.] A quittance by the king made to John Sapcote upon the receipt of £116 13s 4d for the half year's farm of my lord Fitzwarren's lands by the hands of Master Chaderton. Given at Pontefract, 23rd day of June *Anno primo*.

Sir
Richard
Huddilston

[23.] Richard, etc., to our trusty and well-beloved William Griffith, squire, our chamberlain of North Wales, greeting. How be it that we of late commanded you by our other letters of warrant to have paid and delivered of your receipt amongst others but a prest of wages to 40 soldiers being in the retinue of our trusty and well-beloved knight for our body Sir Richard Huddilston, constable of our castle of Beaumaris and captain of our town there, unto the next coming thither of our auditors, yet nevertheless for certain causes us now specially moving we will and straightly charge you that forthwith upon the sight hereof ye pay and deliver to our said knight the wages of the said soldiers being unpaid from Easter last past hitherto, that is to say for every of them four pence by the day and so monthly from henceforth without any obstacle or contradiction unto the feast of All Hallows next coming. Given, etc., *Anno primo*.

John Blekynsop [24.] John Blekynsop hath warrant to the receiver and auditor of Tynedale to forbear and discharge him of 15s rent that he is accustomed to pay for a farmhold that he occupies in Tynedale in recompence of a ground of his which the king occupies beside Carlisle for making of brick. Given the 24th day of June *Anno primo*.

fol. 181v. The abbot of Fountains [25.] A commission directed to Sir William Gascoigne, knight, Nicholas Leventhorpe, squire, Miles Metcalf, Thomas Midilton and Richard Danby where the king by his letters of commission charged them for the inquiry of and upon certain differences betwixt the king's tenants of Knaresborough and the abbot and convent of Fountains and their tenants for the right and title of certain ground bounding upon the forest. Charging to proceed to the same in goodly haste. Given, etc., at York the 20th day of July *Anno primo*.

fol. 204 William Carter [26.] A warrant to John Roberdis, receiver of our duchy of Lancaster within the county of Leicester, to content and pay of such money as is now in his hands or that shall next and first come to the same of the revenues of our said duchy, to pay and content unto our subject William Carter the sum of £13 13s to him by us due for 120 oxen and 6 muttons of him had for the expenses of our Household. Given at Westminster, etc., the 28 day of January *Anno secundo*.

fol. 217 [27.] A commission directed to all mayors, bailiffs, burgesses and inhabitants of the boroughs of New Windsor in Berks., Guildford and Kingston-upon-Thames in Surrey, and to all the officers, farmers, etc., of the lordships, lands and tenements in Amersham in our counties of Buckingham and Hertford, of the lordships, waters, weirs, lands and tenements in Chesham, Langley Marish, Wyrardisbury, Wendover and Datchet in Bucks., of the lordships, etc., in Swallowfield, Cookham, Bray and the 7 hundreds of Cookham and Bray in Berks, and lordships and lands etc., in Bagshot, Worplesdon, Claygate and Pirbright in Surrey, the lordship of Kempton in Middlex., and St Margaret Stratton in Wilts., which, with the feefarms of the boroughs aforesaid, be annexed to the castle of Windsor. Given, etc., the 15 day of May *Anno secundo*.

fol. 217v. [28.] Richard, etc., to our trusty and well-beloved servant Richard Spert, receiver of our lands within our county of Lincoln, greeting. We will and charge you that of the revenues of your office ye content and pay to Sampson Cok the sum of three pounds ten shillings by us due unto him for wheat of him bought for the expenses of our Household. Receiving of him his debenture specifying the said sum, by the which and these our letters ye shall have due allowance at your account for the same. And that this be not stalled nor delayed by any means as ye intend to continue in your office. Any other restraint or commandment to you by us given to the contrary notwithstanding. Given etc., at Kenilworth the 24 day of May *Anno secundo*.

Warrants for the Household Sampson Cok

John Parrowe hath a like warrant to the same receiver for £14 3s for bread of him bought etc., Given *ut supra*.

William Aylest a like warrant to the same receiver for 40s due unto him for hay.

Sir William Husy, knight, a like warrant to the same receiver £40 due unto him for oxen.

John Pulleyn, servant of the cellar and ewery, a like warrant to the same receiver for £16 6s 7d for nappery.

Richard Prior of Aylesbury a like warrant to the same receiver for £9 6s 6d for horsebread.

DOCUMENTS 131

[75 'like warrants' for suppliers of the Household follow, directed to Richard Spert or to other receivers, officers or farmers of the king's lands].

fol. 219 [29.] A commission to all officers, farmers and tenants of
Ulverston the manor of Cravenys in Henham otherwise called the manor of Henham in Suffolk recording that where the same manor and tenement be seized to the king's hands and that upon the claim of John Ulverston, squire, which claimeth the same a perfect examination hath been had by the Council and found his right. Whereupon they be restored to the same John and the duchess of Suffolk amoved of her possession by the king. Writing charging them to be obedient. Given at Kenilworth the 6 day of June *Anno secundo*.

fol. 269v. [30.] Assignment made of divers lordships for the expenses and wages of a household appointed by the king to be holden at Sandal or elsewhere within the county of York, to begin from Michaelmas *anno secundo* to endure for a whole year, after the sum of 2000 marks by year, that is to say

    Barnard Castle with the members £110
    Skipton and Carlton with the
      members   £194
    Cottingham   £152
    Hotham   £20
    Bawtry   £6 13s 4d
    Raby with the members   £66 13s 4d
    Latimer lands   £133 6s 8d
    Thirsk and Hovingham   £72 6s 8d
    Knaresborough, Pontefract and
      Tickhill   £500
    Kirkby Malzeard and Burton in
      Lonsdale   £40
    Caister and North Witham   £49
Total sum of the aforesaid
    assignments   £1344

which makes in marks 2016 marks to be paid at the feasts of Easter and Michaelmas etc.

fol. 270 [31.] Instructions given by the king unto Sir Marmaduke

Constable, knight, steward of the honour of Tutbury. First that the said Sir Marmaduke shall take the oath of all the inhabitants within the said honour that they shall be true and faithful liegemen unto the king, and not to be retained to any lord or other, but immediately to the king's grace.

Also the said Sir Marmaduke shall see that no liveries ne cognizance be given within the said honour contrary to the law and to the statutes thereof made.

Also where heretofore divers extortions and oppressions have been done by the county bailiffs, upon trust that they should continue and not to be removed from their offices, the king will that from henceforth the said Sir Marmaduke put able and well-disposed persons in the said bailiwicks such as be sufficient to answer the king of his duty; and they to be changed from year to year, and that a proclamation to be made at every great court that if any person will come and complain of any of the said bailiffs that they shall be heard, and due reformation and punishment be had according to the king's laws and their demerits.

Also whereas there be certain farmholds let to divers persons which occupy but little or some part thereof to their own proper use and make leases of the residue over unto such as be not the king's tenants, the king, willing his tenants to be preferred to such farmholds and to be farmers immediately to his grace, will that the said Sir Marmaduke discharge all farmers of all such parcels so set over by leases unto other and to let the same farms amongst the king's tenants to such as be able to do the king service and to answer him of his farm.

Also the king will that the said Sir Marmaduke well and diligently survey all his woods within the said honour, and to see that no waste be made in them, ne that no browsing be made in them in the winter season but such as shall be necessary and to the least hurt to the king's woods.

Also the said Sir Marmaduke to see that there be no wood fallen within the said honour for paling but such as is most mete and convenient for the same, and the coppices of the said paling wood with the browsing that is metely for the expenses of the king's

Household or his reparations be kept therefore, the residue to be praised and sold to the king's most advantages.

Also the king will that no livery trees be given within his parks and woods but only under his special warrant or such as have it by special grant of old times past.

Also, where the king hath enlarged the fees of his parkers, to the intent that they should be attending daily in their offices when they await not on his grace, and in their absence make sufficient deputies such as will be of good demeanour to the king's woods and game, the king will that if any such deputy be found not sufficient nor of good demeanour then the said Sir Marmaduke to discharge him and to certify the king's grace, that a sufficient deputy may be put in his room; and also that no parker have of duty in any of the king's parks over 2 kine and two houses.

Also the king will that the herbage of all his parks be let or approved to the king's most advantages, saving sufficient pasture for the deer, and the king's farms not diminished; forseen always that the parkers of the same be neither farmers nor approvers of the said herbage.

Also that the lieutenant, the bowbearer and receivers of wards be such persons as be of good demeanour against the king's woods and game and sworn to the same; and that they and every of them well and duly oversee the game and woods in the parks and wards of the said honour according to their offices as they have been accustomed afore time.

Also the said Sir Marmaduke to put into the office of bailiwicks that be accountants, good and sufficient persons, and such as be able to do the king service and to content the king of such as they shall be charged withal upon their accounts.

fols. 271 –2

[32.] A remembrance made, as well for hasty levy of the king's revenues growing of all his possessions and hereditaments, as for the profitable estate and governance of the same possessions.

First that all the kings' officers of his Court of Exchequer use and execute hasty process against all manner [of] persons accountable, and others being the kings' debtors, as the case shall require; and also to hear and determine accounts of the same, and the issues, profits, and revenues coming thereof to be levied and paid into the king's receipt without delay. Also that no person accountable, nor other person being in debt to the king, have any respite, stallment, or favour in the said court, whereby the king's duties may be delayed over the space of 4 months next after the time that any such person oweth to yield his account, or oweth to pay his debt, whatsoever it be. For it hath been said that many divers officers accountable have been respited of their accounts from year to year and also of their payments by space of many years, to the king's great hurt in times past.

Also that no officers having office in the said Court of the Exchequer have or occupy any office in the Receipt.

Also it is thought that the auditors of the said Exchequer should yearly make a book of all the revenues, issues, and profits growing of all sheriffs, escheators, collectors of customs and subsidies, treasurer of Calais and Guisnes, collectors of dismes, bailiffs of cities, boroughs, and ports, and of all other manner [of] officers accountable of the said Exchequer, with the reprises and deductions thereof, and the same book to declare before such persons as the king's good grace shall like to assign to hear and see it; whereupon his grace may yearly see the profits of the said court.

Also that the Treasurer of England for the time being yearly should make a declaration of all such money as is received or assigned within his office, be it in the Receipt or be it otherwise, for that year before the said years.

Also that the said Court of Exchequer be clearly dismissed and discharged with any meddling with any foreign livelihood in taking of accounts, as Wales, duchies of Cornwall, York, Norfolk, earldoms of Chester, March, Warwick, Salisbury, and of all other lands being in the king's hands by reason of forfeiture; which is thought most behoveful and profitable to be assigned to other foreign auditors for divers causes ensuing, etc.; that is to say:

First, for more hasty levy of money. Also for more easy and less cost of the officers of such livelihood. Also for cause that the lordships may be yearly surveyed by the stewards, auditors, and receivers in the time of accounts of officers of the same for reparations, woodsales, and for other directions to be had among the tenants, with many more causes necessary, etc. And where that many lordships, manors, lands and tenements pertaining to the crown be committed to divers persons for farms in certain, by which the king's woods and his courts, with other casualties, be wasted and lost to his great hurt, and great allowances had for reparations of his castles and manors, and they are not forthy[1] repaired, as it is said; and also the said lordships oft time set within the value; it is thought that a foreign auditor should be assigned for all lordships, manors, lands, and tenements belonging to the crown, and a receiver for the same yearly to ride, survey, receive, and remember in every behalf that might be most for the king's profit, and thereof yearly to make report of the estate and condition of the same; by the which the king's grace should know all the lordships that pertaineth to his Crown, which as now be unknown, as it is said, etc. Also it is thought that such certain auditors as be of good, true, and sad disposition and discretion should be assigned to hear and determine the accounts of all the king's foreign livelihood as is above discharged from the Exchequer, and to have so many auditors and no more but as may conveniently and diligently determine the said livelihood betwixt Michaelmas and Candlemas, with sad and discreet examination of all defaults and hurts of all officers accountable severally in their offices executing, wherein the auditors of the Exchequer can never have so evident knowledge for reformation of the same.

Also that the receivers of good and true disposition, and also of havour of richesse[2] be assigned to the said

---

[1] Obsolete word meaning 'therefore' or 'nevertheless'.

[2] Obsolete expression meaning literally 'possessing wealth', i.e. men of substance.

livelihood; and they to see for reparations of castles, manors, mills, parks, and other, and in the circuit of their receipt they to see the weal of every lordship. Also it is thought that all auditors afore said, as well of the Exchequer as of foreign livelihood, should yearly make declaration of all such livelihood as they have in charge afore such persons as the king's grace will thereto assign at London, alway betwixt Candlemas and Palm Sunday, so that his grace may be ascertained yearly of the whole revenues of all his livelihood, and what thereof is paid and what is owing, and is whose default.

Also, that where lords, knights, and esquires, many of them not lettered, be made stewards of the king's livelihood in divers countries, they taking great fines and rewards of the king's tenants to their proper use, to the king's hurt and poverishing of his said tenants, and also wanting cunning and discretion to order and direct the said livelihood lawfully, with many more inconveniences. Therefore it is thought that learned men in the law were most profitable to be stewards of the said livelihood for many causes concerning the king's profit and the weal of his tenants.

Also it is thought that all lands being in the king's hands by reason of wardship of lords' sons or other noble men should not be let to farmhold for a certain, but that the same lands should remain in the king's hands during the nonage and that auditors of the same lands should yearly determine the accounts thereof and to make declaration as is above said, for the more profit to the king, etc.

Also for temporalities of bishoprics, abbeys, and priories in likewise, etc.

Also it is thought that all the foresaid auditors, every year at the feast of Michaelmas next after the declaration made of all foreign livelihood by for [sic] the said persons by the king so assigned, should deliver or do to be delivered the books of accounts of the same into the king's Exchequer, afore the Barons there after the first year of the premises, there to remain of record, so that the books of accounts of the later year be alway in the hands of the said auditors for their precedence, the duchy of Lancaster, the lordships of Glamorgan and Abergavenny alway except, etc.

[This document is undated, but is entered between documents dated Oct. 2, 1484 and Oct. 23, 1484.]

fol. 290 [33.] [The following is a translation of the Latin of the original]

Assignment made by the special command of the lord king as for the expenses of his most honourable Household as for the wages of his servants with the same Household, that is to say from the last day of March in the second year of his reign to the last day of March the next following, that is to say, for one whole year, to be paid at the terms of Easter and Michaelmas in the manner and form following, beyond the expenses and wages of the chaplains and clerks of the chapel and of the officers and servants of the stable of the same lord king, that is to say:

Of the farms and feefarms pertaining to the king's Crown together with the issues of the sheriffs and escheators of England	£2000 from which in the charge of	The Treasurer of England and John Fitzherbert, receiver of various feefarms p.a.	£1600
		Wiliam Herle, receiver of various crown manors in the circuit of John Stanford p.a.	£800
Of the duchy of Lancaster p.a.	£3000	Hugh Gartside, receiver of Lancaster, Clitheroe and Halton p.a. £123 6s 8d	
		John Agard, receiver of Tutbury p.a. £400	
		Richard Spert, receiver of Long Bennington p.a. £50	

John Dymmok, deputy of Thomas Burgh, knight, receiver of Bolingbroke p.a. £480

Thomas Holbache, receiver of Higham Ferrers p.a. £323 6s 8d

Robert Sharp, receiver in the counties of Norfolk and Suffolk p.a. £500

John Berdefeld, receiver in the counties of Essex and Herts., and elsewhere p.a. £466 13s 4d

Nicholas Brytte, receiver in the county of Sussex p.a. £80

Robert Coort, receiver in the South parts p.a. £666 13s 4d

Of the duchy of Cornwall p.a. £1200, the whole in the charge of John Sapcote, receiver there p.a.

Of the earldom of March p.a. £200, the whole in the charge of Richard Croft, knight, general receiver there.

Of the lands and tenements called Warwick, Salisbury and Spencer lands p.a. } £2000 from which in the charge of

John Hayes, a receiver there p.a. £994

John Cutte, another receiver there p.a. £517

John Agard, a third receiver there p.a. £300

William Hoggesson, bailiff of Saham Toney p.a. £60

Bailiffs of Olney £9, Milton £20, Aston Clinton £20 Singleborough and Buckland Marlow £30 and Quarrendon £50	}	£129

Of the duchy of Norfolk *p.a.* £400, the whole in the charge of Thomas Overton, receiver there *p.a.*

Of the ulnage *p.a.* £300, the whole in the charge of the Treasurer of England

Of the lordships of Kensington and Notting Hill } £41 of which in the charge of { the farmer of Kensington } £26
the farmer of Notting Hill } £15

Of the lands late of lord Fitzwarren *p.a.* £233 6s 8d of which the whole in the charge of John Sapcote, squire

fol. 290v. Of the lands late of Walter Gruffith *p.a.* £66 13s 4d, the whole by Gervais Clifton, knight

Of the lands late of the earl of Essex p.a. £533 6s 8d, the whole by John Plomer, receiver there, paying at the feasts of Michaelmas and Easter

Of the office of Chief Butler of England *p.a.* £100, the whole by Lord Lovel, king's chamberlain

Of forfeited lands in the West parts *p.a.* £300 the whole by John Hayes, receiver there

Of the manor or lordship of Thornbury *p.a.* £200, by the receiver there

Total sum of the aforesaid assignment: £10,574 6s 8d

15. Henry VII informs the Exchequer of their exclusion from land revenue accounting, 1493

FROM The Memoranda Rolls of the Kings Rembrancer, Public Record Office, Exchequer, K.R., E.159/269, 'Brevia directa baronibus', Trinity, m. 1d.

Pro Reginaldo Bray, Henry by the grace of God, king of
Johanno Walshe England and of France and lord of
et aliis Ireland, to the Treasurer and Barons of our Exchequer greeting. Whereas we have ordained made and deputed our trusty and well beloved councillor Reynold Bray, knight, and Hugh Oldeham, clerk, jointly our receivers-general of all our honours, manors, and lordships, lands, and other possessions called Warwicks lands, Salisburys lands, and Spencers lands in all these certain shires of England in which John Hayes was late semblable officer, and where furthermore we have in like wise ordained and made our trusty and well beloved John Walshe, squire, our general receiver of all the said lands in the counties of Warws., Worcs., Staffs., Salop., Gloucs., Heref., Northants., Rutland, Derbys., Cambs., Hunts., Lincs., Leics., Beds., Bucks., Oxon., Berks., Wilts., Norf., Suff., Essex, Herts., Middlx., and Kent, and of certain other lands and tenements which were sometime Richard Beauchamp, sometime earl of Warwick, in the same shires, and also of certain other lands which were late William, late marquis Berkeley, in the counties of Gloucs., and Warws., and of certain other lands which were late the lord Morleys in divers shires of this our realm of England, with the manor of West Thurrock in county of Essex, late the earl Rivers, as in several letters patent and other authorities to our said councillor and Hugh Oldeham jointly, and to the said John Walshe of the premises among other severally made more plainly doth appear. Whereupon as we be certainly informed, ye make yearly execution and and [sic] process for us as well against our said councillor and the said Hugh Oldeham as against the said John Walshe to yield to us at our said Exchequer several accounts yearly of the premises. We, having consideration that the said lands and every parcel of them be not ne have out of time of mind been any parcel of the ancient possessions of our Crown of England, but that they be such lands as have now lately come to our hands by way of our purchase and other wise, intending therefore to have the profits and issues of them only

paid yearly to our own hands and nowhere else, and also to oversee and examine by us and our Council the accounts of the said several receivers from year to year and time to time, therefore we will and straightly charge and command you that ye from the feast of Saint Michael the Archangel the 7th year of our reign, and so yearly from the same feast forward, ne make any process or execution in our said Exchequer neither against our said councillor and Hugh Oldeham ne against the said John Walshe nor any of them nor their heirs ne executors for the said account or any of them by reason of the premises or of any other thing in the said letters patent severally contained, and that ye of the said executions or processes or any other processes, action, executions, suits, and demands made or to be made at our said Exchequer, for the said accounts, or any of them, as well against our said councillor and Hugh Oldham as the said John Walshe, their heirs and executors and every of them, utterly surcease for evermore other than against the auditors of the said lands for the time being for the accounts of the said receivers yearly to be after the determinations of them before us and our Council yearly delivered to you, there to be [Here the clerk enrolling the writ appears to have omitted a line or more] bailiffs and all other occupiers of the said lands of all manner issues, profits, farms, and revenues which shall yearly from henceforth appear to you duly to be answered to us in the said account or accounts, so that no manner farmer, bailiff, sheriff, or any other our minister, whatsoever he be, be charged by reason of any manner execution to be made out of our said Exchequer to make account or payment of any part or parcel of the issues and revenues aforesaid, which by or in the account of our said several receivers and every of them yearly shall be found to us answered, but that ye clearly acquit them and every of them of and for the said accounts, issues, and profits for evermore. Nevertheless we will and charge you that ye against all such bailiffs, farmers, tenants, debtors, and other accountants of the lands aforesaid, which by or upon the said several accounts of our said several receivers from time to time shall appear not to be accounted nor answered unto us, and so in the end of every such account or accounts put to answer unto us by the allegiance[1] of our said several receivers, ye make for us such process as by you shall be thought most requisite, after the course of our said Exchequer, unto such time as we thereof be duly answered, any act, statute, ordinance, provision, or restraint to the contrary hereof made, or any other cause, use, course, or any matter you to the contrary moving notwithstanding. Given under our privy seal at our manor of Sheen, the second day of March the 8th year of our reign.

---

[1] That is, assertion or alleging.

16. Extracts from the General Surveyors' book of declarations of accounts for the twelve month period September 30, 1503–September 29, 1504 (in Latin)

FROM The Miscellaneous Books of the Treasury of Receipt, Public Record Office, Echequer, E.36/213.

[Net amounts ('*et remanet clare*') from current issues, paid to John Heron, treasurer of the Chamber, noted by each separate item in the original]

	£	s	d
Lands late of Queen Elizabeth Richard Decons, receiver	2944	12	7¼
Duchy of Cornwall Richard Nanfan, receiver	3105	11	4½†
Principality of N. Wales John Pyliston, receiver	1213	7	8¼*
Earldom of March Richard Croft, kt., receiver	857	4	5¾*
Palatine counties of Chester and Flint Randolf Brierton, receiver	1351	15	9¼*
South Wales Rees ap Thomas, receiver	459		
Bromfield and Yale[1] Lancelot Lowther, receiver	623	3	7¾
Counties of Chester and Flint[2] William Smith, receiver	132	10	3
Castle of Windsor John Ballson, receiver	55	5	2¾

† £2165 18s 4¼, of this total came from the coinage of tin.
* Including subsidies, i.e. tallage.
[1],[2] Lands late of Sir William Stanley, attainted, 1495.

Chirk
  John Edwarde, receiver   112 4 5¼

Warwick, Spencer and Salisbury lands, etc.
  Thomas Goodman, receiver [lands late of earl of Warwick[1]]   3050 8 3½
  Hugh Oldham, clk, receiver [lands late of countess of Warwick]   1104 19 7¾

Cranbourne and members
  Hugh Oldham, clk, receiver   88 11 3¼

Ditchampton
  Hugh Oldham, clk, receiver   17 12 11

Lands late of the duke of Bedford
  Various receivers [sic.]   1852 15 7
  John Tomson, receiver in Notts. & Derbys.   79 18 4

Usk and Caerleon, lands of earldom of March
  William Harbart, receiver   147 19 9¼

Lordship of Narberth, lands of earldom of March
  Thomas ap Philip, receiver   31 17 8½

Lands late of the earl of Huntingdon[2]
  John Poole, receiver   270 3 6½

Isle of Wight
  John Dawtre, receiver   358 5 8

Blankney and Branston
  Thomas Legh, receiver   40 19 7½

Duchy of York
  Robert Southwell, receiver [Norf., Suff., Cambs., Hunts. Essex, Herts.],
  Edmund Busshy, receiver [Lincs., Rutland, Northants.],
  Robert Pyggot, receiver [Oxon., Bucks.],
  John Grove, receiver [Kent, Surrey, Sussex]   928 5 6

Lordship of Caister
  Ralph Sandeford, receiver   3 15 10½

---

[1] attainted 1503.
[2] William Herbert, died *s.p.m.* 16 July 1491.

Sale of woods			
Richard Empson, receiver	103	–	3
Hunsdon and Eastwick, Herts. [duchy of York]			
William Povington, receiver	41	14	7½
Wanstead			
Williams Tresire, receiver	12	10	7
Lands late of Edmund de la Pole[1]			
Robert Lovell, kt., Henry Reynolde, Geoffrey Darolde, receivers	876	13	11½
Lands late of Lord Audley[2]			
Various receivers [sic.]	473	12	9½
Cheyneys lands			
Richard Elyott, receiver	178	19	8¾
Lands late of Lord Fitzwalter[3]			
Robert Southwell and Thomas Stokes, receivers	647	9	10¼
Tirell's lands,[4] Norf. & Suff.			
Robert Southwell, receiver	119	18	8
[Stoke under Hamdon]			
Giles lord Dawbeney, receiver	32	12	8¾
[Cumberworth]			
Anthony Hansard, receiver	83	14	9¼
Pytchley			
[no receiver named]	16	17	11
Lands late of William de la Pole[5]			
[no receiver named]	477	2	3¾
Lands late of Edward Burgh, kt.[6]			
Richard Leche and William Henage, receivers	482	2	8½
Moor End and members			
John Wykyn, bailiff	19	1	11½

---

[1] Earl of Suffolk, attainted 1503.
[2] John Tuchet, lord A., attainted 1503.
[3] John Radcliffe, lord F., attainted 1495.
[4] Sir James Tyrell, attainted 1502.
[5] Sir William, attainted 1503.
[6] ?Sir Edward Borough, during minority.

Aishleys[1] and Bayleys lands			
Francis Marzen, receiver	8	10	5
Lands late of Lord Hastings			
Benedict Brocas, receiver	214	12	2
Botrigans lands, late Lord Broke[2]			
Lord Broke, receiver [sic.]	19	–	5
Lands late of William Trefrye [?Trefries] in Gloucs.			
Thomas Godeman, receiver	[no sum given]		
Declaration of various farmers			
[including some feefarms and ulnage]	989	15	11¾
Annuities [annual payments]:			
Lands and possessions late lord Roos			
of Thomas Lovell	466	13	4
Lands in Cornwall and Devon			
of Hugh Oldham[3]	100		
Lands of Francis Cheyney in Kent			
of Jacob Archer	100		
Lands late of Catesby			
of Richard Empson	100		
Annuity late Skeltons	40		
Datonslande in Devon			
of Roger Holand	10		
Lands late lord Morley			
of William Parker	120		
[indecipherable]	39		
[„]	26	13	4
[Grand total of the above items, not in the original, £24,620	7	8½]	

Declaration of wards' lands   £6,264 8 10¼
  [on examination this proves to contain some items paid for the previous year and some items paid for the previous two years. Of this total £5173 19s 11¼d remained after the deduction of re-

---

[1] Edward Ashley, attainted, 1495
[2] Robert Willoughby, lord B.
[3] Hugh Oldham crossed out and written over: 'Of the earl of Devon'.

prises. John Heron, treasurer of the Chamber, received £3003 16s 8½d; £168 2s 2¼d was respited to various persons; £990 9s 2¾d was declared to be in the hands of the executors of the bishop of Durham; and £989 9s 4¼d was ordered to be levied, by estimation, from various persons. As often in large calculations of the period, all made in Roman numerals, the totals are not quite accurate.]

17. Extracts from a docket book of the Court of the king's General Surveyors, 1505 to 1508

FROM The Miscellaneous Books of the Augmentations Office, Public Record Office, Exchequer, E.315/263.

fol. 3   *Terminus Purificationis Anno XX^{mo}*   [Hilary Term 1505]

[1.] Memorandum that Robert Skynner and John Skynner not depart from the court to such time they find sufficient surety to the king's grace for payment of the farm of Hadleigh Ray where they get and procure their mussels and likewise John Pope the middler[1] to be bound for that year. Whereupon the said Robert Skynner, John Skynner and John Pope bindeth them and every of them to be bound for others before etc.[2] to pay or cause to be paid to the king's use 20 marks for the farm of the said Hadleigh Ray for the year that shall end at Michaelmas next coming.

[2.] Memorandum that where Hugh Johnes is bound to John Heron and Henry Wyet to pay to the king's use 10 marks yearly for a[3] farm of Thorrington in Suffolk [sic] whereof he asketh allowance yearly of these parcels to this memoradum annexed [details of payments out totalling 62s 2d on an attached slip].

fol. 4   [3.] Memorandum that where certain variances and traverses hang and depend betwixt John Stanley and William Smyth for the payment of certain money, it is now awarded by the court that the said William Smyth shall keep and retain in his hands the said money till the next term and then both the parties abovesaid the first day thereof to appear and to bring the best record they can for their right.

[4.] Memorandum that where John Stanley showeth by

---

[1] The spelling of the original is 'midelir'.
[2] 'etc.' throughout is as it appears in the original.
[3] 'oon' is modernized as 'a' throughout, rather than as 'one', where this makes the better sense.

his bill that the king's grace by his letters patent hath granted to one John Waller esquire the moiety of the manor of Chebsey, it is awarded that he shall appear the first day to Easter and to bring his best record for his right.

fol. 4A [5.] This is the tale of John Stanley for the lands in Chebsey in the county of Stafford. The said John sayeth that the king by his letters patent granted the moiety of the manor of Chebsey to one John Waller esquire, to him and to the heirs male of his body lawfully begotten, as appeareth in the king's Chancery, the estate of the said John Waller the said John Stanley now hath and prayeth that the said John Waller may be sent for to come and make answer to the charge and to bring in the king's letters patent to him in office made etc.

fol. 4B [6.] This is the tale of John Stanley that he maketh to the rent of Tunstall. The said John sayeth that the said rent within the said lordship is payable and ever hath been paid at the feast of the Annunciation of our Lord and that plainly doth appear by the evidence of the tenants there and by the rental of the said lordships, and further all the tenants there know well that it is then payable, and prayeth that the tenants there may be sent for to show the truth or else some man appointed to examine them there upon their oaths, etc.

fol. 4v. [7.] To our auditor for the time being, greeting. We will and also charge you that ye make due and plain allowance unto our trusty and well-beloved servant Richard Sutton our officer and receiver of our lordships of Dedham, Langham and Stratford in his next account of the sum of £37 6s 8d which he hath paid and delivered to our use and this our warrant shall be your sufficient authority and discharge at all times for the allowing of the same. Given in our lodging at Stepney the 13th day of February the 17th year of King Henry VII [1502].

[8.] Memorandum that my Lord Broke hath day to appear for the manor of Trefiw in the month of Easter [*mense Pasche*] and to bring in his best evidence and learned counsel to answer for the same.

fol. 5 [9.] Memorandum that when the executors of William Trefrey thereof of Cornwall *Anno XVII⁰* shall appear, to lay to their charge for the sum of £14 19s 2½d for the arrears the same year of the sheriffwick of Cornwall.

[10.] Memorandum that where William Croke is bound by his obligation to appear the 20th day of February and then to bring in certain books of accounts concerning the lands late the Lady Hastings he hath now the 22nd day to bring the said books being within the city of London; and he hath 4 days after to bring the residue of the land books being in other places. The abovesaid books were delivered to the hands of Master Dudley as he affirms and he has his obligation etc. [in Latin].

fol. 5v. [11.] Memorandum that the late earl of Suffolk hath been accustomed to have in times past his leet and court in Wyton beside Hull; and now the mayor and his brethren there will not suffer the same to be had nor any revenues to come but only to their hands notwithstanding it is come to the king by the attainder of Edmund de la Pole.

[12.] Memorandum that a letter missive is directed to Jasper Philoll that where the king's mills called Whiteley Mills belonging to the manor and lordship of Pimperne within the shire of Dorset were late in the holding of Sir Richard Ragiers, paying yearly during the time he occupied the said mills £6 6s 8d, now it hath pleased the king's Council that a demission be made in John Hotechyns of the said mills and to pay yearly therefor £6 13s 4d and that the said Jasper shall see him put in possession of the same and above that to see the mills at that day be in good and sufficient repair or else to distrain therefor, etc.

fol. 6v. [13.] Memorandum that where Robert Suthill appeared the 8th day of March to have given answer for £100 due by him for the debt of Nicholas Nynys. Now he hath 14th day of March to give a direct answer thereunto. He hath appeared and is committed to the Fleet.

[14.] Litchborough. Valor of the lands and tenements of John Malony in the county of Northampton [Latin heading]. In primis the manor place of Litchborough is now let to farm as it hath been showed with the demesne fee: 8 marks. Item the rent in the same town: 4 marks.
[?signed] Richerd Emson.[1]

fol. 7 [15.] Memorandum that John Grove, receiver of the duchy of York in Kent and Surrey, promiseth to bring in sufficient sureties for his said office the quindene of Easter next coming.

[16.] Memorandum that John Edwards shall send up the names of 6 several men's names for his office of Chirk at the feast of Ascension next coming; and of those 6 persons 4 of them to be bound for his said office.

fol. 8 [17.] Item a letter is directed to my lord president and others of the prince's council that where it hath pleased the king's grace to depute Sir Robert Haid, priest, to be his receiver of his lordships of Acton Burnell with the members, etc., that my said lord and others of the council should take sufficient surety bound in 300 marks of the said Sir Robert for performing of his said office in every behalf etc.

fol. 8v. [18.] Memorandum that Richard ap Pole, receiver of Builth, that he or his sureties appear before us by the commandment of Sir Rees ap Thomas in the rogation days next coming for payment of £24 of his arrears [Anno] XVIII°.

[19.] Memorandum that before the prince's next entry in South Wales that there be given warning thereof to Sir Rees ap Thomas half year before, or at the

---

[1] The whole of this entry is in a different hand.

least seven night before Christmas, when so ever the said entry shall be.

[20.] Memorandum to enquire who holdeth the farm of Daypole in Holderness let for four pounds a year and how the king shall be answered of the arrearage thereof to the sum of £10.

[21.] Memorandum there be a letter sent to the archbishop of York for payment of the farm of the mills and agistment of the park of Macclesfield for the year ending at Michaelmas *Anno XVIII°*.

fol. 9   [22.] Memorandum a letter is directed to the princes' council to take sufficient surety of Philip ap John in £200 to pay to the hands of John Heron at Lammas next coming £50 and at the feast of the Purification of our Lady then next ensuing all such arrears as shall be found due upon the determination of his account ended at Michaelmas last past.

[23.] Memorandum that the reparations of the manor of Webley demanded by Sir Rees ap Thomas amounteth to £65 12s 10d. Memorandum to search in the Chancery for an office found of the said manor of Webley by virtue of any commission.

fol. 9v.   [24.] Memorandum that Richard Hamworthy hath appeared the 9th day of April upon a privy seal unto him directed and the said Richard hath day to appear again the 14th day.

[25.] Memorandum that Chamber the auditor hath injunction to bring in a just and true account of the castle of Windsor in the first of the rogation days next coming sub poena 100 marks.

[26.] Memorandum that a letter is sent to the prince's council by William Tatton that they shall take sufficient surety of James Waghorne for the just executing of the office of receiver of Elvet and then they to deliver to him a bill enclosed in the said letter assigned with the king's hand whereby he may occupy the said office.

fol. 10 [27.] Memorandum that there be certain lands in Carleton Rode of which the king's noble progenitors were seized in the right of their royal Crown and now be occupied by Thomas Pyle of Carleton Rode, son of Richard Pyle late deceased, by what authority or interest it is unknown etc. For which letters of privy seal are sent [note added in Latin].

[28.] Memorandum that the king's letters and letters from the court are directed to the prince's council that they shall attach the receivers of Montgomery and Radnor and to take sufficient surety of them and either of them that they shall appear before us for their account of the year ended at Michaelmas last past and also for their arrearages of other years before; and above that to send hither David ap William Morgan in person for certain duties by him owing. Delivered unto Richard Johnson [marginal note].

fol. 11 [29.] Memorandum that Sir Edmund Hampden hath appeared afore my lord of Carlisle and Sir Robert Southwell the 2nd day of May and hath day to appear upon the 3rd day for the farm of Somerton in county Oxford.

fol. 12 [30.] Memorandum that Sir John Tayte, knight, Mayor of the Staple of Calais, Sir Richard Haddon, knight, and John Thornbourgh, gentleman, of the Fellowship of the Staple aforesaid hath day to appear the first day of the next term and then to make answer how the king shall be contented of all such sums of money as are due unto his grace by the Mayor and Fellowship aforesaid.

fol. 12v. Trinity Term 1505 (*Anno XX^{mo}*)

[31.] Memorandum my lord abbot of Chester hath day to appear upon Wednesday next coming to answer to such things as then shall be objected against him.

fol. 15v.[1] [32.] Memorandum that where Richard Turton of Wake-

---

[1] The last previous term heading was for Michaelmas 1505 at the top of fol. 14.

field was bound by recognizance for the payment £100 12d at three divers days the said Richard hath content and paid to the hands of John Heron the 5th day of November *Anno* 21° for the first of these payments due at Michaelmas last past £43 12d as appeareth a bill of the said John Heron's; in the possession of the aforesaid Richard signed with the hand of the said John [final clause in Latin].

fol. 16v. [33.] Memorandum that Thomas Strange hath entered into this court and promised upon £200 to be forfeited to the king not to depart from this court or else to bring a sufficient discharge from the king's learned council[1] that he is dismissed of all matters laid against him concerning Tylney's lands.

[34.] Memorandum to get a letter from the king to discharge the court of the arrears of my Lady Doune.

[35.] Memorandum to write to the Lord Conyers to know what interest these farmers following hath in these grounds after specified: a close called Estshawes in the holding of my Lady Ratclif and she letteth it her servant called William Bewbank for £5.
Item a close called Harwodshawes set to farm to one hird [sic][2] of Thomas Roulandson for £3 6s 8d
Item a close called Nethershawes and set to one by hald[3] [sic] £4 13s 4d
Summa £13 and Thomas Causfeld would give £15.

fol. 17 [36.] Memorandum that the sheriff's money of Coventry is left in the hands of William Buttelar, grocer, in Cheapside.

[37.] Memorandum delivered to John Houne, pursuivant, 27 privy seals concerning Warwick lands, the names whereof remain in a roll made for the same.

Hilary Term 1506 (*Anno XXI^{mo}*)
fol. 17v. [38.] Memorandum that Robert Ittynghame of Wendover in the county of Buckingham hath injunction to find

---

[1] Spelling of the original is 'counscell'.
[2] ? hired or heard.
[3] Hold or by-hold, meaning a form of tenure.

sufficient surety by obligation within 14 days hereof before Thomas Grenway, bailiff there, or his officer, in £40 under this condition following, or else to keep his appearance in this court at the end of the said 14 days and then to find such etc.

The condition of the obligation is such that if the above named Robert Ittynghame bring before Thomas Greneway or his deputy within 14 days next coming sufficient sureties that the king's mills at Wendover shall be competently repaired at this side Michaelmas next coming that then the obligation be void etc.

[39.] Memorandum that Robert Straugne, esquire hath appeared the 26th day of January upon an obligation of 400 marks as in the same it appeareth;[1] and hath injunction given to him by the said bishop and Sir Robert that he shall be and personally appear before them at any time when he shall be called upon by them upon 14 days warning, failing thereof to forfeit the penalty of his obligation.

fol. 19

[40.] Memorandum that where Henry Stanley standeth bound to Sir Rayndolfe Brearton, knight, in the exchequer at Chester in the sum of £40 upon condition that the said Henry shall appear in his proper person before my lord of Carlisle and Sir Robert Suthwell, knight, at Westminster the 4 day after the feast of the Purification of our Lady, and not to depart from thence without licence etc. He appeared the 5th day of February and injunction is given him to appear here from day to day until he is dismissed by the said bishop and Robert under penalty of £40 [last sentence in Latin].

[41.] Memorandum that when John Clerke, auditor of Warwick lands and Salisbury lands, shall sit upon his account then to send for Sir John Hussy.

[42.] Memorandum for a warrant to be made to William Poyntz, receiver of Essex, and Thomas Everard to make sale of the wood belonging to the lordship of

---

[1] The previous entry but one shows this to have been an obligation 'concerning Tylney's lands'.

Mychleisse in the county of Essex for the kings' most profit and avail etc.

fol. 19v. [43.] Memorandum that where a direction was taken by the prince's council for the reformation of the false making of tin; we by the complaint of divers merchants that now much false tin is made do make a commission to the Lord Broke, warden, Hower, Poullard and Roger Holand to inquire etc.

fol. 20 [44.] Memorandum of a letter sent to this court from W. bishop of Lincoln, remaining in the hands of John Butt, auditor, of which the tenor follows in these words [this clause in Latin]:
My especial good lord etc. As for the fine of Thomas Lee, esquire, truth it is that Master Frost assessed his fine at £10; and so he did assess many more fines with others of the late prince's council such as were with him at that time of assessing at Chester; and this was the order at that time that the prince's chancellor for the time used so to do, and then to call the auditors to allow them, but Master Frost or else the auditor, were negligent and therefore many poor gentlemen be troubled etc.

fol. 22v.

Copy

By the King

[45.] Well-beloved we greet you well; and whereas it hath been complained unto us by our tenants of our lordship of Oddingley in our county of Worcester how that a certain parcel of land called Horam Valet within our said lordship is let by copy to John Broke and Richard Broke for the yearly rent of 13s 4d, which land, as our said tenants allege, was heretofore always wont to be common among them; we let you wit that at the humble pursuit of our said tenants we have granted unto them that they shall have and enjoy the said land like as the said John and Richard had the same, to the intent that for their ease the said land shall be in common among them, paying yearly unto us therefor 13s 4d. Wherefore we will and command you to admit our said tenants unto the said land accordingly by warrant of these our letters which shall be your sufficient discharge in that behalf hereafter. Given under our signet at our Palace of Westminster the 4th day of May the 20th year of our reign.

To our well-beloved the steward and bailiff of our lordship of Oddingley in our county of Worcester.

fol. 23v. [46.] Memorandum that where a privy seal is directed to John Reve and Robert Wall of Oddingley and others of the said town for certain injuries done to the farmers of Horam Valet, if it be found by certain persons to whom a commission shall be directed that the said injuries, besides the stuff, surmount not the sum of 20s or 26s 8d then the said John Reve and Robert Wall shall recompense to the said farmers the sum of 20s so to be dismissed of the appearance of this said privy seal. If the said injuries shall be found to surmount the said sum of 20s or 26s 8d then it is ordered that the said John and Robert shall appear at Westmister before Roger bishop of Carlisle and Sir Robert Southwell, knight, and to abide such order as that court shall award in that behalf, or else content the party sufficiently that no more complaint be made.

The names of such as the commission shall be directed unto:

John Heth of the which [sc. Oddingley] in county Worcester, gentleman.
William Buttelar, senior, gentleman.
George Newporte of the same, gentleman.
John Mores of the same, gentleman.

fol. 24 [47.] Memorandum of the 2nd day of March *Anno* 21 Miles Brown of London and the wife of John Chaffer late deceased, by virtue of the king's commandment, appeared at St John's in London before Roger bishop of Carlisle and Sir Robert Southwell for certain directions to have been taken with them upon certain considerations. There was injunction given to the said Brown and the said Chaffer's wife that they should appear at Westminster the Thursday next after, upon pain of 500 marks. At which day the said wife kept not her appearance. And over that she was warned after to appear at Westminster the 6th day of March upon pain of 500 marks and that notwithstanding she kept not her appearance at the 6 day. Therefore etc.

fol. 26 [48.] Memorandum that Richard Shirley and John Danvers hath appeared before Roger bishop of Carlisle and Sir Robert Southwell, knight, for the jointure of Margaret Farman the 21st day of May etc. The said Shirley and Daunvers is committed to Master Hussey and the king's sergeants for the said matter sub poena 100 marks.

fol. 27 [49.] Memorandum that where John Dalamer is ordered by my lord of Carlisle and Sir Robert Southwell, knight, that he shall appear afore the king's auditor Master Clerke at Warwick and there to answer unto such sums of money as shall be found for the half annuity of rent of Halleplace within the lordship of Elderfelde, which Sir Giles Abrigg was sent to by privy seal for the said sum etc.

fol. 28 [50.] Memorandum that a letter be directed unto Ralph Brikhad, sheriff of Cheshire, and Roger Maneryng, escheator, to certify this court under what title John a Stanley occupieth the manor of Mollington in Cheshire late in the hands of ⁱ Houghton. My Lady Houghton saith that her husband died seized of the same manor of Mollington and that after his death there was an office found that the daughter of the said Houghton which is now the king's ward is next heiress unto the same.

[51.] Memorandum that where Arthur Pilkyngton beside Walkfelde was challenged the king's ward the Abbot of Fountains had sold certain lands belonging to the said ward to one Nicolas Savell etc.

fol. 30 [52.] Memorandum attachment is directed to the sheriff of York commanding him by the same to attach Alexander Landon late of Keynsan in the said

---

[1] Blank in MS.

county, gentleman, for 100 marks sterling by the said Alexander due unto the king as a parcel of debts of Nicholas Mymes late alderman of London, and to cause the said Alexander to find surety to pay the said sum unto Sir Robert Southwell for the king's use, or else to find surety to appear before the bishop of Carlisle and the said Sir Robert Southwell to show why he ought not so to do, on the morrow of the Purification.

[53.] Memorandum to the sheriff of London to attach Edmund Pase for £48 by him due, or to find surety *ut supra*.

[54.] Item another attachment to the sheriff of Essex to attach John Green of Northam for 104 marks by him due or to find surety *ut supra*.

fol. 30v. [55.] Memorandum that a privy seal was directed against the mayor of Bodmin commanding him by the same to pay John Walshe, deputy to the feodary of Cornwall, £5 found by inquisition to be due to the king by the township of Bodmin for the escape of one Welshman, or else to appear before the bishop of Carlisle and the said Sir Robert Southwell on the morrow of the Purification to show cause why they should not so do.

fol. 32v.[1] [56.] Memorandum that John Baynton hath day to appear in the month of Easter next coming to answer to the title that the king maketh to the moiety of the manor of Compton Chamberlain within the county of Wiltshire upon pain of £100. The said John hath appeared the 7 day of May and hath injunction to appear from day to day till he be dismissed by this court.

[57.] Memorandum it is agreed by my lord of Carlisle and Sir Robert Southwell, knight, that Rowland Morton shall appear for William Herbarte of Troy to come in for him in a certain cause concerning an obligation of £22 and 10s wherein Sir David Phelypp, the said William and others were bound to my said

---

[1] The last previous terminal heading was Hilary Term 1507 at the top of folio 31.

DOCUMENTS 159

lord and Sir Robert in the said sum to the king's use.

[58.] Item it is ordered by the king's Council that my Lady Salisbury shall take the fulling mill that Richard Smyth of Denbigh late held, whose term is now expired, and bore the charge thereof, or else that the same fulling mill shall be let to the said Richard to be made a corn mill, and he to bear the charge thereof from henceforth, so he may have timber etc. And the decay assessed thereupon to be assessed where it ought to be of right.

fol. 35[1]   [59.] Memorandum that John ap Madog ap Howell of Carmarthenshire and John Glyne, clerk, Dean of Bangor have day to appear before my Lord Bishop of Carlisle and Sir Robert Southwell, knight, the 15 day of May, upon pain of £100 that they shall appear in the Prince's Chamber at Westminster. On the said day the said John ap Madog ap Howell and John Glyne, clerk, appeared; and had day to day Monday next coming; and appeared on the said Monday, and the aforesaid John Glyne, clerk, was dismissed the court; and the aforesaid John had a day Tuesday next following sub poena £100; and the said John has day not to depart from the court principal without his licence of the court of the lord king *sub poena supradicta*.

[60.] Item that like letters [of privy seal] be directed to Thomas Munke of Markfield in the county of Leicester to show why he hath distrained the cattle of John Parker for occupying of certain land by copy of court roll of the king's manor of Whitwick, sub poena £40.

fol. 46v.   [61.] Item[2] Philip ap John with others is bound in £200 on the condition that he will find sufficient security in £200 before the prince's council that he will well and faithfully pay to the hand of John Heron £50

---

[1] The last previous terminal heading was Easter Term, 1507 at the top of folio 34.
[2] This is the sixth entry in a collection of 125 obligations entered from folio 46 to fol. 53 v. and, after a brief reversion to court proceedings at fol. 54, continuing to fol. 61 v.

at the feast of St Peter ad Vincula next coming and at the feast of the Purification then next following and faithfully pay all other arrears by him owed.

The said obligation is delivered unto the said John by the hands of my lord and Sir Robert Southwell. Trinity Term, Year 21 [1506].

fol. 62[1] [62.] Memorandum there was a privy seal directed to William Bele of Stoke in Climsland in the county of Cornwall, gentleman, commanding him by the same to permit and suffer William Pyper of the same, husbandman, to occupy a corn mill with the appurtenances within the lordship of Climsland aforesaid by him lately made, according to his lease of the same by the prince's late commissioners there for terms of years made; and to recompense him for such hurt and injuries as he hath done the said William Piper in the same, or else to appear afore the right reverend father in God Roger bishop of Carlisle and Robert Southwell, knight, at Westminster within 8 days after the sight hereof, there to answer unto such causes and articles as shall be objected against him for the same upon pain of £40. Therefore William Belle hath appeared the 8th day of May and hath injunction to appear from day to day till he be dismissed.

The said William Bele and William Pyper be agreed and dismissed out of the court.

fol. 65 Placards for Woodsales

[63.] Well-beloved we greet you well and let you wit that the king's pleasure is that Sir John Hussey, knight for his most honourable body, should have the preferment of buying of such his woods as be in your custody in Burne, parcel of his duchy of York, and according to the same we have bargained with him therefor. Wherefore we will and desire you and eftsoons in the king's name charge you to suffer the said Sir John Hussey and his assigns in that behalf to fell, sell, carry and lead away the same wood at

---

[1] On the previous folio (61 v.) is an obligation dated April 14, 1507 to Carlisle and Southwell. Immediately after this William Bele entry is an obligation dated May 12, 1507.

such convenient and seasonable times for the safeguard and good increase of the spring thereof as in such case it appertaineth; and that there be left convenient number of staddles[1] in every acre according to the custom of that country in and of such like woodsales; provided always that the same fell, sale and carriage be done within two years next following the date of these our letters; and that ye see the said woods well and sufficiently enclosed for the defence of the said spring till it may come to such force in growing as it may defend the self; and these our letters shall be your sufficient warrant and discharge in that behalf. Written at Westminster the 10th day of March the 20th year of the reign of our sovereign lord king Henry the VIIth. It is not passed [marginal note].

[64.] Well-beloved etc. And let you wit that the king's pleasure is that Sir David Philipp, knight, should have the preferment of buying of such his woods as be in your custody in Upton called Suthshawe; and according to the same we have bargained with him therefor. Wherefore we will and desire you etc. *ut supra*, provided always that the same fell etc. be done within four years next ensuing the date of these our letters, etc. *ut supra*. Written at Westminster the 28th day of March and 20th year *ut supra*.
It is passed [marginal note].

[1] Young trees left standing when others are cut down.

18. Henry VIII's Council advises the abolition of the 'by-courts', October and November, 1509

FROM Ellesmere MS. 2655, fols. 7, 8, Huntington Library, California.

Acts of the Council of our lord king Henry the Eighth from the first year to the 18th year.

Michaelmas Term in the first year, 11th day of October[1]

[Archbishop of] Canterbury Chancellor [Bishop of] Durham [Bishop of] Norwich [Bishop of] St David's	The matter of the oyer determiner hath been in communication to understand and know what hath been done in every shire upon the same and to the intent that the king's grace may know the perfectness in everything it is ordained a clear book thereof to be made in short parcels to be showed to his highness. Also all such courts as were occupied besides the court of the common law was in likewise had in communication and it is thought by all the whole Council necessary and requisite that all such by-courts which be of no record shall be fordone and that every man from thenceforth may resort to such courts and judges as they did before or such offices were occupied, for if the said by-courts which be of none authority should continue the king's right and title in process of time should perish for lack of matter of record in court of authority, for the king's highness cannot be entitled by record but by matter of record in court of authority. Also all such	Earl of Surrey Treasurer Earl of Shrewsbury Prior of St John's Fineux, Chief Justice Rede, Justice Huddye, Justice Fisher, Justice Bucknell, Justice Butler, Justice Connigsby, Justice Grevell, Justice Sir John Cut Under-treasurer

[1] In Latin to this point.

matters had afore such by-officers be void and of none effect by the king's laws nor none of the king's subjects cannot be discharged by any of the said by-courts. And so the king's subjects be troubled contrary to his laws to their utter undoing, whereof it is thought to all his said Council and judges if it may stand with his pleasure that all such by-courts as have been used of none authority be annulled and fordone. And that it may please his highness of his great goodness by advice of his said Council that the parties which have paid sums of money may be discharged of the same by privy seal or otherwise, for else his poor subjects shall be charged for one thing twice to their utter undoing.

Wednesday 14th November

[Archbishop of] Canterbury Chancellor [Bishop of] Norwich [Bishop of] Rochester	It was had eftsoons in great communication of divers matters of certain courts which in late days were greatly used and none of them was of record ne able after the due course of law to charge or discharge any person coming to the said courts, which was a great abusion, vexation and trouble to the king's people let of the common law and great losses to our sovereign lord of such profits as should grow to his highness by means of his seals in his courts of record if the law might have his due course, for which causes and many reasons there showed it was thought to the said Council and judges expedient and necessary to annul the said courts that they be no more used.	Duke of Buckingham Earl of Surrey Earl of Shrewsbury Lord Herbert Prior of St John's Jerusalem Lord Darcy Thomas Lovell, knight John Fineux and Robert Rede, Justices Thomas Inglefeild, knight Robert Brudenell J. Botler Humphrey Connigsby The king's sergeants, his attorney and solicitor

19. John Heron confirmed in his office by statute, with the new title of general receiver of the king's revenues (Parliament of Jan. 21–Feb. 23, 1510)

FROM *The Statutes of the Realm*, iii, 2, Stat. 1 Henry VIII cap. 3.

Whereas the king our sovereign lord intendeth that divers revenues and duties due and to be due to his highness shall be paid to his trusty servant John Heron, his general receiver, and to other persons by his highness hereafter in like office to be deputed and assigned as in the time of the late king of famous memory Henry the VIIth hath been used, and for that his subjects may be truly and lawfully discharged of payments made or to be made by them of every of the premises to the said John Heron or to other persons thereto to be limited and appointed in form aforesaid; be it therefore ordained, enacted and established, by the authority of this present Parliament, that all acquittances and bills of receipt heretofore made by the said John Heron, in the time of the said late noble king, and in the time of our sovereign lord that now is and hereafter to be made by the said John Heron, and all other the said persons by our said sovereign lord to the said offices to be appointed, and of every of them of any his revenues or duties whatsoever they be, be a sufficient discharge to every such person against the king our sovereign lord, his heirs and successors, as well in the king's Exchequer as in any other of the king's courts, without any other warrant, tally or private seal thereof to be had, obtained or shewed. And that the Treasurer, Chamberlains and Barons of the said Exchequer and every of them, and all other judges, auditors and officers accept, take and allow the said acquittances and bills for a sufficient discharge of the said payments; and this act only to endure to the next Parliament. And over that be it ordained and enacted by the said authority that the same John Heron, and every other person, that shall have the said or like office of receipt, be chargeable and charged to every person and persons spiritual and temporal now having or that hereafter shall have any interest in any part of his or their receipts by title of inheritance or succession or by grant, assignment, act of Parliament or otherwise; and that every of them have like remedy against the said John and every other person that shall have the said or like office of receipt, as they have had or ought to have had against any other person that have received any of the premises, this present act notwithstanding. And that every such person spiritual or temporal for none payment of all such sums of money as they or any of them ought to have of the said receipts, by title of inheritance or succession, or by grant, assignment, act of Parliament or otherwise, have their actions and remedy in every of the king's courts against the said John and every other person having the same or like office of receipt, for the recovery and payment of all sums that shall be so due unto them or any of them after the first day of the present Parliament.

20. The Court of General Surveyors absorbed into the Exchequer from June 1510

FROM The Memoranda Rolls of the King's Remembrancer, Public Record Office, Exchequer, K.R., E.159/290, 'Communia', Mich., m. 26.

Writ of privy seal received, sent to the Barons for divers persons accounting before Robert Southwell, knight, auditor of this Exchequer, of the issues of the king's lordships called Warwick's lands, Salisbury's lands, Spencer's lands and of others enrolled. The lord king formerly sent here his writ of privy seal to the Treasurer and Barons of the Exchequer of which the tenor follows in these words:[1] Henry by the grace of God, King of England and of France and Lord of Ireland. To the Treasurer and Barons of our Exchequer that now be and for the time shall be. And to all and singular our receivers, auditors, bailiffs, surveyors and all other our officers, ministers, true liegemen and subjects and to every of them, greeting. Where we before this time, for divers considerations us and our Council specially moving, have assigned and deputed our trusty and well-beloved servant and councillor Sir Robert Southwell, knight, to be auditor of our said Exchequer, with pre-eminence and superiority above others in the same. To have and occupy the same room with like fees and wages and all other commodities as any other occupying the same room or any other room of auditor in the said Exchequer have had and perceived. And furthermore we willed and have straightly charged you our said Treasurer and Barons that from time to time ye should appoint and assign the said Sir Robert Southwell to take and hear the several accounts of all manner of officers whatsoever they be of all manner [of] honours, lands, tenements and possessions, hereditaments and

---

[1] Marginal note and heading, in Latin to this point.

other revenues whereof we by our letters patent should assign and appoint the said Sir Robert Southwell and others to be our surveyors and approvers, and none other auditor or auditors of the said Exchequer, but if it were desired of you by the said Sir Robert Southwell, as by other our letters of privy seal bearing date the last day of June the second year of our reign to you directed and in our said Exchequer remaining, and also in the other memoranda of our said Exchequer more plainly appeareth.[1] And wherefore we by our letters patent bearing the date the sixth day of February the second year of our reign,[2] for certain considerations in our said letters patent specified, have assigned made and constituted the said Sir Robert Southwell and Bartholomew Westby, one of the Barons of our said Exchequer, to be surveyors and approvers, and to the same Sir Robert and Bartholomew have committed full authority and power to survey and approve all and singular castles, honours, lordships, manors, lands and tenements, feefarms, annuities, possessions and hereditaments whatsoever of our principalities of Wales and of the marches of the same, the duchies [sic] of Cornwall, county palatine of Chester and Flint, the duchy of York, the earldom of Richmond and all and singular castles, lordships, manors, lands, tenements, possessions and hereditaments of the ancient inheritance of our Crown as of others, being in our hands and possession, and in our said letters patent more at large expressed and contained, with divers other authorities unto the said Sir Robert Southwell and Bartholomew Westby given and committed, as by the contents of our said letters patent more plainly appeareth. We let you have knowledge that for divers reasonable considerations us and our Council moving, we be certainly determined and minded, and our pleasure is, that the said Sir Robert Southwell have full authority and power, and by these our letters of privy seal we have committed him full power and authority, that after the general or particular receiver or receivers, accountant, or accountants of every and singular the premises specified in our said letters patent sworn before you, and the same Sir Robert Southwell by you assigned,[3] as is above said, from year to year and time to time, to take, hear, examine, try and discharge and finally determine all and singular the said accounts of every of them, as well of and for the time of the reign of the noble prince of good memory King Henry the seventh, our dear father, whom God pardon, as from the beginning of our reign hitherto and so from henceforth during our pleasure. And

---

[1] See supplementary note 1 at end of this document.
[2] See supplementary note 2 at end of this document.
[3] N.B.—Southwell in consequence henceforward depended on the Exchequer process for summoning accountants before him, as explained below, pp. 175-7, where his use of the privy seal was restored to him.

furthermore we have given and give to the said Sir Robert Southwell by these presents full power and authority as well to charge as to discharge and make plain allowances, deductions and respites to the said several accountants and to every of them from time to time and year to year, as well of all manner [of] payments and sums of money by them or any of them at any time paid unto our said most dearest father in his life into his Chamber by the bills or acquitances of then his trusty and well-beloved servant, and now our trusty well-beloved servant John Heron, as of all manner [of] payments and sums of money paid and hereafter to be paid by any of the said accountants unto us in our Chamber, by the bills or other acquitances or writings of the said John Heron, which bills acquitances and writings of the said John Heron we will be good and sufficient discharge for the payer; and also all manner [of] fees and wages of all manner of officers whatsoever, of any of the premises to them belonging; and also all manner [of] reparations, vacations, new buildings and amendments and other charges whatsoever; and all manner [of] fees, wages and annuities and other charges whatsoever by our said father in his life, or by us in any wise granted or otherwise going out of any of the premises; and all other things to do concerning the nature of account or the faculty or feit[1] of audit without any other writing or warrant to him by us in this behalf to be given or directed; so that all the reparations, vacations, new buildings, amendments and other charges, neither ordinary nor whereof any other letters patent or special warrant may appear unto the said Sir Robert, be allowed not only by his discretion and advice of the said Bartholomew Westby, one of our forenamed commissioners, or of such other our commissioners as we shall at any time hereafter associate unto the said Sir Robert.[2] And that the said Sir Robert Southwell from time to time shall cause the same general or particular accounts and every of them so by him taken, examined and determined, to be written and engrossed in parchment in good substantial hand in due form, as unto him shall be thought by his discretion most convenient. And the same account and every of them so engrossed, the said Sir Robert to deliver from time to time, by virtue of these our letters and by no other commandment or process of our said court, into our said Exchequer, subscribed as well with the hand and name of the said Sir Robert, as with the hand of the said Bartholomew or of such other our commissioners as we shall at any time hereafter associate by our other commissions unto the said Sir Robert, or of one of them at the least, there to remain of record perpetually, as well for the confirmation of

---

[1] Obsolete form of 'feat', meaning act, conduct.
[2] N.B.—This clause takes away his discretionary power of allowance, as explained, and restored, below, pp. 175-7.

our inheritances and rights, as for our subjects' and true liegeners'. And therefore we will and straightly charge you our said Barons that now be and for the time shall be that from year to year and time to time unto such time as ye of us shall have otherwise in commandment by writing ye accept and receive of the said Sir Robert Southwell all manner and every such general and particular receiver's and receivers' account or accounts of the revenues of every of the premises specified and annoted in our said letters patent. And do admit and authorize the same for good, sufficient and lawful account. And also all manner [of] payments, discharges, deductions, allowances, respites whatsoever, by the said Sir Robert Southwell as before is rehersed made and to be made in the same account and every of them, ye also do accept and admit for good, sufficient and lawful without further examination, correction, controlling, changing or other things by you to be used had or done in the same. And that ye cause the same accounts from time to time to be taken and then made up in the pipe roll according to the ancient course of our said Exchequer, without any manner of charges to be borne by any of the said accountants for the same. And that after such account to you in form abovesaid delivered and brought in, ye our said Barons do utterly acquit and discharge against us and our heirs for ever for the time or times of the said account as well all manner [of] the said accountants whatsoever, as [of] all manner [of] bailiffs, reeves, provosts, farmers or occupiers of any of the said lordships, manors, tenements and other the premises, or of any lordships, manors, lands, tenements or other possessions specified and annoted in the said general and particular receivers' accounts or any of them and every of them, how be it that they appear not to you by any matter of record the said lordships, manors, lands, tenements and possessions to be parcel of the receipt or charge of the said accountant, nor parcel of that thing whereof he is deputed receiver, nor that express mention is made in the grant or letters patent thereof made to the said bailiffs, farmers or other officers or occupiers that the said manors, lands, or tenements be or were parcel of the receipts of the said accountants or other cause whatsoever notwithstanding. And that ye surcease for ever of all manner of processes, executions, suits and demands made or to be made for us out of our said Exchequer against them or any of them in or upon the premises for the time that they so have accounted or shall account. Yet nevertheless, we will and straightly command you that against all such bailiffs, reeves, ministers, farmers and other occupiers of any [of] the premises which shall appear unto you by their account not to have paid nor answered unto us of his or their duty accordingly and upon every long [sic] and unde super which shall happen to be set out or charged in the end of any such account or accounts, ye at the request and desire of the said Sir Robert and ellys,[1] do award and make for us such speedy and quick process as by you may be thought most expedient from time to time unto we be truly thereof answered. And after and upon due payment or allowance made to our use in our Chamber or otherwise as is before recited of any of the said debts so set or charged in the end of any such account, we in likewise give full authority to the same Sir Robert to allow the payer or parties thereof upon his or their next account or accounts as he should and might have done by virtue of this privy seal before upon his or their first or former account or accounts. And in case any accountant or accountants of any of the premises specified in our said letters patent appear not to the yielding of his or their said account but therein be remiss and negligent, then we will at the like request and desire of the said Sir Robert Southwell ye from time to time do award and do to be made out of our said Exchequer against all such accountants so defugyng [sic] their account such processes by writs [of] subpoena, distress, attachment or otherwise as after the course of our said court appertaineth and to you shall be thought most expedient unto [the] time the said accountants have yielded themselves to their said accounts.[2] And for as much as we be credibly informed that there remaineth not before you in our said Exchequer any record or remembrance for us of divers lordships, lands, and other things in our said letters patent specified so that no process for us can be made out of our said Exchequer against the receivers [or] other occupiers of the same if need shall require, therefore we will and charge you, upon the information or surmise unto you thereof for us made by John Erneley, our attorney, ye do make against the said receivers or other occupiers like process as is above said.[3] And moreover will and charge you that ye from time to time do receive of the said Sir Robert with the said accounts all such bills and acquittances of the said John Heron as shall be allowed and mentioned in the same accounts and the same to be cancelled and frustrated as well for our surety as for the clear discharge of the said John Heron against us, without any charge or demand whatsoever to be set or demanded upon him by occasions of any [of] the premises, so that the foresaid John Heron never be impeached or impeachable

---

[1] Form of 'else' in the obsolete sense of 'others', meaning here the other commissioners.

[2] N.B.—Southwell now dependent on the Exchequer powers for the summoning of defaulting accountants before him, as explained below, pp. 175-7, where his use of the privy seal was restored to him.

[3] N.B.—An attempt to surmount the deficiencies in the legal processes of the Exchequer caused by the independent operations of Henry VII's Court of General Surveyors, cf. below, p. 175.

thereof against us or our heirs for any receipt of the said sums or by colour of the said bills or acquittances; that express mention of the certainty of the premises herein be not fully had, or that it appeareth not unto you by what warrant the said John Heron doth receive our said money and maketh to the payer bills and acquittances thereof or by what other authority the said Sir Robert Southwell doth make the said discharges and allowances, or any course of our said Exchequer used or had or other cause or matter whatsoever you to the contrary moving notwithstanding. Provided always that for such sums of money as be assigned by authority of Parliament for expenses of our Household or Great Wardrobe or upon the Hanaper or other the revenues of any [of] the premises, whereof tallies be or shall be levied at the Receipt of our said Exchequer for the obtaining of the same, that the said sums be left charged upon the accountants as debts upon the end of their accounts so that the said tallies may thereupon be allowed after the due and ancient course of our said Exchequer. Given under our privy seal at our manor of Richmond the last day of October the 3rd year of our reign.

SUPPLEMENTARY NOTES TO DOCUMENT 20

1. This writ of June 30, 1510 is enrolled on the K.R. Memoranda Roll for 2 Henry VII in Trinity Term, 'Communia' m. 1 d. After stating that there had hitherto been five auditors of the Exchequer it constituted Sir Robert Southwell a sixth, with pre-eminence over all the rest. His charge is there set out as in the present writ and then it is noted that he took the prescribed oaths of office on 16 July 2 Henry VIII (1510).
2. The writ of Febr. 6, 1511 for the engrossing of these letters patent is calendared in *Letters and Papers of Henry VIII*, i (2nd ed.) no. 709 (14). The list of lands, etc. which constituted Southwell's and Westby's charge, is there set out as follows:

1. All lands of the principality of Wales, duchy of Cornwall, county palatine of Chester and Flint, duchy of York, earldom of March, earldom of Richmond.
2. All lands late of Margaret countess of Richmond.
3. All lands late of Jasper duke of Bedford, William viscount Beaumont and Edward earl of Devon.
4. All lands of the following attainted persons: Edward earl of Warwick, John earl of Lincoln, Edmund de la Pole earl of Suffolk, John Ratclyff lord FitzWater, Sir William de la Pole, Francis viscount Lovell, James Tuchet lord Audeley, Sir William Stanley, Sir Richard Charleton, Sir Simon Mountford, Humphrey Stafford,

Sir Richard Emson, Edmund Dudley, Sir Henry Bodryngan, Thomas Kelingworth, William Kendall, Sir Richard Catisby, John Skelton, William Batens, Robert Barley and Richard Assheley.

5. All lands of Anne countess of Warwick, Richard earl of Kent and William marquis of Berkeley, late earl of Nottingham, purchased by Henry VII.

6. All lands held for life by Cecily, wife of Richard viscount Wellis and Eleanor duchess of Somerset, which reverted to Henry VII.

7. All lands of Katharine lady Hastings, Richard viscount Beaumont, William earl of Huntingdon, [Henry Lovell late] lord Morely, Sir Richard Nanfan, Sir Edward Burgh, Sir William Oldehalle, which also came to the king's hands.

8. All lands in the king's hands by reason of entries or alienations without licence, or of minorities, wardships or vacations.

9. The king's lands in the Isle of Wight.

10. The following lands:

Wanstead and West Thurrock, Essex; Cranborne, Dors.; Caister, Lincs.; Swaffham, Norf.; Windsor, Yoxall, Wakering, Cornbrough, Weston by Baldock, West Horsley, Berwick, Blencogo, Ainstable, Lower Whiddon, Grynston and Ditchampton in the counties of Kent, Surrey, Sussex, Hants., Dorset, Devon, Cornwall, Soms., Wilts., Gloucs., Berks., Midd., Essex, Norf., Suff., Cambs., Lincs., Hunts., Yorks., Cumb., Northld., Westmld., Leics., Rutland, Warws., Worcs., Staffs., Derbys., Notts., Heref., Herts., Oxon., Bucks., Beds, or elsewhere in England and Wales and their marches.

11. The ordinary revenues of the town of Calais, Guisnes, Sangatte, Balingham, Marke and Oye and of the Staple of Calais; the surplus of the Staple, Great Wardrobe and Hanaper and the butlerage of 6s 8d. the butt of malvesey.

12. The following lands: Grimston, Norf.; Wormleighton and Fenny Compton [Warws.]; Rochester, Kent; the bailiwick of Winchelsea, Shawe [in Old Windsor, Berks.], Wark and Plainmeller [Northld.], Northstead [by Scarborough, Yorks.], Pencelly and Cantref Selyf [Brecon], Claygate [Surrey], Kenilworth [Warws.], the ulnage in Yorks., Southwold [Suff.], the city of York, Hull, Carlton in Craven, with its members [Yorks.], Penrith [Cumb.], the herbage of Galtres Forest [Yorks.], the lands late of John Mortymer, the office of sheriff of Northumberland, the farm of swans on the Thames, Yoxall [Staffs. already included once in section 10 above].

13. The following lands: lands of Francis Cheyney, Stillingfleet, Dring Houses, Askham Brian and Upton [Yorks.], Norton under Hamdon [Soms.].

All their receipts to be paid to John Heron; the commissioners to have a chamber in the palace of Westminster called the Prince's Council Chamber, with a clerk and an usher there, each to be paid £10 *per annum* during pleasure, by the hands of John Heron. By privy seal at Westminster, 6 Feb., 2 Hen VIII.

21. Statutory authority for the General Surveyors and for the treasurer of the Chamber (parliamentary session of Feb. 4–Mar. 30, 1512)

FROM *The Statutes of the Realm*, iii, 45–7, Stat. 3 Hen. VIII cap. 23.

For Robert Southwell, knight, and Bartholomew Westby

I Forasmuch as in the time of the late right noble and famous prince King Henry the seventh, father unto the right noble king that now is, by his high wisdom, providence and circumspection divers and many his chamberlains of his principalities of Wales and other receivers, feodaries, bailiffs, reeves, farmers, fee farmers and other officers and occupiers of divers his honours, castles, lordships, manors, lands, tenements and other hereditaments, as well in England and in Wales and in Calais and in the Marches of the same, which then were in his hands and possession, as well by the ancient inheritance of his Crown, as by reason of rebellion or forfeiture of divers and sundry persons, or by reason of the nonage of all and singular his wards, or by purchase of himself or of any other his noble progenitors, or by instrusion of any person or persons, or by any other means or occasion of his prerogative royal, did account by his commandment by mouth afore then his trusty servants and councillors Sir Reynold Bray, Sir Robert Southwell, knights, and others whom the said late king in that behalf at several and divers times appointed, as well for the more speedy payments of his revenues to be had and for the accounts of the same more speedily to be taken than his grace could or might have been answered after the course of his Exchequer, as for the greater ease and less charge of all and singular the foresaid accountants, farmers, fee farmers and other officers and occupiers whatsoever of any of the premises; and that divers and many sums of money which were then due by divers and sundry the foresaid accountants, farmers, fee farmers, officers and occupiers upon the determination of their accounts were paid unto the said late king into his Chamber, either to his own hands or to some other person or persons to his use, as it may appear by bills or books signed with his sign manual, or to the hands of then his trusty servant John Heron, as also it may appear by bills signed with the hand of the same John Heron; and that neither those said accounts nor any of them so by the foresaid Sir Reynold Bray, Sir Robert Southwell or by any other taken and determined, nor the said bills or books signed with the hand of the said late king or with the hand of the said John Heron, for any sum or sums of money concerning the premises received, be of any effect or acceptable in the said Exchequer for any record for the discharge of any of the said accountants, farmers, fee farmers, officers and occupiers; by reason whereof all and singular the said accountants, farmers, fee farmers, officers and occupiers be yet chargeable to account and to make their payments in the said Exchequer, as divers and many of the said accountants, farmers, fee farmers, officers and occupiers have been and as hereafter shall be like to be continually vexed and troubled by process made and to be made out of the said Exchequer against them and every of them, their heirs executors or terre-tenants, not only personally to come and appear in the said Exchequer, and thereupon to be compelled there to render their said accounts of new for the premises, but also there to be compelled to make new payments for the same in the king's Receipt of the said Exchequer, as if they never had accounted, nor had made payments of their said duties to their great importable loss, trouble, hurt and damage, against all right reason and good conscience; the high and mighty prince the king that now is the premises well considering, and intending not only the same and similar order of account to continue to be had and used by sufficient and lawful authority from henceforth, both before the said Sir Robert Southwell his trusty knight and councillor and other by his grace appointed and at his pleasure hereafter to be appointed, and to be answered of his revenues in his Chamber in manner and form above said, but also of his godly and gracious disposition intending all and singular the said accountants, farmers, fee farmers, officers and occupiers to be sufficiently discharged for ever for any thing concerning the premises according to right equity and good conscience, did of late direct as well to the said Sir Robert Southwell and also to Bartholomew Westby, one of the Barons of his Exchequer, his special commission to survey and approve his lands and possessions with other divers authorities contained in the same commission, as also divers privy seals to the Treasurer and Barons of his said Exchequer for the discharge of the said accountants and every of them; nevertheless for a further and stronger authority in that behalf to be had and given to the said Sir Robert and Bartholomew and to other persons hereafter to be deputed and assigned in the same room and authority, be it therefore ordained established and enacted by the king's highness and by the assent and consent of his Lords Spiritual and Temporal and of his Commons in this present Parliament assembled, and by the authority of the same, that the said Sir Robert Southwell, knight, and Bartholomew Westby be from henceforth general surveyors and approvers of all and singular the king's honours, castles, lordships, manors, lands, tenements, farms, possessions and other hereditaments whatsoever that now be in his hands or that hereafter may come into his hands by any like or such means or occasion as before is rehearsed; and the approvement of the premises by them be made whereof the king may lawfully approve himself and that they and every of them by the name of general surveyors and approvers of the king's lands be taken accepted named and called; and also that they and either of them by the authority aforesaid have full power and authority to survey and approve by themselves jointly and severally or by the sufficient assign or assigns of them or of either of them by their writing under their seals or under the seal of either of them,[1] all and singular honours, castles, lordships, manors, lands, tenements, farms, possessions and other hereditaments whatsoever now being in the hands of the king that now is or that hereafter lawfully shall come to his hands or to the hands of any person or persons to his use, contained and expressed in the same commission, whereof the king may lawfully approve himself, which commission beareth date the 6th day of February the second year of the reign of the said king that now is to the said Sir Robert Southwell and Bartholomew Westby in that behalf directed...

II [Confirmation of the letters patent of 6 Feb. 1511 and of the privy seals to the Barons of the Exchequer of 30 June 1510 and of 31 October 1511, with the exception of the clause providing for intervention in the Exchequer by the king's attorney John Erneley, now annulled (above p. 169)].

III And forasmuch in the said privy seals is no authority nor power given to the said Sir Robert Southwell to call any of the said officers accountable to make their account nor to make payment of their arrearage but only by process therefore to be made out of the said Exchequer[2] which may nor can be awarded in the vacation time, by the action whereof hath and may ensure long and many delays and losses to the king in and for not making

---

[1] N.B.—They were thus to have their own seal. An example of its use, dated February 15, 1514, is given below (Doc. 23 [23]) pp. 195-6 and cf. pp. 196-7 for a later example (*ibid*. [24]).

[2] See above, pp. 166, 167, 169.

their said accounts and payments in due time; nor also that there is any authority given to the same Sir Robert in the said privy seals to allow any bills, books signed, or tallies, or to be signed, for any receipt or payment concerning any the premises made or to be made, but only the bills signed and to be signed with the hand of the king's trusty servant John Heron; nor that in the said privy seals is any authority or power given to the said Sir Robert Southwell to take and accept the oath and appearance of any accountant or accountants concerning the premises, but that the said accountants and every of them must appear and be sworn before the Barons of the said Exchequer sitting the same court, and then by the same Barons to be assigned to the said Sir Robert Southwell as in one of the said privy seals bearing date the last day of October the 3rd year of the king's reign plainly doth appear;[1] which is not only to the prejudice of them that have accounted, but also to the unreasonable danger, great cost and charge, long attendance and delays of all them and every of them that have or should at any time hereafter account afore the said Sir Robert Southwell or before any other hereafter having like authority. Be it therefore furthermore ordained, established and enacted by authority of this present Parliament that the said Sir Robert Southwell have full power and authority as well to call before him the said officers accountable and every of them by the king's privy seal or seals to appear before him at Westminster in the county of Middlesex in the chamber there only called the Prince's Chamber, at such time as shall be limited and expressed in the same privy seal or seals, at their peril, without any pain of money to be lost for the none appearance of the said accountants to be contained in the said privy seals,[2] as to take the appearance and oath of all and every the said accountants concerning the honours, castles, lordships, etc., in the said commission rehearsed... and to allow in all and every their account or accounts as well all and singular such bills and books as have been signed with the sign manual of the said late king, or that have been or hereafter shall be signed with the sign manual of the king that now is, or that have been or shall be signed with the hand and name of the said John Heron, or with the hand and name of any other person or persons by the king at any time hereafter to be appointed and to be put in like trust and room as the said John Heron now is, by whose hand soever

---

[1] See above, pp. 166, 167, 169–170.

[2] This limitation on their restored power to move the privy seal was to some extent removed by Section II of Stat. 6 Hen. VIII, cap. 24, of 1515, which added a monetary penalty not exceeding £100 at the third summons.

the said sum or sums of money comprised and to be comprised in the said bills or books or in any of them so signed or hereafter to be signed have been or shall be received; as also to allow all and singular such tally or tallies as have been or shall be signed or stricken out of the Receipt of the said Exchequer for any part or parcel of the revenues of any of the lands and hereditaments aforesaid; and also to allow all letters patent and pardons and all other lawful discharges.

VI And also be it ordained, established and enacted by authority of this present Parliament, that the king's forenamed trusty servant John Heron be from henceforth treasurer of the king's Chamber and that he by the name of treasurer of the king's Chamber be named, accepted and called; and that he and every other person whom the king hereafter shall name and appoint to the said room or office of treasurer of his said Chamber be not charged nor chargeable for any such his or their receipt of any part or parcel of the premises as before is expressed, or therefore to account, answer, or make repayment to any person or persons other than to the king or his heirs in his or their Chamber, and not in the said Exchequer [Stat. 1 Hen. VIII c. 3 lapsed with the meeting of this Parliament]. And that the said Sir Robert and all such others that shall have the same room and authority of the said Sir Robert, in the said act specified, have power and authority to make and receive before them all and singular suits or plaints by bills by any person or persons against the said accountants or any of them to be taken, for any assignment of annuities, fees, duties, or debts, to the complainants granted or assigned by letters patent, act of Parliament, tallies granted, or by any other lawful means; and the same suits and plaints by bills so received and taken by or before the said Sir Robert or other that shall have the same authority and room of the said Sir Robert in the said act specified to put and deliver by their hands the same bill or bills before the Barons of the King's Exchequer if it be in the term time within 4 days after such bill before him so received; and if it be out of term, then the first day of the term next ensuing; and to give and prefix the parties the same day of putting and delivering of the said bills into the Exchequer; and that thereupon the said Barons to proceed and determine after the course and order of the said Exchequer in the said suit[1] ...

[1] N.B.—By this provision, appeal against the accountants therefore lay to the Barons of the Exchequer and could not be determined by the General Surveyors.

XII Provided always that if any ambiguity or doubt at any time hereafter shall happen to be found in any of the said act... that then the same ambiguity...be declared expounded, reformed and reduced by the Chancellor of England, the Steward of the King's House, the Keeper of the King's Privy Seal and the 2 Chief Justices of the time being, or any 3 of them. And that this Act endure unto the Feast of Saint Andrew the Apostle next coming [30 November 1512].

XIII Be it also enacted by authority of this present Parliament that the king's auditors and general receiver of his duchy of Lancaster[1] for the time being yearly at the king's pleasure, after the account of and concerning the said duchy heard and by the said auditors viewed and by them declared before the chancellor of the said duchy for the time being, show and declare the said account before Sir Robert Southwell and Bartholomew Westby... And if and upon the said view and controlment it may appear the king be hurted or deceived of any of his revenues of the said duchy that then such reformation to be had therein as by his highness and his honourable Council shall be thought reasonable...

[1] See below, p. 180.

22. The value of the revenues administered by the General Surveyors, 1509 to 1515[1]

FROM three contemporary 'valors' in the Public Record Office and British Museum, compiled by the General Surveyors.

[1] Declaration by estimation made by Robert Southwell, knight, both of the issues and revenues of divers possessions of the lord king of which the current accounts remain with the said Robert Southwell and Bartholomew Westby, commissioners of the said lord king appointed for this purpose, that is to say for three whole years to the feast of St Michael the Archangel 3 Henry VIII, and of arrears outstanding in the accounts of the same possessions to the feast of St Michael the Archangel 24 Henry VII.

Sum of the total charge:
Arrears at Mich. 24 Henry VII £55,069 17s 1¾d

Rents and farms with other issues
 First Year   £55,115   18s   7¼d ⎤
 Second Year   £49,266   1s   1d   ⎬ £138,016   12s   7¼d
 Third Year   £34,633   12s   10⅝d ⎦

Reprises
Fees, wages and other allocations
 First Year   £28,107   12s   1¼d ⎤
 Second Year   £24,676   3s   3¼d   ⎬ £62,484   18s   10¼d
 Third Year   £9,701   3s   5⅝d ⎦

Cash payments:
First Year
 Household   £1,347   17s   8½d ⎤
 John Heron   £14,890   15s   9¾d
 William Compton   £2,328   0s   10¾d ⎬ £19,620   5s   8⅛d ⎤
 Wardrobe   £270   0s   0d
 Thomas Lunam   £783   11s   4½d ⎦

Second Year
 Household   £2,774   4s   4¼d ⎤
 John Heron   £14,827   12s   5¼d   ⎬ £19,314   3s   7d   ⎬ £65,093   16s   6⅛d
 William Compton   £1,406   6s   1¾d
 Thomas Lynam   £306   0s   7½d ⎦

Third Year
 Household   £3,137   15s   6d ⎤
 John Heron   £21,809   3s   1¼d   ⎬ £26,159   7s   2¼d ⎦
 William Compton   £812   8s   7d
 Thomas Lynam   £400   0s   0d ⎦

[1] All three of these documents are in Latin with the exception of the statement of debts at the end of No. 2.

180   THE CROWN LANDS

of which: Remainder £65,507 15s 3½d

Respited to various persons £27,050 5s 3½d
(particulars in the book of possessions)

Charged to various persons [an indecipherable amount
of over £30,000]
(as in the following particulars)
[the rest of this document is missing]

[Public Record Office, Exchequer, K.R., Various Accounts, E. 101/517/16.]

[2] Declaration of the values of all the revenues of lands and other possessions in the hands of the king that now is, Henry VIII, assigned to be declared before Edward Belknap, knight, and other commissioners of the said lord king, that is to say, for one whole year ending at the feast of Saint Michael the Archangel the seventh year of the same king.

[Here follow detailed accounts under 44 group headings, mainly lands in England and Wales, including the duchy of Lancaster,[1] but also including a space left for Calais and including accounts of the Great Wardrobe and the Hanaper.]

Sum of the total charge: £50,283 5s 5¾d
Reprises: £24,814 14s 5½d
  Cash payments:
    Household £7,099 7s 6½d
    Great Wardrobe £2,000 0s 0d
  Accounted for at the Exchequer: 30s 0d
Remainder paid to the king's coffers this year: £16,367 13s 6d

Arrears

The sum total by estimation made of all the arrears of the king's revenues due at Michaelmas in the 8th year of the reign of our sovereign lord king Henry the VIIIth, growing as well in the time of our late sovereign lord king Henry the VIIth as in the time of our said sovereign lord that now is; over and besides the arrears of all the farms, feefarms and annuities in the king's book; and also over and besides the wards and intrusions which be not as yet perfectly known: £60,103 15s 3d

Whereof:
  In debts desperate by estimation: £50,085 11s 9d
  And in money leviable by estimation payable at certain
    days: £10,018 3s 6d

[British Museum, MS. Royal, *Rot. Reg.* 14. B. XI.]

---

[1] Placed under their jurisdiction in February—March, 1512 (see above, p. 178).

[3] Roll of lands and tenements and other possessions assigned, given and restored to various persons by the lord king that now is, Henry VIII, and recovered for various persons against the said lord king, together with fees, wages and annuities newly granted out of the coffers, and of diminished rents and farms granted by the aforesaid lord king, between the twentieth day of April in the first year of the said lord king that now is and the feast of St Michael the Archangel in the seventh year of the same lord king, by reason of which there is less coming to the coffers of the said lord king that now is, Henry VIII, in the seventh year of his reign than in the 24th year of the late king Henry VII, as they are particularly set out below:

[Here follow separate statements under more than 60 group headings, mainly lands in England and Wales, including the duchy of Lancaster,[1] but also including Calais and the Hanaper.]

Castles, lordships, manors, lands and tenements restored to various persons by acts of Parliament	£2,535 5s 0¼d
Various lands and tenements recovered from the king by various persons	£247 0s 0d
Various manors, lands and tenements given by the king to various persons rendering nothing	£7,585 5s 6¾d
Various manors, lands and tenements freed out of the king's hands to the heirs	£447 13s 3½d
Various annuities lately coming from various lands and possessions of various persons paid annually to the lord king and by the present lord king to various persons given, granted and exonerated	£975 13s 4d

Fees and Wages in	England and Wales	£1,959 5s 2¾d	£4,577 11s 10¾d
	Calais with the Marches	£2,618 6s 8d	
Annuities in	England and Wales	£1,109 16s 8d	£1,277 6s 8d
	Calais with the Marches	£167 10s 0d	
Diminutions of farms in	England and Wales	£398 5s 0½d	£430 12s 5½d
	Calais with the Marches	£32 7s 5d	

Money assigned to the king's Household from the revenues of England and Wales	£4,404 9s 5¾d
Money assigned to the king's Wardrobe from the revenues of England and Wales	£1,000 } £1,540
from the revenues of Calais with the Marches	£540

---

[1] See above, pp. 178, 180.

Money assigned for the reparations and fortification of Calais from
the revenues of Calais and the Marches this year   £700

Total sum of the aforesaid excesses . . . . more than in the
24th year of the late king Henry VIIth: £24,719   17s   8½d

[Public Record Office, Special Collections, S.C. 11/837].

23. Extracts from a docket book of the General Surveyors, 1514 to 1537

FROM The Miscellaneous Books of the Augmentations Office, Public Record Office, Exchequer, E.315/313 A.[1]

fol. 8v.　　　　　　Hilary Term 7 Henry VIII (1516)

Duchy of Cornwall	[1.] Memorandum that John Turnor and Gudlack Overton, auditors of the duchy of Cornwall, have delivered into this court afore the general surveyors of the king's lands the 6th day of February the year abovesaid a view of the general receiver's accounts of the same duchy for a whole year ended Michaelmas last past.
Berwick's and Coparceners' lands	Memorandum that John Toly, auditor of the revenues assigned to and for the payment of the soldiers of Berwick, hath delivered in the court afore the general surveyors of the king's lands the 10th day of February the 7th year of the reign of our sovereign lord king Henry VIIIth a view of the general reveiver's accounts of the same lands for a whole year ended at Michaelmas last past. Item the receiver of the coparcener's lands.
Principality of South Wales, lands late of the duke of Bedford, Usk and Caerleon and lands late of the earl of Huntingdon in Somerset and Dorset	Memorandum that Thomas Roberts and John Peryent, auditors there assigned, have delivered in this court afore the general surveyors of the king's lands the 10th day of February the 7th year of the reign of our sovereign lord king Henry the VIIIth a several view of the chamberlain's and receiver's accounts of the same lands for a whole year ended at Michaelmas last past.
Principality of North Wales and the county	Memorandum that Henry Parker and Richard Hawkyns, auditors there assigned, have delivered in this court afore the general surveyors of the king's

---

[1] The book begins with notes in English of 34 privy seals directed to various executors, bailiffs, farmers, receivers etc. At fol. 6 v. is the first date, Trinity Term, 6 Hen. VIII from whence entries, for the most part consisting of appearance in the court, are normally noted in Latin. Exceptions to this are the records of views of account received, of engrossed accounts delivered to the Exchequer and a few decisions of the court, etc., recorded in English.

palatine of Chester and Flint	lands the 6th day of February the 7th year of the reign of king Henry the VIIIth two several views of the chamberlain's accounts there for a whole year ended at Michaelmas last past.
Berkeley's lands Moor End	Memorandum that Thomas Comber and Thomas Roberts, auditors there assigned, have delivered in this court before the general surveyors of the king's lands the 10 day of February the 7th year of the reign of king Henry the VIIIth a view of the receiver's accounts of Berkeley's lands and of Moor End with members for a year ended at Michaelmas last past.
fol. 9	Memorandum that George Quarles, auditor of the lands late in the possession of Margaret late countess of Richmond and Derby, the king's granddam, have delivered in this court afore the general surveyors of the king's lands the 10th day of February the 7th year of the reign of our sovereign lord king Henry the VIIIth a view of the general receiver's account of the same lands for a year ended at Michaelmas last past.
	Item that the said George Quarles hath delivered before the said general surveyors the day and year abovesaid a bill of the said general receiver's account of the lands late put in feoffment by the said countess for a year ended at Michaelmas last past.
	Item that the said George Quarles and John Turnor, auditors of the Warwickslands, Salisburylands and Spencerslands, have delivered in the court the day and year abovesaid a bill of the general receiver's accounts of the same lands for a year ended at Michaelmas last past.
	Item that the said John Turnor and John Wrenne, auditors of the earldom of the Marches, have delivered in this court afore the said general surveyors the said day and year a view of the general receiver's account of the same lands for a year ended at Michaelmas last past.

DOCUMENTS 185

Item the said John Wrenne, auditor of the lordships of Bromfield, Yale, Chirklands and Dyffryn Clwyd within the town of Ruthin and of certain lands which late were Sir William Stanley's, knight, in the counties of Chester and Flint, have delivered in this court afore the said general surveyors the day and year abovesaid 4 views of the receiver's account of the same lands for a year ended at Michaelmas last past.

[2.] Memorandum that it is agreed afore the said surveyors that all the foresaid auditors shall have the said views redelivered to make up the accounts in parchment to be delivered into the Exchequer and at every second year's end to bring in the papers of the receivers of the precedent year etc. and the ministers engrossed.

fol. 9v.[1] [3.] Accounts of sundry receivers and other officers of divers of the king's lands and possessions, engrossed in parchment according to the act of Parliament in that behalf made by the auditors thereunto appointed, and examined by the king's general surveyors of his lands, and delivered into the king's Exchequer for discharge of the said receivers and officers according to the purport of the said act, that is to say:

Account of James Moros and Hugh Edwards, receivers of the lands late in the possession of Margaret late countess of Richmond and Derby, for the 7th year of king Henry the VIIIth, with 3 tallies for the king's Wardrobe contained £1000 and 7 bills signed with the hand of John Heron, treasurer of the king's Chamber, containing £1406 15s 9d.

Account of Thomas Goodeman, receiver of Barkleys lands, for *Anno VII^{mo}* without any bill or tallies.

Account of Robert Neswyke, bailiff of the lordship of Moor End and other, for *Anno VII^{mo}* Henry VIIIth, with £13 19s 2½d in a bill signed with the hand of the said John Heron.

Account of Edward Croft, knight, receiver-general of the earldom of March in the counties of Hereford

[1] Trinity Term, 8 Hen. VIII (1516).

and Salop, the lordships of Wigmore, Radnor, Clifford and Ewyas Lacy, members of the same earldom, for *Anno VII^{mo}* with a tally for the king's Household containing £100 and 2 bills signed with the hand of the foresaid John Heron containing £157 7s and a third part of a farthing.

Account of the earl of Worcester, receiver of divers parcels of the same earldom, for *Anno VII^{mo}* abovesaid, with 2 bills signed with the hand of the said John Heron containing £49 17s.

fol. 10

Account of Sir Rice ap Thomas, knight, chamberlain of South Wales, for *Anno VII* Henry VIII, with a bill signed with the hand of the foresaid John Heron containing £467 14s ¼d.

Account of William Compton, knight, receiver of the lordships of Stoke under Hamdon, Curry Malet and other parcels of the lands late the earl of Huntingdon, for *Anno VII^{mo}*, with a bill signed with the hand of the foresaid John Heron containing £265 19s 10¾d.

Account of Thomas Goodeman, receiver of Warwickslands, Salisburyslands and Spencerslands, for *Ann VII^{mo}*, with a tally for the king's Household containing £1500 and 2 bills signed with the hand of John Heron containing £461.

Account of the said Thomas, receiver of the lordships of Swaffham, parcel of the honour of Richmond, for *Anno VII^{mo}* with a bill signed with the hand of the said John containing £52 2s ¼d.

Account of William Pawne, receiver of the lands assigned to Berwick for *Anno VII^{mo}* with 2 bills signed with the hand of the said John Heron containing £184 3s 4d.[1]

---

[1] N.B.—Entries up to this point are mere routine, but new compared with the docket book for 1505-8 above (Doc. 17). Their appearance here was due to the fact that books of summaries of receivers' accounts (Doc. 16) were no longer being compiled, as a result of the increased dependence on the Exchequer.

| | DOCUMENTS | 187 |

fol. 12 Easter Term 9 Henry VII (1517)

Richmonds lands [4.] Edward Dygby has appeared here in court on a writ of privy seal on the 4th day of May in the ninth year to answer for £4 10s 10d of the arrears of William Bedill late bailiff of Relyngton and he has day to the 6th day of May next to pay the aforesaid debt to the king's Chamber under penalty of £20.[1] Christabel Appulby, executrice of the will of Richard Appulby, has appeared here in court on a writ etc. on the same day to answer for £7 7s of the arrears of the said Richard, late bailiff of Morton, and she has day to Monday next to appear again under penalty of £20. At which day she appeared and has further day to Wednesday next under the aforesaid penalty.

Duchy of Cornwall [5.] Thomas Wastlyn, gentleman, John Wastelyn and Richard Gryme have appeared here in court before the surveyors of the lands of the lord king in the month of Easter this term in their own persons on a writ of privy seal to answer concerning certain articles contained in the same writ and they have day to Friday next.

Earldom of March [6.] Walter Badham has appeared here on the same day on a writ to pay to the lord king £93 6s 8d by him received and he has day to the morrow of the Ascension next at his peril.

Duchy of Cornwall and Suffolks lands [7.] Georgina Hynd has appeared here on the same day for the debts of Henry Reynold and has day to the morrow of the Ascension next at her peril to pay the aforesaid debts or to appear in her own person; and afterwards she came into the court at the aforesaid day and she has further day on the consideration of the court to the octave of Trinity at her peril.

fol. 14 [8.] Memorandum that Richard Gere of Acton Reynold in the county of Salop. giveth information to the king's general surveyors that one Peter Newton, gentleman, late of the king's council in Wales had of the said Richard Gere in ready money £40 to

---

[1] This entry and the following 4 entries are all in Latin.

stand good master unto him and that he might peacefully enjoy the manor of Acton Reynold, by reason whereof the said manor was long concealed from the king by reason of the untruth of the said Peter; and this information was made and reported in the presence of Sir John Daunce, Sir E. Belknapp, knights, Gerard Danet, esquire, and other persons in the court.

fol. 16v.[1]   [9.] Memorandum that upon the matter in variance of long time depending between the Abbot of Tewkesbury and Thomas Spicer on the other part it is determined decreed and discussed before the king's general surveyors the 10th day of July the 10th year of king Henry the VIIIth by the assent of the counsel of the said abbot upon the sight of such grants as the said abbot hath for the demand of his party, that where the said abbot and his predecessors by the space of 7 years hath wrongfully occupied and exercised the haywardship of Barton and Mythe within the lordship of Tewkesbury and Mythe by colour of the king's grant, which grant hath been shewed afore the said surveyors ordained, that the said grant extended not to the said office nor to no parcel thereof and therefore it is ordained that the said Thomas Spicer shall occupy and enjoy the said haywardship from henceforth without any let or hindrance of the said abbot or any in his name, according to the king's grant made to the said Thomas Spicer in that behalf; and furthermore that the said abbot shall pay to the king's use where the said general surveyors shall appoint the sum of £35 which he hath taken of the profit of the said office after 100s by the year for the said 7 years afore All Souls day next coming without delay.

fol. 19   Hilary Term 10 Henry VIII (1519)

[10.] Memorandum that the morrow afore the feast of St Andrew the 10th year of the reign of king Henry the VIIIth it was decreed, ordained and concluded afore the king's general surveyors in this court that Anthony Malory of Bassingbourn in the county of

[1] Trinity Term, 10 Henry VIII (1518).

Cambridge, gentleman, shall content and pay to Roger Swetdew of Bassingbourn aforesaid and Alice his wife the sum of 10 quarters of barley and 20s in ready money in full recompense of all such variances and wrongs which the said Anthony had done to the said Roger; and further that upon the delivery of the said corn and money the said Roger Sweetdew and Alice his wife to seal and deliver to the said Anthony a general acquittance of all manner of accounts, etc.

fol. 20[1]   [11.] The king to all to whom etc. greeting. Know that we by the advice and assent of our well-beloved John Daunce, knight, one of our councillors, Bartholomew Westby and Robert Blagge, Barons of our Exchequer, general surveyors of our lands, and for sufficient mainprize taken before our chamberlain of Chester, have granted and demized at farm to the reverend father Thomas, abbot of the monastery of the Blessed Mary of Basyngwerk, and Thomas Salysbery, gentleman, the keeping or farm of the manor of Coleshill in the county of Flint, lately in the tenure of the said abbot, together with the court leet, tourn, view of frankpledge and their perquisites, with all other issues, commodities and profits pertaining or belonging to the same keeping or farm, to have and to hold the said keeping or farm together with the leet, tourn, view of frankpledge and their perquisites, with all other issues, commodities and profits pertaining to the same keeping or farm, to the said abbot and Thomas Salisbery and other respective executors and assigns, from the feast of St Michael the Archangel in the tenth year of our reign to the end and term of twenty eight years next following and fully completed, rendering annually therefrom to us and our heirs fifty three shillings and eight pence as has been rendered to us, and eight pence further in annual increment at the feasts of St Michael the Archangel and Easter by equal portions, to the hands of our chamberlain of Chester or to the hands of the treasurer of our Chamber for the time being; and if it happens that the said

[1] Easter Term, 11 Henry VIII (1519). A draft or copy of letters patent in Latin.

annual rent or the aforesaid increment shall be in arrears for ten weeks at least in part or in whole after any feast of the aforesaid feasts on which it ought to be paid as stated, that then it is and shall be fully lawful for us and our heirs to re-enter into the aforesaid keeping or farm and the rest of the premises with their appurtenances and to resume and receive them into our hands, these our present letters patent in any way notwithstanding. In [witness] of which etc.

fol. 25v.[1] Lenten appearances in the 11th year of King Henry VIII at the Friars Preachers, London (1520).

[12.] Edward Doun, knight, appeared here before the surveyors of the lord king's lands on 15th day of March in the aforesaid year on a writ of privy seal to pay £50 5s 5d owed to the king as appears in the same writ and has day to the month of Easter next to appear as above under penalty of £100; and afterwards he has day to the quindene of Michaelmas next under the aforesaid penalty.

[13.] John Mores of Princes Risborough in the county of Buckingham appeared as above the aforesaid day and year on a writ of privy seal to answer concerning certain articles charged against him on the king's behalf and has day until the morrow under the penalty contained in the writ; and afterwards he has day to the morrow of the Ascension next.

[14.] Henry Bryse servant of Edward Doun appeared as above the aforesaid day and year on a writ of privy seal to pay 20s owed to the king for his fines and has day until tomorrow under the penalty contained in the writ, and afterwards he gave security by recognizance to pay the said 20s before Christmas next.

[15.] John Bowler, lately bailiff of Princes Risborough in the county of Buckingham, appeared as above the day and year abovesaid on a writ of privy seal to answer concerning certain articles charged against

---

[1] All these entries are in Latin.

him on behalf of the lord king; and has day to the morrow of the Purification and thus from day to day etc., under penalty of £100; and afterwards he has day by the court to the quindene of Michaelmas next to answer as above under the aforesaid penalty; and he then appeared and injunction was given him to appear from day to day until dismissed by the court; and afterwards he made a fine in settlement for the value of trees cut down by him of £10 to be paid on the feast of St Andrew the Apostle next under the abovesaid penalty; and afterwards, namely on 21 November in the 12th year of the aforesaid king,[1] John Boller paid the said £10 to John Heron, treasurer of the lord king's Chamber, as by a bill signed with the hand of the said John and in the possession of Guthlac Overton, auditor of the duchy of Cornwall, and thus the said John left the court *sine die*.

fol. 41[2] [16.] Memorandum it is ordered and decreed the 16th day of July the 15th year of King Henry the VIIIth afore the kings' general surveyors in the Prince's Council Chamber by the assent and advice of the king's learned counsel that Robert Dolbyn of Denbigh shall be and personally appear afore the said surveyors on the morrow of All Souls next coming and in the mean time not to take nor perceive at the half year's court any fees of 2d for the general appearance of the county at the same court upon pain of a hundred pounds.

fol. 42[3] [17.] Memorandum it is ordered by the court that where there is variance for a copyhold betwixt John Barkett and John Cheshire of Tewkesbury that Master Umpton and Master Wye shall have the hearing of the same and the parties be bound to bide such award as they shall make in that behalf upon pain of £40 to be paid to the king if they do not hold the same award.

[18.] John Burt of Papworth in the county of Cambridge,

---
[1] 1520.
[2] The last previous terminal heading was on fol. 40, i.e. Easter Term, 15 Henry VIII (1523).
[3] Terminal heading Hilary, 15 Henry VIII (1524).

of the age of 21 years, sworn and examined, saith that Thomas Aleyn of the same town entered not into the tenement in variance betwixt William Tadlow and William Hichyn by force but only at the request of Master Malary and at that time of his entry which was the Wednesday afore Michaelmas there was not person there to let him nor no resistance to the contrary, but that he quietly entered as tenant to William Tatlow.

Geoffrey Maddy of Papworth aforesaid, of the age of 40 years and more, sworn and examined, affirmeth all the saying of the foresaid John Burt and further he sayeth he was hired to carry the stuff of the said Thomas Aleyn to the foresaid house and he lay there all the night and was there the morrow to 10 of the clock the foresaid Wednesday afore Michaelmas.

fol. 43v.[1] [19.] In the Star Chamber the 26th day of October in the 12th year of King Henry VIIIth [Latin heading].[2]

Memorandum where heretofore variance hath depended between the earl of Derby and his tenants of Holland for certain leases, farms and others liberties, which the same tenants pretend to have within the said lordship of Holland and the which the same tenants did use and enjoy whilst the same lordship was in the king's hands. It is ordered etc. that for as much as it is thought that the said earl by the rigour of the common law might put the said tenants from their said leases and liberties without any offence doing to the said law, that the said tenants in their most humble manner shall make suit and petition to the said earl for the continual enjoying of their said farms, leases and other liberties accustomed. Upon the which their humble suit and petition the said earl shall peacefully suffer the said tenants to enjoy the same leases, farms and other liberties in such wise and manner as they did whilst the same lordship was in the king's hands. And whereas the tenants claim to have the custody of the

---

[1] The last previous terminal heading was on fol. 43, i.e. Easter Term, 15 Henry VIII (1523).
[2] October 26, 1520.

court rolls of the said lordship, which is not thought convenient, it is ordered that they shall leave their hands of them and deliver them into indifferent hands.

fol. 44 [20.] In the Star Chamber the 13 day of February in the 14th year of King Henry the VIIIth above written [Latin heading].[1]

Memorandum that where there was the 26th day of October in the 12th year of the king our sovereign lord an order taken between the late earl of Derby and his tenants of Holland, as in the same order more at large it doth appear, it is now condescended by the most reverend father etc. and the other etc. that notwithstanding the same manor be now in the kings' hands by the nonage of the young earl of Derby that the same order and direction shall stand in like force and strength as to the advantage of the tenants of Holland aforesaid as it did in the same earl's days. And that the same tenants shall in ample manner enjoy their said leases, farms and liberties as they did at any time other, the same manor being in the said earl's hands or in the king's hands.

fol. 51v.[2] [21.] Memorandum it is ordered, ordained and decreed afore the king's general surveyors in the Prince's Council Chamber the 30th day of November the 16th year of King Henry the VIIIth[3] that Sir Roger Pyllisden, David Holand and other sureties of William ap John ap Merydith, late receiver of Ruthin, shall have and perceive all the issues, profits and revenues of the lease of certain parcels of land in Ruthin made and granted by the king's grace to the said William Ap John to such time as the sum of £130 be paid to the king's grace in his Chamber for the debt of the said William and to such time as all other debts hanging and depending before the said surveyors in the auditor's books of Ruthin aforesaid, which the said sureties be become debtors to

---

[1] February 13, 1523.
[2] The last previous terminal heading was on fol. 46, v. i.e. Michelmas, 16 Henry VIII (1524).
[3] November 30, 1524.

the king for by recognizance afore the said surveyors, yielding and paying yearly to Agnes Vergh Symond yearly for the finding of her children 40s at the feast of Midsummer and Christmas by even portions and what time all and every the foresaid debts be by the said sureties fully content and paid to the king's use then it is further ordered and decreed that the said lease and all the profits thereof shall return and revert to the children of the said Agnes Vergh Symonde during the residue of the years therein and at that time to be unexpired, in consideration that the said children be brother children to the foresaid William; and further that the said sureties shall not enter into the said farm nor any parcel thereof afore Christmas next coming.

fol. 87v.[1]   [22.]   By the king.

Right trusty and right well-beloved cousin we greet you well and where we be entitled and ought of right to have the wardship and custody of the body and lands of George Harbotell son and heir of Guycherd Harbotell during the nonage of the same George for as much as the said Guycherd at the time of his death held of us certain lands and tenements *in capite*, as well within our county of Sussex as within our county of Nottingham, as by several offices thereof found and returned into our Chancery more at large it doth appear of record; and where also as our servant Baldwin Willoughby hath seized to our use the said George Harbotell, our ward, we be informed that at the same seizure made one   [2] Loveday, which hath married the Lady Ougle, in your name made a rescue upon our said servant and with force took from him our said ward contrary to our laws and peace. Wherefore we will and desire you and not the less command you that incontinent upon the sight of these our letters ye in our name give in commandment to the said

---

[1] The terminal headings end with Trinity, 19 Henry VIII (1527) at fol. 64. At fol. 65 v. begin entries under 28 Henry VIII (1536-7), mainly recognizances, but the last folios, 87 v.— 90 v., revert to much earlier dates and appear to be a kind of formulary.

[2] Blank in MS.

fol. 88

Loveday to be and personally appear before our right trusty and right well-beloved knight and councillor Sir Edward Belknapp and other the general surveyors of our lands at Westminster in the chamber there called the Prince's Council Chamber *mense pasche* next coming to show why he ought so to do. And furthermore we will and desire you and not the less command you that with diligence upon the sight of these letters ye deliver or cause to be delivered to our said servant or to this bearer all such sums of money as ye or any other person or persons by your commandment of the rents and profits of the lands which late were the said Guycherd Harbotell's there since the death of the same Guycherd hitherto, taking of our said servant or of the said bearer a bill specifying as well the receipt of the said George as of the said sums of money, which bill with these our letters shall be your sufficient warrant and discharge in that behalf; or else that ye or your learned counsel in the law be and personally appear before our said surveyors at the place and above limited [sic] to show cause reasonable why ye ought not this to do. Fail ye not this to do as ye tender our pleasure and will avoid the contrary at your peril. Given under our signet at our manor of Greenwich the 6th day of April the 8th year of our reign [1517].

To our right trusty and right entirely-beloved cousin the earl of Northumberland.

fol. 89v.

[23.] Robert Southwell, knight, and Bartholomew Westby, one of the Barons of the lord king's Exchequer, general surveyors of the lands, tenements and other possessions being in the lord king's hands, to the abbot of Stratford, John Banfford, knight, John Heron, esquire, John Roke and John Skyll, greeting. Know that we, fully considering your fidelity and prudent circumspection shown and to be shown towards our lord the king, have assigned and deputed you five, four, or three of you to survey and inquire by the examination and recognition of good and lawworthy men of the lordship and manor of Wanstead in the county of Essex and of the towns and townships adjacent or lying round about the same lordship how the truth can best be known concerning the state and condition of the woods and underwoods within the precincts of the aforesaid lordship and manor, and how much can be sold there for the profit of the lord king and also the value or price of the said woods and underwoods, either by metes and bounds, or by acres, or otherwise, according to the use of the aforesaid lordship and manor, and also to survey and inquire concerning wastes, destructions and other damages made or perpetrated by any person or persons in the said lordship to the woods or underwoods, when, by what right, and how, and at what loss to the lord king. And therefore we faithfully desire you on the lord king's behalf by the authority committed to us in this matter that you will diligently make surveys and inquisitions concerning the premises according to your wise discretion so that you send us knowledge of the same as quickly as possible and not later than the morrow of the Annunciation of the Blessed Virgin Mary next coming under your seals or under the seals of four or three of you, together with these our letters sent to you in this behalf; commanding moreover by our aforesaid authority that all and every officer and minister of the aforesaid lordship and manor shall be duly obedient and assisting to you in the execution of the premises. In witness of which we have set our seal to these presents.[1] Given in the chamber called the Prince's Council Chamber at Westminster the 15 day of February in the fifth year of the reign of the said lord king that now is, Henry VIIIth [Latin].

fol. 90v.   [24.] John Daunce, knight, one of our sovereign lord the king's councillors and John Hales, one of the Barons of the king's Exchequer, general surveyors of our said sovereign lord the king's lands, to Thomas Slade, general receiver of our sovereign lord the king's lands called Warwickslands, John Ketylby, esquire, steward of the lordship of Elmley Lovett in the county of Worcester, and Richard Caine, gentleman, greeting. We, trusting in your fidelity, circumspec-

---

[1] Authorized by Stat. 3 Henry VIII cap. 23, see p. 175 above. cf. below, p. 197.

tion, wisdom and industry have appointed, assigned and by authority to us given have authorized you to sit and examine and inquire of and upon all and singular articles, causes and matters comprised and specified in the bill of complaint, answer, replication and rejoinder unto this commission annexed, and also to survey and view all and singular woods and underwoods within the precincts of our lordship of Elmley Lovett aforesaid and what the said woods and underwoods be worth by the acre or in gross, forsaying that ye make no sales of any of the same woods or underwoods. And therefore we desire you and in our said sovereign lord's name command you that ye diligently do sit, examine and inquire of and upon all and singular the premises and that that ye do therein to certify unto us, by your writing signed and sealed with your hands, at Westminster in the Prince's Council Chamber in the morrow of the Ascension of our Lord next coming with this our commission. Desiring also and in our said sovereign lord's name commanding the sheriff of the said county of Worcester and all other bailiffs and ministers to whom it shall appertain that, at certain days and places which ye shall give them knowledge of, to cause to come afore you such and as many good, sad and lawful men of their bailiwicks as shall be right and necessary for the sure and true knowledge in and of the premises. Given under our seal[1] and sign manual the 5th day of April the 16th year of King Henry the VIIIth [1525].

[1] cf. above, pp. 175, 196.

INDEX

Abergavenny, lordship of, 46, 62, 64, 122, 125, 137
Abrigg, Sir Giles, 157
Acton Burnell, lordships of, 150
Acton, Reynold, 187-8
Agarde (Agard), John, receiver, 124, 128, 137, 138
Ainstable, 171
Aleyn, Thomas, auditor, 109, 118
Aleyn, Thomas, of Papworth, 192
Alien priories, lands of, 32, 38, 39
Allington, castle and lordship of, 126
Amersham, 130
Anne (Neville), queen of Richard III, 46, 62, 64
Appulby, Richard, bailiff, 187; Christabel, executrice of, 187
Archer, Jacob, 145
Ashley (Aishley) Edward, lands of, 47, 145
Askham Brian, 171
Assheley, Richard, lands of, 171
Aston Clinton, 139
Attainders, 46, 68, 72, 149; and see Forfeitures; Parliament, acts of attainder in
Attorney, king's, 163 and see Erneley, John
Audley, lord, see Tuchet
Augmentations, court of, 81
Aumale, countess of, see Redvers
Aylesbury, 130
Aylest, William, 130

Badham, Walter, 187
Bagshot, 130
Ballson, John, receiver, 142
Banfford, John, kt., 195
Barkett, John, 191
Barley, Robert, 171
Barnard Castle and members, 131
Barnet, battle of, 57
Barton, 188

Bassingbourn, 188-9
Basyngwerk, Thomas, abbot of, 189
Batens, William, lands of, 171
Bawtry, 131
Bayleys lands, 145
Baynton, John, 158
Beauchamp, Eleanor, duchess of Somerset (died 1467), lands of, 171
Beauchamp, Richard, earl of Warwick, lands of, 140
Beauchamp of St Amand (Seinteourbant), Richard, kt., lands of, 121
Beaufitz, John, receiver, 59, 110
Beaufort, family, lands of, 57
Beaufort, Henry, cardinal, 26, 32
Beaufort, Margaret, countess of Richmond and Derby, (mother of Henry VII), 46, 68, 170, 184, 185
Beaumaris, castle of, 61, 129
Beaumont, Richard, viscount, 171
Beaumont, William, viscount, 170
Bedford, county of, 121, 140, 171
Bedford, duchy of, 46
Bedford, duke of, see Lancaster; Tudor
Bedill, William, bailiff, 187
Bedminster, lordship of, 122
Bele (Belle), William, gent., 166
Belknap, Edward, kt., general surveyor, king's councillor, 180, 188, 195
Benet, William, 100
Berdefeld (Bredefeld, Bredefelde, Bardfeld), John, receiver, 124, 125, 138
Berkeley, William, marquis, earl of Nottingham, lands of, 140, 171, 184, 185
Berkhamstead, lordship & castle, 92
Berkshire, 33, 111, 130, 140
Berwick, 48, 171, 183, 186
Bewbank, William, 153
Black Prince, see Edward of Woodstock

Blackmere, 112
Blackstone, Sir William, *Commentaries on the Laws of England*, 16
Blagge, Robert, Baron of Exchequer, general surveyor, 189
Blankney, 143
Blekynsop, John, 129
Blencogo, 171
Blount, Walter, lord Mountjoy, auditor, 103
Bodmin, mayor of, 158
Bodryngan (Botrigan), Sir Henry, lands of, 145, 171
Bohun, Humphrey de, earl of Essex, Hereford and Northampton, 31
Bohun, Humphrey de, Joan, wife of, 32
Bolingbroke, honour of, 138
Bonerston or Boverston, 122
Bosley, manor of, 32
Bosworth, battle of, 66
Bourchier, Fulk, lord Fitzwarren, lands of, 128, 139
Bourchier, Henry, earl of Essex, lands of, 139
Bowler (Boller), John, bailiff, 190
Brackenbury (Brankenber, Brakenber) Robert, squire of the body, receiver, 126-7
Branston, 143
Brasted, lordship of, 126
Bray, 7 hundreds of Cookham and Bray, 130
Bray, Reginald, kt., receiver, 71, 140, 141; general surveyor, 173-4
Brecon, county of, 171
Brecon, lordship of, 98
Brierton (Brearton), Randolf, kt., receiver, 142, 154
Brikhad, Ralph, sheriff, 157
Bristol, customs of, 122
Brittany, counts & dukes of, earls of Richmond, 32
Brocas, Benedict, receiver, 145
Broke, John, 155
Broke, lord, see Willoughby
Broke, Richard, 155
Brokhall in Dersingham, manor of, 112
Bromfield, lordship of, 142, 185
Broughton, manor of, 111
Broun, John, keeper of the king's bears & apes, 126
Brown, Miles, 156
Browne, Robert, auditor, 122
Brudenell, Robert, justice, 163
Bryse, Henry, 190
Brytte, Nicholas, receiver, 138
Buckingham, county of, 121, 130, 140, 143, 153, 171, 190
Buckingham, duke of, see Stafford
Bucknell, justice, 162
Buckland Marlow, 139
Builth, lordship of, 98, 123, 150
Burgh, Edward, kt., lands of, 144, 171
Burgh, Thomas, kt., receiver, 138
Burgundy, duchy of, 26
Burne, 160
Burstwick-in-Hoderness, lordship of, 23, 32
Burt, John, 191-2
Burton-in-Lonsdale, 131
Bushey, manor of, 125
Busshy, Edward, receiver, 143
Butler, Chief, of England, 139; and see Southwell, Robert
Butler, James, earl of Wiltshire, lands of, 57, 113, 125
Butler (Botler), justice, 162, 163
Butt, John, auditor, 155
Buttelar, William, grocer, of Cheapside, 153
Buttelar, William, senior, gent., 156

Caerleon, 98, 143, 183
Caine, Richard, gent., 196
Caister, 131, 143, 171
Calais and Guînes (Guisnes), accounts and revenues of, 48, 62, 77, 84, 134, 171, 173, 180, 181
Calais and Guînes (Guisnes), acts of resumption in, 93, 103
Calais and Guînes (Guisnes), reparations and fortifications of, 182
Calais and Guînes (Guisnes), Staple of, 77, 171

Calais and Guînes (Guisnes), Staple of, Mayor and Fellowship of, 74, 152
Cambridge, county of, 57, 140, 143, 171, 189, 191
Caniziani, Garard, of London, merchant, 110
Canterbury, Archbishop of, see Stafford, John; Warham, William
Cantref Selyf, 171
Carleton Rode, 152
Carlisle, 157
Carlisle, bishop of, see Layburne, Roger
Carlisle, king's brickworks at, 129
Carlton in Craven, 131, 171
Carmarthen, county of, 159
Carter, William, 129
Castle Rising, manor of, 32
Catherine of Aragon, queen of Henry VIII, 46
Catherine of Valois, queen of Henry V, 26, 39
Catesby, lands of, 145
Catisby, Sir Richard, lands of, 171
Causfeld, Thomas, 153
Cedewain, 97
Chaderton (Chatterton), Edmund, king's clerk, chaplain, treasurer & receiver of Chamber, 68, 119, 124, 127, 128
Chaffer, John, 156-7
Chamber, 22-3, 46, 50, 54, 62, 63, 66, 77, 78
Chamber, revenues and accounts in, 42, 44-5, 48-50, 56, 57, 58, 59, 60, 64, 65, 68-70, 71, 72, 73, 74, 77, 79, 80, 83, 85, 86, 88, 100-1, 110, 112, 113, 114, 119, 120-39 *passim*, 151, 152-3, 159-60, 164-5, 167, 169, 173, 174, 180, 185, 187, 189, 191, 193
Chamber, treasurer of, see Chaderton, Edmund; Heron, John; Lovell Thomas; Vaughan, Thomas
Chamber, ushers of, 60, 121, 122
Chamber,—, auditor, 151
Chamber des comptes, 22

Chancellor of England, 79, 80, 178; and see Stafford, John; Warham, William; Wolsey, Thomas
Chancery, 33, 39, 57, 79, 80, 105, 110, 148, 151, 194
Chancery, Hanaper in, 77, 170, 171, 180, 181
Charleton, Sir Richard, lands of, 170
Chebsey, 148
Cheney, John, squire, 121
Chertsey, abbot of, see Maye John; Pigot Thomas
Chertsey, convent of, temporalities of, 113
Chesham, 130
Cheshire, John, 191
Cheshire, sheriff of, 157
Chester, abbot of, 152
Chester, county of, 123, 142, 157, 185
Chester, earldom of, 24, 31, 38, 62, 103, 134
Chester, prince's council at, 74, 155
Chester, and Flint, palatine counties of, 23, 46, 72, 142, 165, 170, 184
Chester, and Flint, palatine counties of, chamberlain of, 41, 189
Chester, and Flint, palatine counties of, exchequer of, 74, 154
Cheylesmore, manor of, 32
Cheyney, Francis, lands of, 144, 145, 171
Chirk and Chirklands, lordship of, 32, 91, 143, 150, 185
Chichester, temporalities of bishopric, 71
Cholmeley, Richard, receiver and surveyor, 71
Cilgerran, lordship of, 32
Cinque Ports, Warden of, 33
Clarence, duchess of, see Lancaster
Clarence, duke of, see Lancaster; Plantagenet
Claygate, 130, 171
Clerk, Robert, king's servant, 128
Clerke, John, auditor, 154, 157
Clifford, lordship of, 98, 186
Clifton, Gervais, kt., 139
Clitheroe, 137

O

Cobham, John de, 32
Cok, Sampson, 130
Coleshill, manor of, 189
Colt, Thomas, 57; chancellor of earldom of March, 99
Combes, Thomas, auditor, 184
Compton Chamberlain, manor of, 158
Compton, William, keeper of privy purse, 179; receiver, 186
Connigsby, Humphrey, justice, 162, 163
Constable, Mamaduke, kt. of the body, 132-3; steward of honour of Tutbury, 61; steward of honour of Tonbridge, 126
Conyers, lord, 153
Cookham, 130 Cookham & Bray, 7 hundreds of, 130
Coorte (Coort, Court), Robert, auditor & receiver, 71, 118, 125, 127, 138
Coparcener's lands, 183
Corbridge, 48
Corfham, 112
Cornborough, 171
Cornbury, park of, 109
Cornwall, county of, 23, 113, 122, 123, 143, 149, 160, 171
Cornwall, duchy of, 23, 24, 31, 38, 39, 46, 48, 55, 59, 62, 64, 70, 72, 103, 134, 138, 142, 166, 170, 183, 187, 191
Cornwall, duchy of, receiver general of, 41, 67, 183; and see Nanfan, Richard; Sapcote, John
Cornwall, duchy of, coinage of tin in, 142
Cornwall, duchy of, feodary of, 202
Cornwall, duchy of, tin and lead mines in, 48, 53, 122, 155
Cornwall, earl of, see John of Eltham
Cottingham, 131
Council, 26, 27, 35, 36, 37, 39, 42, 51, 52, 54, 61, 62, 76, 78, 92, 95, 104, 131, 149, 159, 165, 166, 178
Council, committees of, 42, 45, 71-3, 80, 135, 141
Council, in Star Chamber, 82, 192, 193

Council, in Wales, 187
Council, Learned, 76, 153, ?191
Council, memorandum of, on crown lands (1484), 45, 55, 62-3, 133-7
Council, minutes of (1509), 162-3
Courtenay, Edward, earl of Devon, 145, 170
Courtenay, family, (Devonshire) lands of, 63, 113
Coventry, acquittance given at, 100
Coventry, sheriff of, 153
Cranbourne & members, 143, 171
Cravenys in Henham, see Henham
Croft, Edward, kt., receiver, 185
Croft, Richard, esq., receiver, approver and surveyor, 58, 108-9; kt. and receiver, 57, 112, 126, 138, 142
Croke, William, auditor, 122-3, 149
Cromwell, Ralph, lord, Treasurer of England, 37, 38, 48, 69
Cromwell, Thomas, 88
Croyland, chronicler of the abbey of, 40, 53, 63, 104-5
Cumberland, county of, 123, 171
Cumberworth, 144
Curry Malet, lordship of, 186
Customs (and subsidies on wool, etc., tunnage and poundage), see Taxation in Parliament
Customs, surveyors of, 105
Customers in the ports, 39, 70, 134
Cutfold, Thomas, scholar, 114
Cutte (Cut), John, receiver, 138; kt., under-treasurer, 162

Dalamare, Sir Thomas, 121
Dalamer, John, 157
Danby, Richard, 129
Danet, Gerard, esquire, 188
Danvers, John, 157
Darcy, Thomas, lord, 163
Darolde, Geoffrey, receiver, 144
Dartington, lordship of, 123
Datchet, 130
Datonslande, 145
Daunce, John, kt., king's councillor, general surveyor, 188, 189, 196
Dawbeney, Giles, lord, receiver, 144

Dawtre, John, receiver, 143
Daypole in Holderness, 151
Dean, forest of, 99
Decons, Richard, receiver, 142
Dedham, lordship of, 148
Denbigh, 97, 126, 191
Derby countess of, see Beaufort
Derby, county of, 103, 123, 140, 143, 171
Derby, earl of, see Stanley
Dersingham, 112
Devon, county of, 113, 123, 145, 171
Devon, earl of; Devonshire lands; see Courtenay
Dialogus de Scaccario, 19
Ditchampton, 143, 171
Dolbyn, Robert, 191
Domesday Book, 18, 21
Domesday Book, *terra regis* in, 15, 19, 20, 24
Don, Sir John, 121
Dorset, county of, 113, 123, 149, 171, 183
Dorset, marquis of, see Grey
Dorstone, 98
Doun, Edward, kt., 190
Doune, Henry, receiver, 99
Doune, John, receiver, 98
Doune, lady, 153
Dring Houses, 171
Dudley, Edmund, 76, 149; lands of, 171
Durham, warrant dated at, 100
Durham, bishop of, see Ruthall, Thomas
Durham, temporalities of bishopric of, 48, 57, 146
Dyffryn Clwyd, in Ruthin, 185
Dygby, Edward, 187
Dymmock, John, deputy receiver, 138
Dynham, John, lord, Treasurer of England, steward and surveyor of duchy of Cornwall, 70

East Dereham, 112
Eastwich, 144
Ecclesiastical temporalities, see Temporalities

Edingworth, 122
Edward I, 17, 23, 24, 32
Edward II, 17, 23, 50, 51
Edward III, 17, 23, 24, 32, 33, 35, 51, 68
Edward IV, 23, 26, 27, 28, 31, 40, 44, 51, 52, 53, 54, 55, 56, 57, 58, 59, 62, 63, 64, 65, 96, 97, 99, 100, 102, 103, 104, 106, 108, 110, 111, 112, 113, 115, 116, 124, 127, 151
Edward V, 117
Edward of Woodstock, prince of Wales, 32; lands of, 24
Edwards, Hugh, receiver, 185
Edwards (Edwarde), John, receiver, 143, 150
Edyall, Henry, clerk of general surveyors, 73
Elderfelde, lordship of, 157
Elizabeth of York, queen of Henry VII, 68; lands of, 45-6, 72
Elizabeth (Wydville), queen of Edward IV, Dame Elizabeth Grey, 68, 125, 142
Elmley Lovett, lordship of, 196-7
Eltonhead, John, auditor, 55
Elvet, receiver of, 151
Elyott, Richard, receiver, 144
Empson (Emson), Sir Richard, 150; king's councillor, 76; receiver, 145; receiver-general of woodsales, 47, 144; lands of, 171
Enderby, Sir Richard, 121
Erneley, John, king's attorney, 77, 169, 175
Erpingham, family, 33
Escheators, 33, 39, 79, 134, 137
Escheats, 18, 20, 34, 38, 91
Essex, county of, 123, 124, 138, 140, 143, 154, 155, 171, 195
Essex, earl of, see Bohun; Bourchier
Essex, sheriff of, 158
Estates, seigniorial, accounts of, 43-4
Estates, seigniorial, management of, 42-3, 54-5
Everard, Thomas, 154
Evesham, monastery of, 120
Ewyas, 98

Ewyas Lacy, lordship of, 186
Exchanges, the king's, in London, 80
Exchequer, 18-9, 22, 28, 33, 34, 36, 37, 38, 39, 40-1, 42, 47, 50, 53, 54, 55, 56, 57, 58-9, 61, 62, 66-7, 69, 70, 71, 74, 77-8, 79, 81, 82, 83, 94, 108, 109, 112, 133, 134, 135, 140, 141, 164, 165-70, 174, 175, 177, 180, 185, 186
Exchequer, as a court of record, 117, 136, 141, 167-8, 169
Exchequer, Barons of, 58, 67, 71, 77, 78, 79, 118, 136, 164, 168, 176, 177; and see Blagge, Robert; Hales, John; Westby, Bartholomew
Exchequer, chamberlains of, 164
Exchequer, declaration of account in, 53, 58-9, 95, 106-7, 113-4
Exchequer, financial estimates in, 37-9, 48-9, 92-3
Exchequer, foreign accounts in, 41, 67
Exchequer, Ordnance of 1323, 67
Exchequer, pipe rolls in, 18, 19, 41, 67, 96, 168
Exchequer, receipt and issue rolls in, 27, 45, 66-7
Exchequer, summons of the pipe in, 41, 96
Exchequer, writs of the Treasurer and Barons of, 94, 95, 96, 106, 107, 108, 110, 111, 112, 113, 115, 116, 117, 140, 165, 175
Exeter, bishop of, see Lacy, Edmund; Neville, George
Exeter, duke of, see Holand

Farman, Margaret, jointure of, 157
Fastolf, John, kt., 56
Fenny Compton, 171
Ferrers, Henry, auditor, 103
Ferrers, lands of, 23
Fiennes, James, lord Say and Sele, Treasurer of England, 25
Fineux, John, Chief Justice, 162-3
Fisher, John, bishop of Rochester, 163
Fisher, justice, 162
Fitzherbert, John, receiver, 137

Fitzwalter, lord, see Radcliffe
Fitzwarren, lord, see Bourchier
Flanders, 85
Fleet prison, 150
Flint, county of, 142, 185, 189
Flint, palatine county of, see Chester
Fogge, John, kt., treasurer of Household, 56, 57, 107
Forfeitures, 57, 62, 72, 84-5, 113, 134, 173; and see Attainders; Parliament, acts of attainder in
Fortescue, Sir John, L. C. J., *The Governance of England*, 16, 26, 27, 32, 36, 40, 91
Fotheringay, acquittance given at 100; writ dated at 107
Fountains, abbot of, 61, 129, 157
Fowler, Richard, 57
Fowler, Thomas, squire, gentleman usher of Chamber, receiver, 121, 125
Framsden, manor of, 32
France, 26, 36
France, kings of, see Francis I; Louis XI
Francis I, king of France, 87
Franke, Geoffrey, squire of body, receiver, 120
Fransham, Great, manor of, 112
Fransham, Little, 112
Frebody, Thomas, receiver, 124
Friis, James, 99
Frost, Master, 155

Galtres Forest, herbage of, 171
Gartside, Hugh, receiver, 137
Gascoigne, William, kt., 129
Gere, Richard, of Acton Reynold, 187
General Surveyors, 23, 42, 45, 46, 59, 60, 76-7, 78, 79, 80, 81, 84-6, 88, 165-172, 173-8
General Surveyors, accounts of, 47, 48, 71-2, 73, 83, 84, 142-6, 179-82
General Surveyors, as a 'by-court', 75, 76
General Surveyors, clerk of, see Edyall, Henry

General Surveyors, docket books of, 73-5, 81-2, 85, 147-61, 183-97
General Surveyors, obligations and recognizances before, 71, 74, 79, 80, 82, 152-4, 158, 159-60
General Surveyors, right of traverse against, 80
General Surveyors, seals of, 78, 175, 196, 197
General Surveyors, sign manual of, 197
General Surveyors, meeting places of, 73, 78, 156, 159, 172, 176, 190, 191, 193, 195, 196, 197
General Surveyors, see also Bray, Reginald; Daunce, John; Hales, John; Layburne, Robert; Southwell, Robert; Westby, Bartholomew; Belknap, Edward; Blagge, Robert
George, Mary, wife of Walter, 112
George, Walter, esquire, 112
Glamorgan, lordship of, 46, 62, 64, 122, 137
Glasbury, 98
Glyne, John, clerk, dean of Bangor, 159, 205
Gloucester, county of, 111, 140, 145, 171
Gloucester, duke of, see Lancaster; Plantagenet
Goodman (Godeman, Goodeman), Thomas, receiver, 143, 145, 185, 186
Goodrich, 112
Governance of England, see Fortescue
Gower, 99
Great seal, 73, 80, 92, 94
Great Wardrobe, see Wardrobe
Green, John, of Northam, 158
Green wax, fines of, see Law Courts
Greenwich, writs dated at, 99, 111, 113, 195
Grenebanke, Miles, of York, saddler, 120
Greneway (Grenway), Richard, auditor & receiver, 111, 112, 115, 125
Grenway, Thomas, bailiff, 153-4
Grevell, justice, 162

Grey, Dame Elizabeth, see Elizabeth, queen of Edward IV
Grey, (of Groby), Thomas, marquis of Dorset, lands of, 63, 121, 122-3
Grey, Richard, (of Ruthin), earl of Kent, 171
Griffith, William, squire, chamberlain of N. Wales, 128
Grimston, 171
Grove, John, receiver, 143, 150
Gruffith, Walter, lands of, 139
Gryme, Richard, 187
Grynston, 171
Guienne, 88
Guildford, 130
Guînes (Guisnes), see Calais
Gwyntlwg, 98

Habsburgs, loans to, 87
Haddon, Richard, of the Fellowship of the Staple, kt., 152
Hadleigh Ray, 147
Hadlow, lordship of, 126
Haid, Robert, priest, receiver, 150
Haldall & East Serikkes in East Dereham, manor of, 112
Hales, John, general surveyor, Baron of Exchequer, 196
Hallamshire, lordship of, 115
Halleplace, 157
Halton, 137
Hampden, Edmund, kt., 152
Hampshire, 32, 113, 123, 171
Hamworthy, Richard, 151
Hanaper, see Chancery
Hanborough, manor of, 108
Hansard, Anthony, receiver, 144
Harbart, Willian, receiver, 143
Harbotell, George, 194-5
Harbotell, Guycherd, 194-5
Harecourt, John, receiver, 125
Haresfield & Eastington, manor of, 122
Harle (Herle), William, receiver, 122, 125, 137
Hastings, John, earl of Pembroke, 32
Hastings, John, earl of Pembroke (son of John), 32
Hastings, Katherine, lady, see Neville

INDEX

Hastings, lord, lands of, 145
Hastings, William, lord, 61
Haverfordwest, 99
Hawarden, manor of, 32
Hawkyns, Richard, auditor, 183
Hawte, Martyn, receiver, 124, 125
Hay, 98
Hayes (Heys, Hays), John, receiver, 59, 113, 114, 123, 125, 138, 139, 140
Hebyn, John, receiver, 97
Henage, William, receiver, 144
Henham, manor of, 130
Henry I, 20
Henry II, 18, 19, 20, 22
Henry III, 23, 24
Henry IV, 23, 24, 25, 26, 31, 32, 39, 51
Henry V, 25, 31, 32, 33, 38, 39, 51
Henry VI, 25, 26, 27, 31, 32, 33, 35, 36, 39, 46, 51, 52, 53, 54, 56, 67-8, 69, 72, 92, 95, 103
Henry VII, 29, 37, 39, 40, 41, 42, 44, 45, 46, 47, 48, 49, 50, 53, 56, 58, 59, 64, 65, 66, 67, 68, 69, 70, 72, 73, 74, 75, 76, 77, 78, 79, 80, 81, 82, 83, 84, 85, 86, 87, 140, 164, 166, 169, 171, 173, 180, 182
Henry VIII, 29, 44, 46, 60, 75, 76, 78, 81, 82, 85, 86, 87, 88, 162, 165, 174, 180, 181, 194
Herbarte, William, of Troy, 158
Herbert, Thomas, squire, 100
Herbert, William, lord, 98, 99, 100
Herbert, William, earl of Huntingdon (son of William lord Herbert), 64, 143, 171, 183, 186
Herbert, Katherine, wife of William earl of Huntingdon, see Plantagenet
Herbert, lord, see Somerset
Hereford, 57
Hereford, county of, 97, 112, 140, 171, 185
Hereford, earl of, see Bohun
Hereford in Hoo, manor of, 112
Heron, John, treasurer of Chamber, 44, 45, 47-8, 72, 74, 77, 79, 80, 83, 86, 142-6, 147, 151, 152, 159-60, 164-5, 167, 169, 170, 172, 173, 174, 176, 177, 179, 185, 186, 191

Heron, John, esquire, 195
Hertford, county of, 124, 130, 138, 140, 143, 144, 171
Hertford, earldom of, 127
Heth, John, gent., 156
Heton, family, 55
Hewik, John, auditor, 103
Hichyn, William, 192
Higham Ferrers, 138
Hiotte, Robert, receiver, 99
Hobson, Thomas, 71
Hoggesson, William, bailiff, 138
Holand, David, 193
Holand, John, duke of Exeter, 92
Holand, Roger, 145, 155
Holbech (Holbache), Thomas, receiver, 125, 138
Holderness, see Burstwick; Daypole
Holland, lordship of, 192, 193, 266
Hospitallers, Hospital of St John, lands of, 32
Hospitallers, Hospital of St John, prior of, 210, 212
Hotechyns, John, 149
Hotham, 131
Houghton, lady, 157
Houne, John, pursuivant, 153
Household, 25, 26, 31, 39, 40, 52, 53, 56, 64, 83, 84, 93
Household, appropriations and assignments for expenses of, 27, 52, 61, 64, 94, 96, 133, 137-9, 170, 179, 180, 181, 186
Household, provisions, etc. bought for, 100, 129, 130-1
Household, chamberlain of, see Lovell, Francis
Household, cofferer of, 108; and see Kendal, John
Household, controller of, 57, 94, 108
Household, patronage in, 54
Household, steward of, 79, 94, 178
Household, treasurer of, 57, 94; and see Fogge, John; see also Sandal
Hovingham, 131
Howard, John, lord, 57, 112; earl marshal, duke of Norfolk, 64

Howard, Margaret, wife of John lord Howard, 112
Howard, Thomas, earl of Surrey (son of John Howard, duke of Norfolk), 64, 65; Treasurer of England, 162, 163
Howell, John ap Madog ap, 159
Howell, Walter ap David ap, receiver, 98
Howes,—, 155
Huddilston, Richard, kt. of the body, constable of Beaumaris castle, 128-9
Huddye, justice, 162
Hugford, John, squire of the body, constable of Warwick castle, 128
Hull, 149, 171
Hundred Rolls, 18
Hungerford, Edmund, kt., king's carver, 92
Hungerford, Walter, esquire, 121
Hunsdon, 144
Huntingdon, county of, 57, 124, 127, 140, 143, 171
Huntingdon, earl of, see Herbert
Huntley, Hugh, receiver, 99
Hussey (Hussy) John, kt. of the body, master of the king's wards, 154, 157, 160
Husy, William, kt., 130
Hynd, Georgina, 187

Inglefield, Thomas, kt., 163
Inquisitions, 33, 34
Irchenfield, 112
Ireland, act of resumption in, 93, 103
Isabella, queen of Edward II, 23, 32
Isham, (Issham), John, receiver, 124, 125, 127
Ittynghame, Robert, of Wendover, 153-4

Joan of Navarre, queen of Henry IV, 26, 39
John, abbot of monastery of Evesham, 120
John, king of England, 17, 22
John of Eltham, earl of Cornwall, lands of, 24, 32

John, Philip ap., 159
Johnes, Hugh, 147
Johnson, Richard, 152
Justices, Chief, 79, 178

Kelingworth, Thomas, 171
Kempton, 130
Kendal, John, treasurer and household cofferer of Richard duke of York, cofferer of Household, 44
Kendale, John, king's secretary, 121, 126
Kendall, William, 171
Kenilworth, 171; warrants dated at, 130-1
Kenninghall, manor of, 32
Kensington, lordship of, 139
Kent, county of, 30, 60, 126, 140, 143, 145, 150, 171
Kerry, 97
Kessingland, manor of, 32
Ketylby, John, esquire, steward, 196
Keynsan, 157
Kidwelly, 99
Kidwelly, family, 55
Kilvey, 99
Kingston-upon-Thames, 130
Kirkby Malzeard, 131
Kirkeham, manor of, 127
Knaresborough, 129, 131

Lacy, Edmund, bishop of Exeter, keeper of shrine of, 114
Lancaster, 137
Lancaster, duchy of, 31, 38, 39, 41, 44, 45, 50, 53, 54, 55, 60, 61, 62, 72, 83, 84, 93, 97, 99, 103, 124, 127, 129, 136-7, 180, 181
Lancaster, duchy of, chancellor of, 178
Lancaster, duchy of, receiver-general of, 43, 71, 78, 94, 178
Lancaster, royal county and honour of, 23
Lancaster, Edward of, prince of Wales, 27
Lancaster, Humphrey of, duke of Gloucester, earl of Pembroke, 26, 35, 38

Lancaster, John of (Gaunt), duke of, 23
Lancaster, John of, earl of Richmond, duke of Bedford, 26, 38
Lancaster, Thomas of, duke of Clarence, 26
Lancaster, Thomas of, duke of Clarence, widow of, 39
Lancaster, Thomas of, earl of, 42, 51
Land revenues, 38, 47-9, 64, 67, 69, 70, 71-2, 77-8, 83-5
Landon, Alexander, gent., 157-8
Langham, 148
Langley, Edmund of, duke of York, 68
Langley Marish, 130
Latimer lands, 131
Law Courts, fines of green wax in, 38
Laws of Edward the Confessor, 17
Layburne, Roger, bishop of Carlisle, general surveyor, 71, 73, 152, 154, 156, 157, 158, 159, 160
Lea, manor of, 32
Leche, Richard, receiver, 144
Lee, Thomas, esquire, 155
Legh, Thomas, receiver, 143
Leicestershire, 103, 106, 123, 129, 140, 159, 171
Leicestershire, sheriff of, 95
Leventhorpe, family, 55
Leventhorpe, Nicholas, squire, 129
Leybourne, Juliana de, countess of Huntingdon, 32
Lincoln, bishop of, see Smith
Lincoln, earl of, see Pole
Lincoln's Inn, 55
Lincolnshire, 116, 130, 140, 143, 171
Lincolnshire, sheriff of, 57
Litchborough, 150
Liverles, 126, 132, 133
Lloyd, Howell ap. Jevan, receiver, 98
Lloyd, Philip ap. Griffith, receiver, 98
Loans by the king, 87
Loans to the king, see Taxation
London, 34, 52, 62, 136, 149, 156, 190
London, sheriff of, 158
London, writs etc., dated at, 96, 112, 114, 116, 117, 122
Long Bennington, 137

Louis XI, king of France, 104
Loveday, —, 194-5
Lovell, Daincourt & Gray, Alice, lady, 110
Lovell, Francis, viscount, king's chamberlain, 110, 139, 170
Lovell, Henry, lord Morley, lands of, 140, 145, 171
Lovell, Robert, kt., receiver, 144
Lovell, Thomas, kt., treasurer of Chamber, 68, 69, 145, 163
Lowther, Lancelot, receiver, 142
Ludlow, 64
Luthington (Lathington), John, auditor & receiver, 55, 57, 116, 125
Lychfelde, William, receiver-general of wards' lands, 47
Lydney, manor of, 111
Lynam, Thomas, 179

Macclesfield, 151
Maddy, Geoffrey, of Papworth, 192
Maelienydd, 97
Magna Carta, 105
Malary, Master, 192
Malony, John, 150
Malory, Anthony, gent., 188-9
Maneryng, Roger, excheator, 157
March, earl of, see Plantagenet
March, earldom of, 31, 42, 44, 46, 50, 55, 57, 62, 72, 97-8, 126, 134, 138, 142, 143, 170, 184, 185-6, 187
March, earldom of, chancellor of, see Colt, Thomas
Marden, lordship of, 126
Margaret of Anjou, queen of Henry VI, 26, 27
Margaret, daughter of Edward III, countess of Pembroke, 32
Markfield, 159
Martin, Master Richard, auditor, 103
Marzen, Francis, receiver, 145
Maye, John, B.D., abbot of Chertsey, 113
Menrek, Trahairon ap. Jevan, receiver, 98
Merydith, William ap. John ap., receiver, 193-4

Metcalf, Miles, 129
Middilton (Midilton), David, receiver, 97, 126
Middleham, lordship of, 120
Middlesex, county of, 124, 130, 140, 171, 176
Midilton, Thomas, 129
Milewater, John, receiver-general, 44, 55, 56, 57
Milewater, John, receiver-general, account of, 97-101
Mills, 149, 151, 154; fulling and corn, 159; corn, 160
Milton (Lincs.), 116; (Bucks.), 139
Milton, lordship of (Kent), 126
Mold, lordship of, 32
Mollington, 157
Molyneux, Hugh, auditor, 48
Monmouth, 99
Montalt, Robert of, lands of, 32
de Montfort lands, 23
Montgomery, 97, 152
Moor End and members, 146, 184, 185
More, Sir Thomas, *Richard III*, 63, 64
Mores, John, 190
Mores, John, gent., 156
Morgan, David ap William, 152
Morganok, lordship of, 122
Morley, lord, see Lovell
Moros, James, receiver, 185
Morton, 187
Morton, Rowland, 158
Mortymer, John, 171
Mountford, Simon, kt., 170
Mountford, William, kt., sheriff of Warws. and Leics., 95
Mountjoy, lord, see Blount
Mowbray, John, duke of Norfolk (died 1432), lands of, 38
Mowbray, John, duke of Norfolk (died 1461), lands of, 97, 99
Munke, Thomas, of Markfield, 159
Mychleisse, lordship of, 154
Mymes, Nicholas, alderman of London, 158
Mythe, 188

Nanfan, Richard, kt., receiver, 142, 171; receiver-general, duchy of Cornwall, 48, 71-2
Narberth, 98, 143
Neston, manor of, 32
Neswyke, Robert, bailiff, 185
Neville, Anne, countess of Warwick, lands of, 143, 171
Neville, George, late bishop of Exeter, archbishop of York, 52, 58, 108, 109
Neville, Katherine, wife of William lord Hastings, lands of, 149, 171
Neville, Richard, earl of Warwick, 52, 57
Neville, family, 32
Neville (Warwick, Salisbury and Spencer) lands, 46, 58, 59, 62, 73, 113-4, 123-8, 134, 138, 140-1, 143, 154, 165, 184, 186, 196-7
Newport, 98
Newporte, George, gent., 156
Newton, Peter, 187-8
Nomina villarum (1316), 18
Norfolk, county of, 112, 138, 140, 143, 144, 171
Norfolk, duchy of, 62, 134, 139
Norfolk, duke of, see Mowbray; Howard
Norrey, William, kt., 121
Norstead (by Scarborough), 171
Northam, 158
Northampton, county of, 106, 123, 124, 127, 140, 143, 150
Northumberland, 103, 171
Northumberland, earl of, see Percy
Northumberland, sheriff of, 171
North Witham, 131
Norton under Hamdon, 171
Norwich, bishop of, see Nykke
Nottingham, county of, 115, 143, 171, 194
Nottingham, earl of, see Berkeley
Nottingham, writ dated at, 119
Notting Hill, lordship of, 139
Nykke, Richard, bishop of Norwich, 162, 163
Nynys, Nicholas, 150

Oddingley, 155-6
Offices, royal, in England and Wales, 34, 36, 39-40, 62
Ogmore, 99
Oldehalle, William, kt., 171
Oldham (Oldeham) Hugh, clerk, receiver, 71, 140, 141, 143, 145
Olney, 139
Ordinances of 1311, 17, 24-5
Osmund, St., bishop of Salisbury, keeper of shrine of, 114
Osney, monastery, writ dated at, 92
Ougle, lady, 194
Overton, Gudlack, auditor, 183, 191
Overton, Thomas, receiver, 139
Oxford, county of, 58, 108, 140, 143, 152, 171

Palmer, Thomas, receiver and approver, 106-7
Papworth, 191
Par, Gilbert, squire of the body, 92
Parker, Henry, auditor, 183
Parker, John, 159
Parker, William, 145
Parkers, the king's, 133
Parliament, 24, 26-7, 31, 37, 51, 52, 68, 102, 116, 164-5, 170, 175, 177, 178, 185
Parliament, acts of attainder in, 46, 57, 58
Parliament, acts of resumption in, 27, 33-5, 36, 39-40, 41, 46, 52, 53, 54, 67, 70, 72, 84-5, 92-3, 102-3, 105
Parliament, knights of the shire in, 24
Parliament, legislation of Edward I, in, 33
Parliament, legislation of Henry VIII in, 77-81, 83, 84
Parliament, Speaker of the House of Commons, see Say
Parrowe, John, 130
Pase, Edmund, 158
Paston, John, executor of Sir John Fastolf, 56
Pawne, William, receiver, 186
Peerage, creations to and elevations in, 35

Pembridge, Richard de, 33
Pembroke, county and lordship, 32, 38, 46
Pembroke, earl of, see Lancaster; Tudor
Pembroke, earldom of, 38
Pencelly, 171
Penler, John, receiver, 125
Penrith, 171
Penshurst, lordship of, 126
Percy, Henry, earl of Northumberland (died 1461) lands of, 57
Percy, Henry, earl of Northumberland (died 1537), 82, 195
Peryent, John, auditor, 183
Philipp (Phelypp), David, kt., 158, 161
Philip, Thomas ap., 143
Philoll, Jasper, 149
Pigot, Thomas, abbot of Chertsey, 113
Pilkington, Arthur, 157
Pimperne, lordship of, 149
Pirbright, 130
Plainmeller, 171
Plantagenet, Cecily da. of Edward IV, wife of Richard (*recte* John) viscount Welles, lands of, 171
Plantagenet, Cecily, duchess of York, 68, 72
Plantagenet, Edward, earl of March, duke of York (Ed. IV), 42, 50, 51, 56
Plantagenet, Edward, prince of Wales (Ed. V), council of, at Ludlow, 64
Plantagenet, Edward, earl of Warwick, 113, 143, 170
Plantagenet, George, duke of Clarence, 46, 52, 53, 57, 58, 63, 103, 113, 125
Plantagenet, Katherine, countess of Huntingdon, illeg. da. of Richard III, 64
Plantagenet, Margaret, da. and heir of George, duke of Clarence, lady Salisbury, 159; widow of Sir Richard Pole and later countess of Salisbury, 87
Plantagenet, Richard, duke of Gloucester (Rich. III), 42, 46, 60, 64, 71

Plantagenet, Richard, duke of York, 25, 27, 43, 44, 52
Plomer, John, receiver, 139
Pole, lady Margaret, see Plantagenet
Pole, Richard ap. receiver, 150
de la Pole, Edmund, earl of Suffolk, lands of, 47, 72, 144, 149, 170, 187
de la Pole, Elizabeth, duchess of Suffolk, 131
de la Pole, John, earl of Lincoln, 170
de la Pole, William, kt., lands of, 47, 72, 144, 170
de la Pole, William, duke of Suffolk, 25
Pontefract, 131; acquittance, etc., dated at, 100, 127, 128
Poole, John, receiver, 143
Pope, John, 147
Porter, family, 33
Poullard, —, 155
Povington, William, receiver, 144
Poyntz, William, receiver, 154
Prince's Council Chamber, see Westminster
Princes Risborough, 190
Prior, Richard, of Aylesbury, 130
Privy seal, 39, 59, 73, 77, 78, 79, 80, 82, 104, 107, 108, 110, 111, 112, 113, 114, 116, 117, 118, 141, 151, 152, 156, 157, 158, 159, 160, 163, 165, 166, 169, 170, 172, 175, 176, 183, 187, 190
Privy seal, keeper of, 79, 104, 178
Pulleyn, John, servant of cellar and ewery, 130
Purveyance, 17, 24, 52, 53, 54, 61, 93, 94
Pyggot, Robert, receiver, 143
Pyle, Thomas, son of Richard Pyle of Carleton Rode, 152
Pyliston, John, receiver, 142
Pyllisden, Roger, kt., 193
Pyper, (Piper) William, 160
Pytchley, 144

Quarles, George, auditor, 184
Quarrendon, 139

Raby, 131

Radcliffe (Ratclyff) John, lord Fitzwalter (FitzWater), lands of, 47, 144, 170
Radnor, lordship of, 97, 152, 186
Ragiers, Richard, kt., 149
Ratclif, lady, 153
Rede, Robert, justice, 162, 163
Redvers, Isabella de, countess of Aumale, 31-2
Relyngton, 187
Resumptions, see Parliament, acts of resumption in
Reve, John, 156
Revenues, classification of, 15-7, 66
Revenues, French pension, 56, 105
Revenues, see also Taxation; Land Revenues
Reynold (Reynolde) Henry, receiver, 144, 187
Richard II, 23, 24, 46, 65, 68
Richard III, 42, 46, 55, 56, 58, 59, 60, 61, 62, 63, 64, 65, 67, 68, 70, 71, 73, 117, 119, 120, 121, 122, 123, 124, 125 126 127, 128, 130
Richmond, countess of, see Beaufort
Richmond, earl of, see Lancaster; Brittany; Tudor
Richmond, earldom of, 32, 38, 55, 57, 166, 170
Richmond, honour of, 57, 116, 125, 126, 186, 187
Richmond, writ dated at, 170
Richmondsfee in Lincs., 116
Rivers, earl, see Wydeville
Roberdis, John, receiver, 129
Roberts, Thomas, auditor, 183, 184
Rochester, 171
Rochester, bishop of, see Fisher
Roke, John, 195
Roos, Thomas, lord, lands of, 57
Roos, Edmund, lord, lands of, 145
Rosser, Thomas ap., receiver, 98
Roulandson, Thomas, 153
Ruthall, Thomas, bishop of Durham, 162
Ruthin, 185, 193
Rutland, county of, 106, 123, 140, 143, 171

Saham Toney, 138
St Albans, 2nd battle of, 52
St David's, bishop of, see Vaughan
St John's in London, 73, 156
St John of Jerusalem, prior of, 162-3
St Margaret Stratton, 130
Salisbury, shrine of St Osmond at, 114
Salisbury, writ dated at, 121
Salisbury, countess of, see Plantagenet
Salysbery, Thomas, gent., 189
Sandal, Richard III's northern household at, 61, 64, 131
Sandeford, Ralph, receiver, 143
Sapcote (Sapcotte) John, squire, receiver-general, duchy of Cornwall, 117-8, 121, 122, 128-38, 139
Sapcote, family of, 55
Savage, Thomas, archbishop, of York, 151
Savell, Nicholas, 157
Say, John, Speaker of the House of Commons, 102
Scarborough, 171
Scotland 88
Scottish campaign of 1496-7, 70
Scorpe (Scrop) John, lord, 123
Seintleger, Thomas, kt., 121, 123
Sergeants, king's, 163
Sharp, Robert, receiver, 138
Shaw, Edmund, kt., of London, merchant, 127
Shawe (in Old Windsor), 171
Sheen, manor of, writ dated at, 141
Sheffield, 57
Sheffield, castle of, 115
Sheriffs, accounts of, 18, 28, 38, 53, 95, 134
Sheriffs, duties of, 28, 41
Sheriffs, farms of the shires of, 19, 30, 62, 67, 69, 95, 137
Sheriffs, proffers of, 49
Sheriffs, rewards of, 70
Shilbottle, 48
Shirley, Richard, 157
Shrewsbury, earls of, see Talbot
Shrivenham, manor of, 111
Shropshire, 98, 112, 140, 186, 187

Sign manual, the king's, 41, 56, 68, 72, 119, 173, 176
Signet, the king's, 36, 59, 73, 81, 82, 92, 156
Signet, the king's, docket book of, 40, 41, 59-64, 66, 120-39, 195
Singleborough, 139
Skelton, John, 171
Skeltons, annuity late, 145
Skipton in Craven, 131
Skyll, John, 195
Skynner, John, 147
Skynner, Robert, 147
Slade, Thomas, receiver, 196
Smith, William, bishop of Lincoln, 155
Smith, William, receiver, 142
Smyth, Richard of Denbigh, 159
Smyth, William, 147
Snettisham, manor of, 32
Solicitor, king's, 163
Somerset, Charles, lord Herbert, 163; earl of Worcester, 186
Somerset, county of, 113, 123, 171, 183
Somerset, duchess of, see Beauchamp
Somerton (Oxon), 152
Somerton, castle, manor and lordship of (Lincs.), 116
Southampton, county of, 32, 113, 123, 171
Southwold, 171
Southwell, Robert, receiver, general surveyor, auditor of Exchequer, Chief Butler of England, 48, 71, 73, 77, 78, 79, 143, 144, 152, 154, 156, 157, 158, 159, 160, 165-70, 173, 174, 175, 176, 177, 178, 179-80, 195
Spert, Richard, receiver, 130-1, 137
Spicer, Nicholas, gentleman usher of Chamber, receiver, 122, 125
Spicer, Thomas, 188
Stafford county of, 103, 140, 148, 171
Stafford dukes of Buckingham, 55
Stafford, Edward, duke of Buckingham, 84-5, 163

Stafford, Henry, duke of Buckingham, 61, 64, 121
Stafford, Henry, duke of Buckingham, rebellion of, 63
Stafford, Humphrey, lands of, 170
Stafford, Humphrey, duke of Buckingham, 97, 98
Stafford, John, archbishop of Canterbury, Chancellor of England, 92
Stanford, John, auditor, 137
Stanley, Edward, earl of Derby, 193
Stanley, Henry, 154
Stanley, John, 147-8
Stanley, John a, 157
Stanley, Thomas, earl of Derby, 192, 193
Stanley, William, kt., 68; lands of, 47, 72, 142, 170, 185
Staple, see Calais
Star Chamber, see Council
Stephen, king of England, 18, 23
Stepney, acquittance dated at, 74, 148
Steward of the honour of Tutbury, duties of, 161-4
Stidolff, Thomas, steward and receiver, 57, 111
Stillingfleet, 171
Stoke in Climsland, 160
Stoke under Hamdon, lordship of, 144, 186
Stokes, Thomas, receiver, 144
Stonesfield, manor of, 108
Stonor, William, kt., 121
Stradlynge, John, receiver, 99
Strange, Thomas, 153
Straunge, Robert, esquire, 154
Stratford, 148
Stratford, abbot of, 195
Suffolk, county of, 131, 138, 140, 143, 144, 147, 171
Suffolk, duchess of, see de la Pole
Suffolk, duke of, see de la Pole
Suffolk, earl of, see de la Pole
Surrey, county of, 123, 124, 130, 143, 150, 171
Surrey, earl of, see Howard
Sussex, county of, 32, 138, 143, 171, 194

Suthill, Robert, 149
Sutton, Oliver, receiver, 125
Sutton, Richard, receiver, 148
Swaffham, lordship of, 171, 186
Swallowfield, 130
Swansea, 99
Swetdew, Roger, of Bassingbourn, 189
Swetdew, Alice, wife of Roger, 189
Swift (Swyft), John, receiver, 57, 115
Swindon, manor of, 111
Symond (Symonde) Agnes Vergh, 194
Symond, Sir John, priest, receiver of bishopric of Exeter, 123

Tadlow (Tatlow), William, 192
Tailboys, Robert, kt., sheriff of Lincoln, 116, 117
Talbot earls of Shrewsbury, estates of, 57, 111-2
Talbot, family, 33
Talbot, George, earl of Shrewsbury, 111, 115, 162-3
Talbot, John, earl of Shrewsbury, 111, 112, 115
Talgarth, 98
Tatton, William, 151
Taxation, benevolence, 56, 88; clerical, 87, 105; forced loans, 88; in Parliament, 21, 25, 26, 32, 37, 38, 69, 87, 93, 134; sales tax, 26, 28; scutage, 20; tallage, 20-1, 54
Tayte, John, kt., mayor of Staple of Calais, 152
Tedirton, 122
Temple, Order of, lands of, 32
Temporalities, 30, 47, 48, 57, 67, 69, 73, 77, 105, 113, 120, 123, 136
Tenby, lordship of, 32
Tenure, burgage, 20; by courtesy of England, 31; by-hold, 153; by military service, 20, 29; copy-hold, 79, 155, 159, 191; in ancient demesne, 20; socage, 20
Terrae datae, 18, 19, 95
Tewskesbury, 188, 191
Tewskesbury, abbot of, 188
Tewskesbury, battle of, 57

Thames, farm of swans on, 171
Thirsk, 131
Thomas, Rees ap. kt., receiver, cham-, berlain of S. Wales, 142, 150, 151 186
Thornborough, John, of the Fellowship of the Staple, gent., 152
Thornbury, lordship or manor of, 122, 139
Thorrington, 147
Tickhill, 131
Tiptoft, John, earl of Worcester, Treasurer of England, 104
Tiverton, manor and lordship of, 113
Tokotts, Roger, kt., 121
Toly, John, auditor, 183
Tomson, John, receiver, 143
Tonbridge, honour of, 126
Totothe, Thomas, receiver, 126
Towton, battle of, 52
Treason, 22, 30, 32, 91
Treasurer of England, 17, 54, 58, 92, 94, 134, 137, 139, 164; and see Exchequer, writs to; Cromwell, Ralph; Dynham, John; Fiennes, James; Howard, Thomas; Tiptoft, John.
Trefiw, manor of, 148
Trefrey (Trefrye), William, lands of, 145, 149
Tresire, William, receiver, 144
Tuchet, John, lord Audley, lands of, 47, 72, 144, 170
Tudor, Arthur, prince of Wales, 72
Tudor, Edmund, earl of Richmond, 26, 27, 67
Tudor, Henry, earl of Richmond (Henry VII), 63, 65
Tudor, Henry, duke of York, prince of Wales (Henry VIII), 46, 150
Tudor, Jasper, earl of Pembroke, duke of Bedford, 26, 27, 46, 68, 72, 143, 170, 183
Tunstall, 148
Turnor, John, auditor, 183, 184
Turton, Richard, of Wakefield, 152-3
Tutbury, honour of, 61, 124, 132, 137
Tylney's lands, 153, 154

Tynedale, 129
Tynedale, receiver and auditor of, 129
Tyrell, James, kt., lands of, 47, 72, 144

Ulnage, 96, 139, 145, 171
Ulverston, John, squire, 131
Umpton, Master, 191
Upton, 171
Upton, Suthshawe in, 161
Usk, 98, 143, 183

Vaughan, Edward, bishop of St David's, 162
Vaughan, Thomas, treasurer of Chamber, 56
Vaughan, Thomas ap. Rosser, receiver, 98
Venice, correspondence with, 86, 88
de Vere, family, lands of, 63
Veyne, Rees ap. David ap. Howell, receiver, 97

Wadley & Wicklesham, manor of, 33
Wagette, Master William, canon of Exeter, 123
Waghorne, James, receiver, 151
Wakefield, 125, 152-3
Wakering, 171
Wales (Principality and Marches), 84, 123, 166, 171, 173, 180
Wales (Principality and Marches), acts of resumption in, 39, 93, 103
Wales (Principality and Marches), king's council in, 187
Wales (Principality), 23-4, 31, 38, 39, 46, 62, 64, 72, 103, 134, 142, 150-1, 170, 183
Wales (Principality), chamberlains of North and of South, 33, 41, 173, 183, 186; and see Griffith, William; Thomas, Rice ap.
Wales, prince of, see Edward of Woodstock; Lancaster; Plantagenet; Tudor
Wales, prince of, chancellor of, 155
Wales, prince of, commissioners of, 160

INDEX

Wales, prince of, council of, 64, 73, 150, 151, 152, 155, 159-60
Wales, prince of, patrimony of, 23-4, 31, 35, 38, 39, 46, 62, 72, 103, 134, 142, 150, 159, 166, 170, 173, 183
Wales, Statute of, 23
Walkfelde, 157
Wall, Robert, 156
Wall, John, esquire, 148
Walshe, John, deputy to feodary of Cornwall, 158
Walshe, John, squire, receiver, 71, 140, 141
Walton-on-Trent, manor of, 32
Wanstead, lordship & manor of, 144, 171, 195-6
Wardrobe, Great, 77, 83, 84, 170, 171, 179, 180, 181, 185
Wards' lands, 18, 20, 30, 34, 38, 47, 48, 55, 57, 60, 62, 69, 73, 77, 79, 84, 97, 113, 115, 136, 145, 157, 171, 173, 180, 193, 194-5
Wards' lands, master of, see Hussey, John
Wards' lands, receiver-general of, see Lychefelde, William
Warham, William, archbishop of Canterbury, Chancellor of England, 162-3
Wark, 171
Warwick, 60-1, 128, 157
Warwick, countess of, see Neville
Warwick, county of, 106, 123, 140, 171
Warwick, earl of, see Beauchamp; Neville; Plantagenet
Warwick, Salisbury and Spencer lands, see Neville
Warwickshire, sheriff of, 95
Wastlyn, John, 187
Wastlyn, Thomas, gent., 187
Webley, manor of, 151
Welby, Richard, receiver, 116, 117, 125
Welles (Willis), Cecily, wife of Richard viscount Welles, see Plantagenet
Wendover, 130, 153-4

Westby, Bartholomew, general surveyor, Baron of Exchequer, 77, 78, 166, 167, 170, 173, 174, 175, 178, 179, 189, 195
West Horsley, 171
Westminster, 59, 154, 156-7, 160, 172
Westminster, Prince's Council Chamber at, 73, 78, 159, 172, 176, 191, 193, 195, 196, 197
Westminster, writs and commissions, etc. dated at, 94, 95, 100, 106, 108, 110, 111, 118, 125, 127, 129, 156, 167, 196
Westmoreland, county of, 171
Weston by Baldock, 171
West Thurrock, 171
Wheathampstead, John, abbot of St Albans, 36
Whiddon, Lower, 171
Whitwick, manor of, 159
Wicklesham, see Wadley
Wight, Isle of, 143, 171
Wigmore, 97, 186
Wilkokes in Little Fransham, manor of, 112
William I, 19, 20, 24, 31
Willoughby, Baldwin, 194
Willoughby, Robert, lord Booke I (Died 1502), 145
Willoughby, Robert, lord Booke II (son and heir of I), warden of the stannaries, 145, 148, 155
Wiltshire, 111, 113, 123, 130, 140, 158, 171
Wiltshire lands, see Butler
Winchelsea, bailiwick of, 171
Windsor, 171
Windsor, castle of, 130, 142, 151
Windsor, estates, 38
Windsor, New, 130
Windsor, Old, 171
Winforton, 98
Woderowe, John, receiver, 125
Wolsey, Thomas, Cardinal, Chancellor of England, 29, 79, 84, 85, 86, 87, 88, 193
Woodsales, 30, 47, 73, 79, 133, 134, 144, 154-5, 195-7

Woodsales, placards for, 160-1
Woodsales, receiver-general of, see Empson, Richard
Woodstock, manor and lordship of, 108, 109
Wootton, manor and hundred of, 108
Worcester county of, 140, 155, 156, 171, 196
Worcester, earl of, see Tiptoft; Somerset
Worksop, lordship of, 115
Wormleighton, 171
Worplesdon, 130
Wrenne, John, auditor, 184, 185
Wydeville, Anthony, earl Rivers, lands of, 63, 140
Wydeville, Elizabeth, see Elizabeth, queen of Edward IV
Wydeville, family, 63
Wye, Master, 191

Wyet, Henry, 147
Wykyn, John, bailiff, 144
Wyrardisbury, 130
Wyton beside Hull, 149

Yalding, lordship of, 126
Yale, 142, 185
York, 171; commission dated at, 129
York, archbishop of, see Neville, George; Savage, Thomas
York, county of, 64, 115, 123, 131, 171
York, duchess of, see Plantagenet
York, duchy of, 31, 42, 46, 50, 57, 62, 72, 134, 143, 144, 150, 160, 166, 170
York, duke of, see Langley; Plantagenet; Tudor
York, House of, 50, 65, 68
York, sheriff of, 157
Yoxall, 171
Ystlw, lordship of, 32

For Product Safety Concerns and Information please contact our EU representative GPSR@taylorandfrancis.com
Taylor & Francis Verlag GmbH, Kaufingerstraße 24, 80331 München, Germany

www.ingramcontent.com/pod-product-compliance
Lightning Source LLC
Chambersburg PA
CBHW061826300426
44115CB00013B/2267